THE RELEVANCE OF THE NEW TESTAMENT

HEINRICH SCHLIER

THE RELEVANCE
OF THE
NEW TESTAMENT

HERDER AND HERDER

1968

HERDER AND HERDER NEW YORK
232 Madison Avenue, New York, N. Y. 10016

BURNS & OATES LIMITED
25 Ashley Place, London S. W. 1

PALM PUBLISHERS
1949–55th Avenue, Dorval-Montreal

Original edition:
"Besinnung auf das Neue Testament",
Herder, Freiburg, 1964. Translated by W. J. O'Hara.

Nihil Obstat: Lionel Swain, STL., LSS., Censor
Imprimatur: † Patrick Casey, Vic. Gen.
Westminster, 18th August 1967.

The Nihil Obstat and Imprimatur are a declaration that a book
or pamphlet is considered to be free from doctrinal or moral error.
It is not implied that those who have granted the Nihil Obstat and Imprimatur
agree with the contents, opinions or statements expressed.

Library of Congress Catalog Card No. 67—21849
First published in West Germany © 1967, Herder KG
Printed in West Germany by Herder

Contents

Abbreviations

BZ	Biblische Zeitschrift
JBL	Journal of Biblical Literature
LTK	Lexikon für Theologie und Kirche (2nd ed., 1957—65)
MTS	Münchener Theologische Studien
MTZ	Münchener Theologische Zeitschrift
PL	J. P. Migne, ed., Patrologia Latina (1878 ff.)
RB	Revue Biblique
TLZ	Theologische Literaturzeitung
TQ	Theologische Quartalschrift
TWNT	Theologisches Wörterbuch zum Neuen Testament (1933 ff.)
ZNW	Zeitschrift für die neutestamentliche Wissenschaft und die Kunde der älteren Kirche
ZTK	Zeitschrift für Theologie und Kirche

Foreword

The modern Catholic Scripture movement in America has, to a large degree, received its guiding impulse from France and Belgium rather than from Germany. (There are various reasons for this: French and Belgian scholarship is largely Catholic, while German biblical scholarship is predominantly Protestant; in the formative years, the 1940's and the 1950's, German Catholic scholarship had not yet recovered from the War; French is more easily read than German, especially for those trained in Latin; etc.) De Vaux, Benoît, Boismard, Cerfaux, Coppens, Robert, Cazelles, Feuillet, Lyonnet, and de la Potterie are among the names that appear most frequently in the indexes of American Catholic biblical works, both scientific and popular. The *Bible de Jérusalem* has had enormous influence, as one series of biblical pamphlets after another has popularized opinions taken verbatim from the footnotes and introductions of that Bible. Although this influence has been somewhat lopsided, its effect was providential; for in the "bad years" of biblical progress in this country (1958—63, when the orthodoxy of Catholic biblical scholars was often questioned), the day was saved by the irenic quality of this French-speaking scholarship, translated to the American scene. Less trenchant and disturbing than German criticism, this biblical interpretation had a positive and constructive tone and was benignly sensitive to doctrinal implications.

Now, however, the influence of German scholarship is being felt more and more on the American Catholic biblical scene. In part this may be attributable to the ecumenical movement. If American Catholic scholars speak of their teachers at the École Biblique of Jerusalem, the Pontifical Biblical Institute of Rome, or the University of Louvain, their Protestant counterparts are likely to speak of the professors of Heidelberg, Marburg, or Tübingen. American Protestant biblical scholarship has been very heavily influenced by Germany and not at all by France and Belgium. And so, in the interests of meaningful dialogue, as well as in the interests of their own scholarship, American Catholics are being forced to familiarize themselves with German criticism, especially in the New Testament field.

Here the German Catholic exegetes are serving as a bridge, for they have had the possibility and the reason to come to terms with Bultmannian criticism and have found a way to combine what is truly scientific in that criticism with the fundamentals of Catholic theology. The names of Wikenhauser and Schnackenburg are already well known on the American scene, but many other important German Catholic scholars are not generally known because their works remain untranslated. One of these is Professor Heinrich Schlier of Bonn. His short work *Powers and Principalities in the New Testament* has appeared in the *Quaestiones Disputatae* series (of which he is co-editor with Karl Rahner), but this is no adequate reflection of his importance in New Testament scholarship.

Born in 1900 and reared a Lutheran, Schlier received his theological training in Leipzig, Marburg, and Jena. Bultmann was his teacher and later his faculty colleague when Schlier came back to Marburg as *Privatdozent* from 1930 to 1935. During the Hitler years Schlier served as a pastor; and only after the War did he return to teaching, receiving the chair of New Testament in the Protestant Faculty at Bonn. His conversion to Catholicism came in 1953. Because of the custom in Germany that Catholic laymen do not teach in a theological faculty (a custom strange to Americans who tend to think of the German Church as liberal), Schlier has served since that time as an honorary professor in the Faculty of Philosophy and has lectured in the field of Early Christian Literature.

Schlier's conversion produced a theological debate in Germany, for here was a Bultmannian critic who found no contradiction between Catholicism and the Bible. His critical abilities were beyond question. In his early days he had written on the religious background of the Ignatian Epistles, and he was a specialist in the question of Gnostic influence on Early Christian Literature. He had contributed the commentary on Galatians to the *Meyer Kommentar,* the most prestigious of the Protestant New Testament commentary series. He was acknowledged as an authority on Ephesians, the New Testament book that brings up acutely the problem of the Church. Yet it was precisely his study of that Epistle that had been influential in leading him to Catholicism! (His commentary on Ephesians, published by him as a Catholic in 1957, is an important work.) Schlier's position, combined with the emergence of other first-rate modern German Catholic exegetes, has shattered the image of a Catholicism that could not tolerate biblical criticism or hold its own in the exegetical field.

Only if Schlier's commentaries and monographs become available in English will the American public have the opportunity of evaluating his work in its most scientific form, but the present essays allow, at least, a sampling of its richness. Some of the essays are more formally scholarly than others, but all should be easily readable to those interested in biblical work. The perceptive reader should be able to find echoes of Schlier's career and principal interests in the essays chosen. My own favourite is the one on "The State according to the New Testament"—it is a superb bit of Johannine exegesis, and its relevance is frighteningly apparent when one thinks of the Hitler state. Schlier's sensitivity to the theological and spiritual implications of the New Testament should open the eyes of all readers to the positive aspects of truly critical scholarship.

Raymond E. Brown

St. Mary's Seminary,
Baltimore, Maryland.

CHAPTER I

The Meaning and Function
of a Theology
of the New Testament*

The notion of what a theology of the New Testament, or a biblical theology, should be has often changed in the two hundred years of its history. Even today there is no general agreement,[1] though the field is being intensively cultivated, as is shown by the appearance of a number of works covering the whole subject and countless monographs on particular items. The considerations which follow can only be a supplement to the discussion which is already taking place,[2] a contribution

---

* This essay first appeared in English in *Dogmatic versus Biblical Theology*, ed. by H. Vorgrimler, translated by Kevin Smyth (1964), pp. 87—113. It is reprinted here by permission of the publishers, Helicon (Baltimore), Burns and Oates (London).

[1] F.-M. Braun (see next footnote), p. 221, remarks: "The terms 'biblical theology' and 'New Testament theology' have now become common expressions. However, those who use them attach such widely different meanings to them that they run the risk of nourishing serious confusion." Cf. C. Spicq, p. 564, V. Filson, pp. 71, 80, in the works cited in the next footnote.

[2] Cf. A. Bea, "Der heutige Stand der Bibelwissenschaft" in *Stimmen der Zeit* 153 (1953), pp. 91—104; R. Bultmann, *Theology of the New Testament*, vol. II (1955), "Epilogue", pp. 237—51; F.-M. Braun, "La théologie biblique" in *Revue Thomiste* 61 (1953), pp. 221—53; C. T. Craig, "Biblical Theology and the Rise of Historicism" in *JBL* 62 (1943), pp. 281—94; V. Filson, "Biblische Theologie in Amerika" in *TLZ* 75 (1950), pp. 71—80; W. Hillmann, "Wege zur neutestamentlichen Theologie" in *Wissenschaft und Weisheit* 14 (1951), pp. 56—67, 200—211; 15 (1952), pp. 15—32, 122—36; M. Meinertz, "Randglossen zu meiner Theologie des Neuen Testamentes" in

from an author—and this is their advantage and disadvantage—
to whom the question itself is still open.

I

The name of our field of works has indeed hardly changed
at all, and today it is by general consent the title for very different types of books. This shows that the name has obviously
anticipated for a long time the nature of the undertaking. Thus
the title can be a sort of guiding star for our enquiry, the
means of clarifying the principles and of grasping the meaning and task of a general presentation of New Testament
theology.

As the name implies, indicating the subject beforehand, this
is a theology of the *New Testament*. This brings in elements
which should tell in its general presentation. At the very least
it means that our work deals with the concepts, expressed or
implied, of the New Testament and with others. It is based
exclusively on texts taken from the New Testament. They are
put before the biblical theologian by the Church as part of the
inspired and sacred scriptures. They dominate, at various levels,
in her preaching, her catechism, her liturgy. Dogmatic theology
is constantly preoccupied with them because they are the
primary source of its information. Exegesis strives to disclose
the meaning of each particular text, and the 'Introduction to

TQ 132 (1952), pp. 411—31; id., "Sinn und Bedeutung der neutestamentlichen Theologie" in *MTZ* 5 (1954), pp. 159—70; Bo Reicke, "Einheitlichkeit
oder verschiedene 'Lehrbegriffe' in der neutestamentlichen Theologie" in *TZ* 9
(1953), pp. 401—15; R. Schnackenburg, "Die Botschaft des Neuen Testamentes" in *Heilige Schrift und Seelsorge* (1955), pp. 110—27; C. Spicq,
"L'avènement de la Théologie Biblique" in *Revue des sciences philosophi-
ques et théologiques* 35 (1951), pp. 561—74; E. Stauffer, "Prinzipienfragen
der neutestamentlichen Theologie" in *Evangelische Lutherische Kirchenzeitung* 4 (1950) 327—29; V. Warnach, "Gedanken zur neutestamentlichen
Theologie" in *Gloria Dei* 7 (1952), pp. 65—75; A. N. Wilder, "New Testament Theology" in *Transition in Study of the Bible Today and Tomorrow*, ed. by H. R. Willoughby (1947), pp. 419—36.

the New Testament' tries to throw light on their history and literary forms, by tracing the course of the earliest transmission of the texts. Since it is the theology of scripture which presents itself in such an ecclesiastical and theological context, its procedures, its set of concepts, its methods, its themes and even the basic structure of its presentation must be derived from its object and from nowhere else.

This means first of all that a New Testament theology questions the various books, or groups of writings, of which the New Testament consists, as to their theology. For the New Testament is composed of writings whose origin, contents, forms, intentions and meaning are very different, as exegesis and 'Introduction' show. The nature of the matters treated make it therefore preferable to begin, when seeking the basic theological principles of the New Testament, by investigating it in the light of the manifold diversity of the books. This naturally demands the procedure which has been eleaborated in exegesis, and in general in the explanation of historical texts.[3] This is the philological and historical method, which has as its object the straight-forward delineation and description of the theological contents of each particular book. To live up to its name, a theology of the New Testament must allow its concepts to be formed for it by the New Testament. This will always be a matter of approximation, for its world of concepts can only impose itself on the interpreter in so far as they silence his own, once the contents are really grasped. But on principle, a theology of the New Testament must tend towards a set of concepts suited to it, which are not scholastic or idealist, nor those of modern philosophy. They are pre-philosophical and pre-theological, and yet not just naïve. Their simplicity is radical, and couched in a language which is often worn with use. Literal translation will not do the job, and the speech of biblical theology cannot be just the 'language of Canaan' or popular piety,

[3] A. Bea, "Stand der Bibelwissenschaft", p. 100.

as is clear. This would merely show that the intention of the New Testament has not been grasped.

Further, theology of the New Testament means that the themes must be presented by the New Testament itself,[4] with all the variety and all the limitations which appear there. No doubt all the basic themes of theology are touched on somehow or other, and many are developed in different sets of variations. Thus for instance Christology, ecclesiology and eschatology come to mind. Other themes appear only marginally, as for instance creation; and for others only the key-word is given, as for instance in the weighty theme of offices in the Church. All this must be taken into consideration in a theology of the New Testament. At any rate, its subjects will not be imposed on it by a mature, that is, a highly developed dogmatic theology.

Finally, a theology of the New Testament will prove itself to be such by handling the themes set it by the New Testament in the way indicated to it in each case by the various books of the New Testament. It will pay attention to the basic movement of thought in each book or group of books, and try to integrate their intention into the structure of its presentation. Thus, to my mind, the theology of the New Testament, when dealing with St Paul, will develop his theology as a function of the Event, in whose basic traits he sees comprehended the history and existence of mankind. This is the resurrection of Jesus Christ, the crucified Lord, who has been exalted in view of his Coming, so that his being raised up was an eschatological or final act.

If one tries to meet all these demands, which the New Testament itself—as exegesis, form-criticism and history of tradition have taught us to understand it—imposes on its theology, the theology of the New Testament presents at first a very remarkable picture. It is composed of a whole series of theologies, each with very different horizons, stand-points and ways of

---

[4] Van der Ploeg in *RB* 55 (1948), pp. 108 ff., (quoted in F.-M. Braun, *Revue Thomiste* 61 [1953], p. 224).

looking at things, with concepts developed in very different ways and often diverging in content, with themes of many kinds, or simply hints of themes, and with basic structures which vary widely. On the whole, it is a theology, or rather a collection of different theologies, of a markedly fragmentary character. Often the lines are not fully drawn. A theological statement is intoned, it rings out here and there, and then suddenly is buried again in deep silence. A presentation of New Testament theology will have to pay particular attention to this, even though in consequence subjects may appear to be treated with little regard to their true proportions. However, this character of the fragmentary is shared by New Testament theology, as a matter of principle, with dogmatic or speculative theology. This latter is indeed systematic, but this does not mean that it could, somewhat like a system of philosophy, offer a system that would be in any way comprehensive and complete. In this sense the words of 1 Corinthians 13:9, "We know ... in part", hold good for dogmatic theology too.

But let us look at the other element. A New Testament theology is by virtue of name and concept also a *theology* of the New Testament. That means firstly, as regards tendencies that are still at work to-day, a very formal contrast. New Testament theology does not set out to be the presentation of a historical process. It is not at all a history of the religion of primitive Christianity. Nor is it a history of New Testament theology. From the standpoint of a history of primitive Christianity, and indeed from a purely 'historical' stand-point in general, a theology of the New Testament is an absurdity, first of all because it is 'theology' and then because historically there is no justification for restricting it to the collection of books in the New Testament.[5] Such a restriction is already a piece of theology, and the starting-point of New Testament theology. E. Stauffer

[5] Cf. W. Wrede, *Über Aufgabe und Methode der sogenannten neutestamentlichen Theologie* (1897).

indeed maintains that this is what entitles it to the name of theology.[6] But this is a mistake. He has indeed taken the title 'theology' seriously, because in his *New Testament Theology* he does not describe a process immanent to history, the 'development' of a religion. He tries to give the transcendent process of salvation and its Christocentric history. But history, even the theology of history, is not enough to make up a theology, not even the theology of the theology of the New Testament. It fails most completely when this "theology of history"—as the benevolent critic J. Jeremias remarked about Stauffer—is in danger of becoming a "Gnosis of the process of salvation".[7]

However, the name 'theology of the New Testament' of course means more than a formal contrast to any sort of presentation of history, important though this demarcation may be. As we have seen, when the New Testament is interrogated for its theology it answers first of all by giving various theologies, according to each group of writings and, indeed, according to individual books. There is for instance a distinctive theology of the Letter to the Hebrews. But the name of our discipline, and therefore the concept foreshadowed by it, is not concerned merely with a number of different theologies. It has *one* in view, *the* theology of the New Testament. This it claims to produce because there exists a previous theological conviction of the unity of the New Testament, which has in the course of a long process impressed itself on the mind of the Church and received its approbation.

The claim to unity is also based on the concept and essence of theology. It is true that theology, meaning primarily dogmatic theology, is never more than a fragmentary presentation. But just as surely, it presupposes a hidden, inner unity which is always present. This is precisely what is indicated by its systematic character. The end and object is to draw the hidden unity out of its concealment as much as possible, and to make it

[6] Cf. "Prinzipienfragen", p. 328.
[7] *Evangelische Lutherische Kirchenzeitung* 4 (1950), p. 157.

known. And only so far as it is *en route,* so to speak, to this inner unity, do its particular propositions show themselves in their full light. For the place they have in this inner unity is given them by God. The same holds good for a theology of the New Testament. Hence its presentation must always look to the inner unity and take the way to this goal. The task must not be performed too hastily; the immediate discrepancies in theological views must not be overlooked or passed by. But the more the presentation penetrates into the central unity of the theology of the New Testament, the more it will be theology.

How is it possible to penetrate through all its variety to the unity of the theology of the Testament? At this point New Testament theology shows clearly that it needs not only the methods of history and philology, but also a method of theology. Such a method is of course always needed, but here the question as to its nature beomes more acute. Indeed, it would perhaps be better not to say 'method', and rather ask: by what route shall we gain entrance to the real content; on what road does the reality spoken of by the New Testament disclose itself? The way is open to one only in so far as one actually marches along it. And by this we mean that while one must make full use of historical criticism and linguistic research, one must also be involved in the reality which confronts one in the texts of the New Testament. But this involvement takes place in the act of faith!

In any case, the historical and philosophical approach is never enough to disclose the sense of a historical text. To confine oneself to history and linguistics when reading Plato, without ever giving oneself over to his thought, which means—since his thought is no isolated process—without ever trying to share his experience, would be to miss for ever the vision of reality which Plato discovered and from which he lived and thought. Something of the same kind is true of all historical texts. Interpretation, when it really reaches the heart of the matter, is never just a technique: it is a vital process. One could apply all the instruments available from history and linguistics to interpreting the New Testament, but never yield oneself to the basic experience out of which the New Testament itself speaks, that is, faith. If so, one would never recognize the reality which finds utterance in the New Testament.

In saying this, we do not mean to disregard the demand which the New Testament, as a document from ancient times, makes upon us, namely that we translate it objectively, using the means offered by historical science and philology. And likewise, we do not thereby mean to turn the faith into a method. But we mean that the interpretation of the New Testament is also to become part of our own real experience, as should all interpretation. The historical and linguistic explanation of the New Testament must be at the service of faith, if it is to reach through the text to the thing itself and the intrinsic connexions of things. Here this means to have insight into the links of salvation, as described in the theology of the New Testament.

The theology of the New Testament, like every theology which presents the faith, is a matter of the *intellectus fidei*. As C. Spicq says: "The object of this theology is not the words nor even the thoughts of the inspired writers, but the reality itself to which they bear witness. The theologian, convinced of the objectivity of revelation and of its radical unity, scrutinizes the divine mystery in its biblical expression. He discerns for example all the components of a certain theme, gives precisions about their articulation and development, allots full value to its multiple aspects, displays its connexions with other themes, and using its enunciations but reaching beyond them, gives the believer the possibility of attaining the divine object itself" (*Revue Biblique*, 1951). The *intellectus fidei*, therefore, penetrates to the thing itself *(res)*, and its unity, and so constitutes itself as theology. Thereby the theology of the New Testament proves itself to be an involvement of the person in history, not just a historical science.

This means here that it is a science where the personal history

of him who practises it is involved, a science in whose exercise
the practitioner must let his own history, his 'existence', be determined and moulded by that which is disclosed in the course of
interpretation. One cannot practise a science which has to do
with history, unless one surrenders one's own personal history
to the word which confronts him, from the pages of a history
which at first was external to him. Faith is the necessary self-
surrender to the history which addresses us from the New
Testament. In faith I tread the path upon which the Church,
always going before me, has met his history, in order to meet
it ever anew. The theology of the New Testament presses on to
the reality of the matter, there thought of and expressed,
reaches its unity and so raises itself to be a theology, if and in so
far as it is itself a personally historical process, none other than
the movement of the *intellectus fidei,* the thinking of the faith.

II

From this way of understanding New Testament theology,
there now follow certain consequences for its structure. Where
is this theology to make a start if it is to realize its concept?
M. Meinertz says that "by the nature of things", the presentation
of Jesus and his doctrine must come at the beginning of New
Testament theology.[8] Hence the first major section of his book
(*Theologie des Neuen Testaments*, 1950) deals with the teaching
person and history of Jesus. R. Bultmann (*Theology of the New
Testament*, 2 vols., 1958–9) says that New Testament theology
begins only with the Kerygma, the preaching of the primitive
community, so that Jesus' own proclamation cannot be part of
a theology of the New Testament, though as a presupposition
it must be allowed its say. So he puts it as the first chapter of the
first part of his *Theology*, where he develops the "Presupposi-

[8] Cf. *MTZ* 5 (1954), p. 163.

tions and Motifs of New Testament Theology". The second chapter deals with "The Kerygma of the Earliest Church", a third with "The Kerygma of the Hellenistic Church aside from Paul". But is this not to let historical view-points dominate theology; or, as the case may be, is not to introduce the *genre* of history into theology?[9] What has a history or a 'picture' of Jesus to do with the presentation of the theology of the New Testament? Jesus, after all, did not begin the theology of the New Testament; and the theological reflexions of the New Testament writers are not continuations of the theological reflexions of Jesus. Of course, the Event of Jesus, his person, actions and words, preceded the theology of the New Testament writers, so that there is no such thing as New Testament theology apart from his Event. But in what way did it precede the theology of the New Testament?

Briefly, in this way: the history of Jesus, which called forth faith, makes the theological enunciations of the New Testament possible, being their *raison d'être* in every way. It is "the Call, the answer to which is first represented by the testimony to faith, given by the primitive community". Thus far J. Jeremias, from whom this formulation is taken, and Bultmann, who means the same thing, are correct. But Jeremias apparently means by the Call only the preaching of Jesus. And Stauffer is therefore correct in countering him—and thereby Bultmann—by saying: "To the self-revelation of Jesus belong not only his word but his actions, his life and his death". Since the whole history of Jesus is involved, Stauffer says that he sees no possibility of "presenting Jesus Christ, really and fully, within the framework of a biblical theology" (*Evangelische Lutherische Kirchenzeitung*, 4 [1950] pp. 157, 329).

But is there not also a reason why on principle we should not insert the history of Jesus into the presentation of the theology of the New Testament, not even as its presupposition? Have

---

[9] Cf. Bo Reicke, *TZ* 9 (1953), p. 407.

we any access at all to Jesus and to his history, except by means of the 'personal-historical' approach, that is, by means of an interpretation of the gospels which is given by faith, and therefore through the witnesses who are the authoritative interpreters of the life of Jesus, and who alone can reveal it? We ask this question not merely on the practical grounds that form-criticism and history of tradition have shown how inextricably narrative and interpretation, story and message, are interwoven. The historical interpretation which prescinds from the interpretation and the message of the evangelists leaves scarcely anything over!

However this negative result, which comes from very careful investigations of acknowledged worth, is only a symptom of the reason given by the nature of the matter itself, that is, by the person and the history of Jesus. We put the question therefore also on theological grounds. Is the Jesus of whom the gospels speak, is the 'real' Jesus, the Jesus Christ of this earth in his history, accessible to us in any other way, except as he was known and attested by the witness in the light of the faith of Easter? Is the real Jesus ever disclosed to us, except in the interpretation of the witnesses, who objectively refuse to disregard faith as the presupposition of their knowledge? Has the real Jesus ever been anyone but he who was so known and attested? Is there an 'historical' Jesus, to be grasped by 'historical' means? Is not the so-called 'historical' Jesus either the real challenging (*geschichtlich*) Jesus of the gospels—or one disclosed in a fundamentally inappropriate way, namely, apart from the *intellectus fidei*? Such a Jesus would not be truly disclosed but only invented, thought out that is, by historical fantasy. Here then is the theological reason for our question, a reason however which is precisely proved true by historical research. Is there a Jesus except as he comes by the word of the Church, from the very beginning and by the nature of things?

The meagre success of every effort at arriving at a 'life of Jesus', their heavy-handed psychology and fantasy confirm the fact that from the very start and by his nature Jesus only exists for us through and throughout the gospels, that is, in the voice of the Church, which alone renders his reality as it is. However, we must go back a little. The history of Jesus is the presupposition, not a part of New Testament theology. Here we mean his whole history, the event of his person, his deeds and his word. The whole event however reaches us in its full and undisguised reality only in the answer which the gospels, and indeed the whole testimony of the New Testament give. The gospels, which embraced and expounded that history (rhema: 'word') in their 'word' (rhema) must be the first to be interrogated as to their exposition, so that their theology may be quarried out.

It is significant therefore that Stauffer, Meinertz and Bultmann, each for different reasons, omit all systematic treatment of the theology of the synoptic gospels. As we have already pointed out (see pp. 9 f.), Bultmann's outline in the first part of his work confines itself to history, as even the titles of the sections show. It is the same in the third part of the work, which bears the very revealing title: "The Development toward the Ancient Church". Here the discussion ranges for the most part outside the New Testament writings. Only the second part of his work has as headings, "The Theology of Paul", "The Theology of John". And this is the only part where theological content dominates the arrangement. Thus the very outline of the whole work makes it clear that, according to Bultmann, only St Paul and St John have theologies in the proper of the word.[10]

Admittedly, there is a question here. Can a New Testament theology begin with a presentation of that of the synoptics, without more ado? Chronologically—though that does not matter—and even causally, was it not preceded by another theology, because the synoptic testimony was preceded by another? When one interrogates the New Testament, do there not exist before

[10] J. Bonsirven in his instructive work, *Theology of the New Testament* (1963), at first develops a Christology on the basis of the four gospels, and in doing so hardly gives a treatment of Johannine theology at all.

all its books and all its theology, certain concrete testimonies, which already contain theological enunciations, and indeed precisely those which were to dominate the whole theology of the New Testament as it took shape in the books? Even before there were any New Testament writings, had not the 'word' of the history of Jesus Christ crystallized into formulations and did these not impose themselves in various ways on the New Testament writings, in the form of the confession of faith of the primitive Church? These formulas are the primary utterance of the revelation of Jesus Christ as it voiced itself. They are the primary response of the Community as it threw itself open to him. Do they not therefore carry within them the primary explanation of the salvific act of God in Jesus Christ, an explication which is then developed in the New Testament writings and their proclamation and their theology?[11]

In fact, the history of New Testament tradition has shown us with ever-increasing clarity that the New Testament writings enshrine a number of fixed traditions of the faith, and in particular formulas of the faith, which give a stamp to the books and to their proclamation, consciously or unconsciously.[12] A fixed form of transmission, for instance, decisively influenced the formation of the Passion narrative and the theology behind it. Outlines of the original proclamation of the faith and certain formulas of belief come up constantly and at decisive moments in the Acts of the Apostles and the New Testament epistles, and then make themselves felt as the rule of faith developed in the

[11] See the author's *Die Zeit der Kirche* (3rd ed. 1962), pp. 214 ff.; Schnackenburg, "Botschaft des NT", p. 113, speaks of the 'primitive apostolic preaching of salvation' and the 'community theology based upon it' as the 'first steps of primitive Christian theology'.
[12] Cf. R. Bultmann, *Die Geschichte der synoptischen Tradition* (2nd ed. 1931), pp. 297 ff., E. T.: *The History of the Synoptic Tradition* (1963); M. Dibelius, *Die Formgeschichte des Evangeliums* (2nd ed. 1933), pp. 178 ff., E. T.: *From Tradition to Gospel* (1933); W. Hillmann, *Aufbau und Deutung der synoptischen Leidensbriefe* (1941); K. H. Schelkle, *Die Passion in der Verkündigung des Neuen Testaments* (1949); J. R. Geiselmann, *Jesus der Christus* (1951).

texts. Thus, to take one example which may stand for others, the normative 'good word' which St Paul cites in 1 Corinthians 15:3—5, is used by the Apostle himself as the basis of his theological explanation of the resurrection of the dead in 1 Corinthians 15. In the Letter to the Hebrews, a confession of faith is expounded by texts of scripture used in an esoteric way (*Schriftgnosis*). Must not a theology of the New Testament take this fact into account and therefore try first of all to present the archaic theology of these authoritative primary forms of the Message, the theology which is unfolded in the writings of the New Testament?

This is of course a very difficult undertaking. For it includes working out on different levels those traditions and formulas of the faith which were minted in the primitive Church, and which then continued to colour the expositions which followed. This study would leave many questions open simply on account of the state of our sources, but it is above all the extremely fragmentary character of the relatively few recognizable primitive formulas of revelation which makes it hard to grasp the theological thoughts which find expression in them. All the same one will be able to ascertain theological principles which form the effective basis of the theology of the New Testament writings, a theology which is both bound by them and develops them. This makes it clear that the theology which expresses itself in the New Testament writings already implies the presence before its eyes of the apostolic tradition, as the proximate source of faith. To expound the theology of this proximate source of faith for New Testament theology would not be to import a foreign body.

With this as a starting-point, the theology of the New Testament writings could then be presented as the exposition of these basic traditions. And here the sequence of the writings and groups of writings to be interrogated for their theology will play a role. This sequence is hard to fix clearly. But at any rate, the date of origin of this book or that cannot be accepted as the decisive word. Nor will one be able simply to follow the order of the books in the Canon, for this order had other than theological causes. Undoubtedly, the Acts of the Apostles will be investigated along with the Gospel of St Luke, and the Letters of St John along with his gospel. To organize the work, one could perhaps take the proximity of content in a given book or group of books, with regard to the underlying formulated traditions of faith, and likewise the degree of development in the theology in question.

At any rate, one will first treat the theology of each of the synoptic gospels. For these are, if one may say so, none other than an interpretation and expansion, from their several proper theological stand-points, of a common tradition of faith, and preaching, somewhat in the form which Acts 10: 36-43 still preserves for us. In all the synoptic gospels the Lord Jesus Christ is meant to speak, he whose death and resurrection (and manifest Coming) were a certain truth of faith, and who spoke in his whole historical coming—in his word and in his deeds, which were already gathered and circulated orally, and to some extent in writing. The theology of these gospels may be deciphered above all from the manner in which they interpreted, arranged and modified each item of the contents of tradition.[13] The 'studies in the theology of St Luke' by H. Conzelmann[14] are exemplary from the point of view of method in such work. But even his work shows how much a theology of the New Testament has still to accomplish at this point. The theology of St Luke could of course only be derived from the whole gospel, including therefore chapters 1 and 2, and from the Acts of the Apostles. Part of the theology is precisely the fact that the evangelist St Luke takes the salvific history of the Lord Jesus Christ back even to his birth, and continues it in the history of his 'Name', which is also the history of the Holy

[13] Cf. Hillmann, "Wege zur neutestamentlichen Theologie", p. 57; Schnackenburg, "Botschaft des NT", p. 114.
[14] H. Conzelmann, *The Theology of St Luke* (1960).

Spirit in the Apostles and in the Church till its constitution in Rome.

It is hard to decide whether the theology of the individual synoptics, including the Acts of the Apostles, should be followed by the theology of the Pauline or of the Johannine writings. For taking the latter first, we have grounds in the fact that it too seems to offer a theological interpretation of the basic preaching, in the form of a gospel. But if one looks closer, one recognizes how far the Gospel of St John has departed from the synoptic concept of how a basic outline of the preaching may be expanded and filled out from historical material still available. The fourth gospel is very deliberately an interpretation of the well-worked-out gospel matter which lay before him, very like that of our synoptics, but not identical with it. And the interpretation which follows is given from the stand-point which was already authoritative, but which is now made express and thought out in its consequences: that the history of Jesus is the history of the Word, and must also be presented as such. The Logos (Word) in its action, and the action of the Word, must be presented in a gospel. This the Gospel of St John shows clearly on every page, so that it is monstrous, for instance, to separate the so-called prologue from the rest of the gospel when handling the theology of this gospel.

But the theological reflection of this gospel is also strongly developed in other respects. This can be seen for instance in its doctrine of the Spirit, and above all from something that is mostly under the surface but is very active, namely its reflexion on the sacraments and on the Church. Finally, the Johannine theology, if we take in also the Johannine epistles, already casts its net very wide. The salvific action of the Word is expressly and frequently considered in its effects on the existence of man, whom the Word has assumed. And if the Apocalypse, which at any rate shows objective points of contact with the Gospel of St John, is to be dealt with here also—and I do not know where else it can be placed—then the scope of Johannine theology becomes even greater. For the so-called revelation of St John continues, if one looks at it from a theological standpoint, the history of the Word made flesh, in so far as it uncovers the process of his Coming in the fate of the world, through and throughout its history, and thereby shows itself to be a prophetic gospel.

With these peculiar properties of the Johannine writings in mind, one will rather develop the Pauline theology in the second section, in a theology of the New Testament. The Apostle St Paul writes no gospel. But from a theological point of view, he is closer to the synoptic gospels than the Gospel of St John. His epistles let us see how closely he in particular links up with the formulas of faith of the primitive Church and its other traditions. The basic experience which he had on the road to Damascus provided for him personally the certainty of the legitimacy of his gospel and his apostolate. Theologically it marked out for him his horizon, and determined his outlook. Still, it is not for him the source and object of his theology. What he thinks over theologically, in the certainty and illumination communicated to him at Damascus and by the light there received, are the traditions of faith handed on by the primitive community, in which traditions the Lord speaks for St Paul. (This remains true, even if one does not accept entirely the explanation of 1 Corinthians 11:23 put forward by O. Cullmann, *Tradition* [1954], pp. 9–12).

St Paul links up with the traditions by a manifold interpretation of the Christological message, and in manifold ponderings of its consequences for the existence of man and the history of the world. And this link-up, as it does its work of interpretation and develops its consequences, is accomplished often by him in conscious theological argumentation and in relatively developed theological concepts. All this is precisely the reason why the Pauline theology is the easiest to grasp, and occupies spontaneously the major portion of a theology of the New Testament. The Letters of St Paul, the legacy which has been preserved to us in writing, are also the only writings of the New Testament which allow us to place this or that item of theology in something like a line of development; or better, which allows us to see traces of different levels of theological thinking.[15]

The Pauline theology, on account of its close links with the tradition of the community which, to be sure, it unfolds on the basis of a personal experience and in a theology developed independently, may then be placed before the Johannine. And if this be accepted, one will continue it with the theology of the other New Testament epistles which remain. Here of course the First Letter of St Peter and the Letter to the Hebrews are the most weighty. The theology which is at work in them and which they put forward also rests on acquired and developed traditions of faith. The smaller epistles of the New Testament have likewise their own place within the totality of New Testament theology. But this still does not mean that they offer even remotely a complete theology, so that for instance one would be entitled to speak of a 'concept of doctrine' in the Letter of St Jude. Investigating these epistles for theological propositions will heighten our awareness that New Testament theology is composed primarily of a number of fragments of theology.

To be sure, with this presentation of the theological structure of the individual books or groups of writings in the New Testament, the task of writing a theology of the New Testament has not been performed. And if what has been said above about the nature and exigencies of a 'theology' is to be observed carefully even in the investigation of the theology of individual books and groups of writings, it is all the more important when we come to the point where we must leave individual items and come to the theology of the whole, of the New Testament. The task of composing such a theology is only done when we

[15] A clear impression of this is given by L. Cerfaux, *Christ in the Theology of St Paul* (1962).

have succeeded in showing the unity of the different 'theologies'. Only then does the name make sense and the concept of 'a theology' find verification. That there is such a unity, that ultimately there is no contradiction between the various theological principles and utterances, is from the point of view of theology a presupposition which derives from the inspiration and canonicity of the New Testament or the Bible. The unity thus envisaged is however a real one, not one so mysteriously hidden that it cannot be made known at least at a certain level. The structure of this unity may already be glimpsed in the elementary theology of those formulas of faith which have influenced to a greater or lesser extent the whole of the New Testament. And now, when the theology of the individual sources has been brought to light, its unity must be made as explicit as possible.

How is this to be done? The best way, no doubt, is to take some major themes, such as God, the Reign of God, Jesus Christ, his death and resurrection, the Spirit, the Church, the new life, the faith and so on, and use them to indicate how the various theologies are intrinsically related to each other. In this way the hidden basis and the mysterious bond of the single New Testament theology will be illuminated. This is a difficult undertaking, and one which must skirt many dangers. One such danger is that the individuality of the theological conception of a given book may lose again the contours which have been drawn for it, when the unity of New Testament theology is put too much into the foreground. For this unity is a background. Another danger is that we might—expressly or otherwise—make the theology of one book or group of books the norm of what is 'Theology of the New Testament' and try to arrange all other theological concepts to fit it.

The theology of the New Testament is built on the basis of all the New Testament writings, though of course not all of them contribute in the same proportion.

One must also avoid the temptation of trying to find the unity of New Testament theology merely in the unity of a single

basic theme, as for instance in the so-called 'Event of Christ'.
Here misgivings should arise, not only because the theology of
the New Testament would thus be reduced to Christology, but
because the real task would be lost sight of, which is precisely
to show the unity of the different interpretations of the 'Event
of Christ'. Finally, one will try to avoid leaving the unity of
New Testament theology too much to generalities. Like every
real theology, it must be concrete to be authentic.

Here I might add my own opinion that one must not let it
all come down to the developed credal formulas of the ancient
Church, as though the Creeds were the result of New Testament
theology and the title-deeds of its unity. These formulas have
been discussed very helpfully by Stauffer and Meinertz. But we
must remember that the primitive formulas of faith were at
hand in the Church even before the New Testament, and that
the ancient Creeds do not derive solely from the New Testament.
The historical process was more or less that both oral and
written traditions came together and were crystallized in the
Creeds, and that the apostolic heritage was committed independently in each case to scripture and to the Creeds. The processes influenced each other reciprocally.

For an integral theology of the New Testament one more
thing is wanted. We must demonstrate its basic unity with that
of the Old Testament, or show its relation to Old Testament
theology. After all, it is only in combination with the Old Testament that the New has the character of sacred and canonical
scripture. As things are to-day, however, it will be a long time
before such a condition is more than a wish. For here too over-
hasty and patch-work solutions will not do. And why should
not a theological science confess its limitations and its deficien-
cies in a given epoch? It must only keep in mind, recalling it
constantly by means of individual investigations (as is in fact
done), that the theology of the Old Testament, in general and in
particular, has been taken up into the theology of the New
Testament in such a way that they mutually determine and

illuminate each other. Thus only a biblical theology can bring into full light of day the fulness of a New Testament theology.

III

Such a theology of the New Testament has much significance for theology in general. It is of course most fruitful for the discipline out of which it grew, the exegesis of the New Testament. And here it is well to add that there are various reasons why Catholic scientific cooperation on the theology of the New Testament came so relatively late. (Meinertz, introducing his *Theologie des Neuen Testaments* in 1950 could say with reason: "This is the first general presentation of New Testament theology from the Catholic side, that makes any claim to fulness".) One reason is that even in the nineteenth and the beginning of the twentieth century, sacred scripture was rather in the background in Catholic theology. One can adduce the fact that "Catholic exegesis stood too long on the defensive, and so neglected too much the rich exegetical results of which it could have made use." [16] One can also emphasize the priority—justifiable in itself—of dogmatic theology. [17]

But there is another decisive reason, as it appears to me. For a long time, biblical or New Testament theology felt itself, by reason of origins, to be expressly opposed to Orthodox Protestantism and to its dogmatic theology. This opposition was understood differently during the 'Age of Enlightenment', of 'Idealism', of 'Positivism'. But in any case it marked off biblical theology from the orthodoxy of Protestantism. This polemical attitude, which went back of course to the Reformation principle of *sola scriptura*, went so far in certain circumstances that biblical theology looked on itself as a substitute for dogmatic

[16] Bea, "Stand der Bibelwissenschaft", p. 101.
[17] Cf. Meinertz, "Sinn und Bedeutung", p. 161.

theology. But the work of biblical theology on the New Testament made it clear that a New Testament theology was to be justified, not by its opposition to Protestantism, but by the necessities of exegesis and dogmatic theology. And only then could the misgivings of Catholic theology be overcome. First came monographs on individual subjects of biblical theology, then partial presentations of biblical theology, and finally general coverage. Biblical or New Testament theology had discovering its objective starting-point.

Exegesis is presupposed by a theology of the New Testament; and exegesis needs such a theology. Without it, exegesis will not for instance easily find the correct basis for the exposition of an individual book of the New Testament. And without it, the work of interpretation easily succumbs to the danger of isolating individual texts from the whole. For instance : if one knows, from a presentation of the theology of the New Testament, St Paul's general attitude toward the Law, one will not miss the fact that his statements in the Letter to the Galatians are to some extent one-sided. And if one knows the Pauline theology of the Law, one will not be liable to misundstand the Law as a code of morals or as a past historical situation. This contribution of a theology of the New Testament to exegesis is also one of the reasons for its existence. In the long run, it came to be because of the *excursus,* added to the commentaries with regard to individual theological concepts and themes, out of which grew monographies. On the other hand, a careful and clear-sighted exegesis will always be able to check critically any theology of the New Testament, as indeed it will always wish to. All New Testament disciplines are in the end at the service of New Testament theology; so too exegesis, the more it penetrates to reality at particular points, the more it will put its results at the disposition of New Testament theology as a whole, and thus help it to launch ever further into the deep.

The 'History of Dogma' as it is called, will also benefit by a theology of the New Testament, for in such history are debated the theological considerations in which the faith of the primitive Church ponders the claims of the foundation of the faith. The faith of the primitive Church is the faith of the Church at its origin, and this, even from the purely historical point of view, is something unique. But its chief distinction is that it remains decisive, as the divinely-constituted and permanent source, for the later development of the truths of faith.[18]

New Testament theology has special significance for dogmatic theology, and so for the theological effort whereby, when the faith of the Church has been collected from all its sources, theological decisions are taken with regard to present-day concepts. Dogmatic theology is not confined to the New Testament as such for its information; it has before it a New Testament which has been illuminated, even with regard to its theological intentions, by an objective development of its theology. When the Bible or the New Testament, as the case may be, has thus been rendered transparent, the dogmatic theologian is forced to a much more radical re-thinking of the truths of faith than he is used to when reading the New Testament merely in the light of his own theological questioning and his own theological answers.

Sacred scripture, propounded according to its theology, demands for instance of the dogmatic theologian a constantly new effort to pinpoint certain fundamental concepts of faith.[19] It reminds the theologian of the basic scriptural concepts of the nature of man, which have long fallen into oblivion, and calls for new efforts of discussion. Or it brings up certain fundamental concepts which have often become blurred, such as 'Kingdom of God', 'Saviour', 'Grace' (*Charis*), and forces the theologian to clarify his notions and enunciate their truths more in accordance with the primary and objective sense. It urges dogmatic theology to take some theological notion and work

[18] Cf. K. Rahner, *Inspiration in the Bible* (2nd rev. ed. 1964), esp. pp. 43, 44.
[19] Cf. Schnackenburg, "Botschaft des NT", pp. 117 ff.

it out more deeply than hitherto by showing its presence and proportion in the totality of New Testament theology. What 'Glory' (*Doxa*) means, for instance, precisely when considered in the context of its manifold shades of meaning, is as yet relatively virgin soil to dogma.

And the theology of the New Testament can also put before dogmatic theology certain comprehensive themes, in whose theological explanation the biblical foundations have hitherto counted far too little. For instance, what the theology of the New Testament has been working out with regard to 'History as a process of salvation' or 'Eschatology', or the sacramental foundations of the new life and so on, will surely affect the dogmatic explanations. It is well known, for instance, that what has been worked out with regard to the Church has already borne fruit for theology, and even for the authentic decisions of the teaching authority. The gaps that may be noticed in dogmatic theology will also be pointed out by a New Testament theology. Must not dogmatic theology begin to consider, in all its ramifications, what the 'Word of God' implies as a means of salvation, and ask itself in what sense it is a means of salvation?

Finally, a thoroughgoing presentation of the theology of the New Testament, especially as a whole, is a challenge to the dogmatic theologian to investigate and check the formal structure of theology as a whole. Dogma is unchangeable, but that does not imply that the outlines of dogmatic theology are unchangeable. It must think over anew the process of its presentation, which is not merely conventional or technical, if biblical theology on the whole shows a general structure so different from that of dogmatic theology.[20] After all, biblical theology is not merely the theology of the original faith of the Church. It is also the theology of the inspired scriptural testimony, and therefore the main source of dogmatics. There are signs that dogmatic theology is already taking up the duties imposed on

[20] Cf. Geiselmann, *Jesus der Christus*, pp. 171 ff.

it by the theology of the New Testament (though not by it alone), as is shown by the new outline of theology offered for instance by Karl Rahner.[21]

Thus the theology of the New Testament, expressly or otherwise, puts many urgent questions to dogmatic theology. But this is not from any secret, perhaps unconscious will to replace dogmatic theology by its own elaborations, nor from any desire to make itself the norm of dogmatic theology. It is still aware of the fact that theological knowledge is finally won, by theological means, in dogmatic theology and finds expression there. For dogmatic theology, based on scripture and tradition (no matter how one determines their relationship more closely), has to think out the whole deposit of faith in the Church and bring it forward in present-day concepts.

But the theology of the New Testament also knows, from an experience gained gradually in painful and often controversial work, what radical and pure power of thought, what riches of basic theological insight and wisdom is given to the Church in the sacred scripture, and especially in the New Testament. It strives, in its own place, to serve dogmatic theology and indeed the Church's thinking in general, by casting light on theology in so far as it is attainable in scripture, particularly in the New Testament, and bringing thereto an expert and immediate knowledge. "Sacred scripture cannot be too highly estimated", says St Bonaventure when discussing the place of its study in theology.[22]

What has been said here does not exhaust the significance of a theology of the New Testament. But to indicate its uses in the preaching and catechism of the Church—and even in its controversies—would take us too far afield.

---

[21] Cf. K. Rahner, *Theological Investigations*, vol. I (1961), pp. 1—37.
[22] Cf. *Wissenschaft und Weisheit* 14 (1951), pp. 1 ff.

CHAPTER II

Biblical and Dogmatic Theology

I

Biblical theology, which we are here considering from the point of view of a theology of the New Testament, presupposes a particular conception of the New Testament. This is provided chiefly by exegesis, literary study and the history of the Canon. These show the New Testament to be in the first place a collection of writings, religious in content and various in scale, from the age of primitive Christianity. The writings come from the hand of various authors, some known, some unknown. They arose in different places within the sphere of the early Christian mission and were intended for different recipients. They speak the Greek of that age, but in very different ways, and belong to different literary genres. Very different situations prompted them, their sources are very various, and they pursue different purposes in very different ways with different ability. On the other hand they all have *one* event before their eyes and seek to bear witness to it. They aim at informing their readers that God has revealed himself in Jesus Christ and thereby has affected in a new way their own lives and those of all men. They all give expression to the mysterious and concrete self-disclosure of God in the person and history of Jesus, his work, cross, resurrection, advent in the Spirit, presence in the Church's word and sign, his coming at the end of the world.

The various writings contained in the New Testament have one theme, God's self-revelation in Jesus Christ. They are entirely writings of their own age. And from the beginning they conceived themselves to be messages or letters from men tho whom the revelation-event was entrusted in a special way and who recognized, formed and proclaimed the true claim made by the tradition of revelation. Because they had met the risen or exalted Christ and by the power of the Holy Spirit manifesting him in his truth, the authors of these writings knew themselves to be authentic and authoritative witnesses of this event, who wrote down authentic, authoritative and "inspired" testimony to it. They claimed despite all their human and historical limitations to present plainly and without distortion, enlightened by the Spirit of truth, what God had delivered in Jesus Christ.

Their claim met with the assent of the Church, which declared precisely these and only these writings to be themselves the rule of faith, the "Canon". These writings themselves elicited that assenting judgment. That happened in a long process of discoveny which is difficult for us now to disentangle. The process involved a gradual sifting of the stock of written tradition. By it the fundamental and authoritative written tradition of he revelation-event imposed itself on the Church's experience.

But for the theology of the New Testament, the New Testament is not merely this historical but at the same time inspired and regulative collection of varied writings on the one theme. For biblical theology, another feature of the New Testament is worthy of note. The book presents the testimony to God's revelation in Jesus Christ in a faith which is already engaged in reflection on itself. It demonstrates that the revelation never occurred or found expression in language in any other way than by kindling both faith and thought in faith and by prompting reflection on that faith. The event came to light in and through the believing interpretation of those who declared and transmitted it. The degree of reflection varies. In this respect, for example, the Gospel according to Mark will not be regarded as standing on the same level as the Letter to the Hebrews. But one of the assured results of the often misunderstood form-criticism and editorial history of the text, is that we can see even in the synoptic gospels a definite conception of the faith at work shaping and arranging. On occasion the believing thought which accompanies the experience of faith may reduce the Jesus-event almost to no more than the cross and resurrection and it may reflect on these only in regard to their cosmic, soteriological, anthropological and ecclesiological consequences. That is of course the case in the Pauline epistles. The very fact, however, that the New Testament witness to the faith is of that kind, instructs the reader to take up the reflection and elucidate the import and interconnections of the explicit or implicit theological considerations of the New Testament and develop them.

In this the biblical theology of the New Testament can appeal to a third characteristic of this writing which is also of importance for its relation to dogmatic theology. It is a question of what we might call the essentially open character of its statements. And this in turn is based on a peculiar plenitude, which consists in the fact that what is said contains things unsaid, and the statement flows from what is unsaid. These writings, we noted, were intended for recipients of their own epoch. But they also in fact make a claim beyond those to whom they were addressed and do so not as general ideas or maxims, but *in* what they actually say to the congregations and faithful of that time. Perhaps for that reason we do not really know, for example, for whom John's gospel was written. At all events the Letter to the Colossians can and is to be exchanged without more ado for one to Laodicea. In the pastoral epistles the Pauline gospel expressly appears as a legacy which God will maintain until the Last Day and which Timothy is to guard as a "pattern of sound words". In these letters it also becomes clear what constitutes this capacity to transcend their original destination, without abandoning it, and how they do in fact go beyond their original purpose. The words in which the revelation-event has found expression, and in which it is preserved by the power of the Spirit, are, if the expression be permitted, primordial, seminal words, spoken for a particular situation, yet from them flow words which throw light on all particular situations at all times. But this takes place in interpretative remembrance, which is a faithful and living repetition of the message for whatever particular present moment is in question. Now this does not apply only to the words of the apostles, but even prior to that, to the words of our Lord. The four gospels themselves are evidence of this. For in them the words (and of course the deeds) of Jesus are given in the interpretation of the evangelists, which often differs considerably. But in each of these expositions, so the evangelists and the Church are convinced, the original utterance is present.[1] This open character of the word of scripture is, therefore, not only the objective ground of the necessity and legitimacy of scriptural preaching, but also justifies the elaboration of a theology of the New Testament. The latter does not merely accept the hint suggested by the reflective character of scriptural revelation, but also obeys the directive implied in the open character of its language, and endeavours to unfold from it, in a new statement, its express or implicit theological content. It is this open character of the words of scripture which also permits and encourages dogmatic theology side by side with, and subsequent to, biblical theology.

[1] This fact is shown by the actual character of the synoptic gospels as they stand. In John's gospel it is also reflected upon. For this gospel claims, of course, to be the anamnesis foreseen by Jesus himself, of his person and life, his words and deeds, through the Spirit, disclosing and interpreting what had truly happened.

II

The theology of the New Testament has therefore to deal with these writings, historically of different kinds but one in theme, which attest the truth of the revelation-event in Jesus Christ and which imposed themselves on the Church as standard of belief. And in the reflection on the faith which they contain, revelation finds primordial and seminal expression. New Testament theology seeks to elucidate the facts of revelation and their interconnections as far as they are comprised in the foreground or the background of the reflective thought, in faith, of the New Testament. It questions the New Testament about its theological subject-matter and statements. If the history of this branch of study is investigated, it will be seen that that is not so commonplace as might appear. New Testament theology is not, for example, a history of early Christian religion or piety. Nor is it, to mention another view, an account of what is called salvation history, that is, a kind of theology of history.[2] Nor is it merely an inventory and description of the propositions contained in the New Testament, a modern form, that is, of the *collegia biblica*. A theology of the New Testament aims rather at grasping the revelation-reality in the light in which the thoughtful belief of the New Testament understood it, and at making it intelligible precisely as the New Testament understood it.[3] What God's rule is, God's

[2] Salvation history is on occasion a theme figuring in the presentation of Pauline theology. It would certainly be appropriate to discuss first what it means in Paul's sense.

[3] Consequently—I insist on this because of the misunderstandings encountered by what I wrote in the *Biblische Zeitschrift* 1 (1957) (cf. above, Essay I)—there does not belong to a theology of the New Testament an account of the preaching and life of Jesus of the kind historical research seeks to draw from the gospels. Of course the life and death of Jesus as well as his words and deeds are directly or indirectly the source of all theological reflection by the New Testament authors. And it is also certainly the case that decisive features of the events concerning Jesus can be historically reconstructed. But the endeavour of a theology of the New Testament,

righteousness, the cross of Christ and his resurrection, the world, man, flesh, sin, conversion, faith, hope, love, spirit, people of God, Body of Christ, the person of the Lord, and much else—these are the plain questions which the theology of the New Testament attempts to answer in the sense of the New Testament. In doing so the endeavour is made to disclose the whole wealth, complexity and, above all, the fundamental import of the statements.

The theology of the New Testament will, however, only inquire into the thought which expresses the belief of the *New Testament*. This again looks like a platitude, but is not so. It means two things. First, that it does not inquire into the theology of the supposed sources of the New Testament or, at all events only does so in order to clarify the theology of the New Testament writings themselves. Secondly, its investigation does not extend beyond the New Testament into early Christian literature generally, or at least, does so only for the same purpose. It accepts the exclusive character of the Canon as an es-

its attempt to elucidate the theological statements of the New Testament proclamation of faith, can prescind from both, and must do so. Otherwise the impression is given that in addition to the only legitimate interpretations of the ῥῆμα χριστοῦ by the four evangelists, there is another, that of the historiographical picture which the historian gives of this reality. And in that case, as the course of New Testament scholarship shows, the statements of the four evangelists may easily come to be judged by this fifth. It is one of the unexplained mysteries of the theological spirit of the age that often those who strictly maintain that access to the redemptive event in faith is ensured through the Church make an exception in the case of the primitive Church and affirm that Jesus is not accessible through the interpretation of the evangelists by entering into their relation to the real events concerning Jesus, but through a reconstruction undertaken by historical research. So great is the need for the certainty which people think is ensured by an "objective" regress to what is intelligible, such as historical research carries out. We need not take up the point here that in this matter those who defend the historicity of the account of the events concerning Jesus given in the gospels, are in agreement with those who contest it. But it would be ill-advised, by such presumptuous insistence on access through "historical research" to the saving event, to sanction a very temporary attitude to past history and by so doing to miss the past reality itself.

sential presupposition of its work. From the standpoint of comparative religion dealing with the history of primitive Christianity or its piety, that is, of course, arbitrary, as W. Wrede clearly said as early as 1897. But without this "arbitrariness" which in the relevant theological perspective reflects a necessary and meaningful datum, the theological character of New Testament theology is abandoned at the very onset.

If in this way the theology of the New Testament directs its attention to the theological data as they appear in the light of the New Testament, and investigates on principle only the New Testament writings as such, then what will first emerge will be a series of different and fragmentary theologies. It will show that just as the New Testament writings display great differences in origin, circumstances and purpose of their composition, language, form etc., so too their theological assumptions, terms, points of view etc. are very different. For example, Luke's theology of the epochs of salvation differs notably from Mark's epiphany-theology. The differences between Pauline and Johannine eschatology are well-known. Moreover, the theology of the New Testament will also show that these various theologies mostly, and really in fact always, represent only fragments of a theology. That also applies to the larger groups of writings. In them the topical character of these writings, the way they are tied to a particular situation, becomes evident. A single theological statement often reveals only one aspect. Seldom are the lines extended, seldom is an inner link visible. And so an account of the thought and belief of the New Testament in fact presents merely a number of theological fragments, varying greatly in content and form and, in addition, often scarcely comparable in scope, degree of theological reflection and intrinsic importance.

The single claim and summons of the revelation which finds expression in the writings of the New Testament, divides in its theological refraction, into very different theological tendencies.

But in that case, what is the position as regards a theology of the New Testament, or of the Bible itself? We have left the latter entirely in the background, but it increases the urgency of the question. It is certainly possible to agree with O. Kuss when he says, "The theological unity of the New Testament is neither a fact nor a problem for the New Testament itself".[4] And it is also possible in a certain sense to say with E. Käsemann, "A single biblical theology springing from one root and pursued in unbroken continuity, is wishful thinking and an illusion".[5] That can be said as regards a ready-made theology. But it is of course a question of how we interpret the fact of the heterogenous and fragmentary character of New Testament theology as we actually find it. And it is a question of whether the New Testament itself does not give us indications that we are to go beyond the fact and problem presented by it. How is the actual pluralist and fragmentary character of the New Testament theologies to be interpreted? Must we stop at this or can we not rather see in it a summons to extend a little the numerous broken lines and to relate the divergent lines to a single point? If in the writings of the New Testament the one revelation-event has projected itself into manifold forms of believing thought, does this thought not address itself to a *single* theology? And are not the various theological tendencies to be developed with reference to this unified theology? It is indeed difficult to say how far this development in relation to one theology is possible without premature harmonization. Trial and error must show. At all events the venture must be made, all the more so as the tendency towards unity in relation to the "truth of the gospel" (Gal 2) the growth of which can be traced in the New Testament, itself implies an orientation towards a unified theology.[6]

---

[4] *BZ* 5 (1961), p. 171, note 5.   [5] *ZTK* 54 (1957), p. 18.
[6] It is also possible to think, as O. Kuss himself does (*BZ* 5 [1961], p. 171), that in the various writings of the New Testament "in each case a clear tendency is visible towards ecclesiastical unity" and "that in the various individual writings of the New Testament, the fact of heresy is quite plainly

But in that case are we not secretly on the way to a dogmatic theology? This brings us to the third decisive viewpoint in our reflections.

III

We have said that in the New Testament the revelation in Jesus Christ is consigned in such a way that it can be grasped from its authors' reflection on their faith. The theology of the New Testament endeavours to elucidate and exhibit in their interconnections the data of revelation as these were understood by that New Testament understanding of the faith. By doing this, the fundamental step is taken towards their interpretation. But this first step is not the last. The theology of the New Testament or, as the case may be, biblical theology, presents the theological datum which it has drawn from scripture and elucidated, for the Church's further meditation in faith. This takes place expressly in dogmatic theology above all. Consequently the process of interpretation of the revelation-event which has entered into scripture proceeds further. But in dogmatic theology it assumes a different character. For dogmatic theology does not seek to meditate the theological data themselves as they appear to the faith and consideration of scripture, but aims at pursuing thought into the reality itself, within the domain which in scripture has been opened out and delimited in principle, and it does so in perpetual discussion with the knowledge, experience and decisions of the Church gained from the same source and preserved in tradition. In this way it seeks to enter into discussion of the subject-matter itself and penetrate the reality itself. Dogmatic theology is no longer concerned, for example, with inquiring what "God's righteousness" means

reckoned with". If these two things are taken together, it is clear that according to the New Testament itself, the Church pursues the path towards a single doctrine. How else could it be explained, for that matter, that early Christian thought about its belief was already supported by common formulas of faith?

according to the Pauline writings, but what it is in itself, as the Church perpetually experiences and meditates it on the basis of those writings. Then it seeks to formulate that reality by listening to the faith and reflection of holy scripture as elucidated by biblical theology and to the tradition of the Church which directly or indirectly unfolds it. By such thinking out towards the reality itself, the Church's reflection on faith does not move away from the data of revelation but comes closer to them. What was thought in the believing reflection of the Bible is considered by biblical theology, in preparation for dogmaic theology, so that this may penetrate it and in certain circumstances think it out to a conclusion. Such thinking out to a conclusion which takes place in the believing consensus of the Church about its belief, can, if the whole spiritual situation of the hour requires and permits, lead to its fixation in dogma.[7] We cannot speak of that now. One point only must be noted. Dogma does not mean the end of reflection, but the elevation of what has been thought out to the rank of what is incontestably and permanently worthy of thought. For biblical theology, dogma means that what has been thought out to a conclusion, but by the very nature of the case to a conclusion which is provisional in form, is directed towards a new elucidation of the original belief and reflection.

Biblical theology presents its exposition of the belief and reflection of scripture to dogmatic theology so that the latter, placed in its very origin in contact with the words which express the data of revelation, may, in the context of the tradition of faith, meditate these in relation to the reality with which

---

[7] This is not the product of the human inclination to dogmatize, as is widely assumed. Nor is it in any way a necessary conclusion of the consensus regarding faith, which in principle when everything had been taken into account, could and did inevitably follow. Dogma arises rather in the freedom, and the necessity, of the situation, which is largely impenetrable to a contemporary or later gaze. For dogma, of course, is an eschatological phenomenon, something which in a special sense is directed towards the end, because in a provisional way it manifests what is final.

they deal. If this is so, there is a much closer relation between the two theologies than the traditional theology of the Schools will in practice admit, or than the present complicated organization of the various branches of biblical study permits. Biblical theology and dogmatic theology both move in the stream of the great process of expounding revelation, and they do so in mutual relation. Dogmatic theology at all events has legitimate questions to put to biblical theology which the latter cannot itself propound yet which serve to throw light on the biblical datum.[8] They are questions suggested by an understanding of the faith which has come to grips with the relevant reality itself and which on that basis addresses an understanding of the faith which remains close to its source. Dogmatic theology does not simply impose on biblical theology the task of providing a scriptural basis for its dogmatic theses, in other words, the task of furnishing the well-known *dicta probantia*. Nor does it prescribe the conclusions to be arrived at. If it did it would have forgotten the intrinsic character of its own critical foundation, which is holy scripture elucidated by biblical theology. It would have overlooked, if the expression is permitted, that a river always includes its well-spring but in the first place owes its origin to it. Nevertheless biblical theology does pursue its tasks to the accompaniment of questions which arise from dogmatic reflection. It does exegesis no harm, for example, if it endeavours to throw light on the Pauline conception in Romans chapter 5 in full awareness of the dogmatic discussion about original sin. On the contrary it will inquire into the text with greater vigour and subtlety in the light of a discussion of the reality itself which is in question.[9]

[8] Cf. K. Rahner, "Exegesis and Dogmatic Theology" in *Theological Investigations,* vol. V (1966), pp. 67 ff.

[9] Naturally this knowledge cannot guide the exegetical inquiry, at least such a pointer from dogmatic theology would have to be willing to allow itself to be destroyed by the question put by the text. And of course an exegesis which is guided or even merely prompted by the question developed in dogmatic theology about reality itself, can make things easy for itself and

But dogmatic theology also must allow itself to be questioned by biblical theology, for the latter after all confronts it with the theological datum of biblical interpretation. In that way recollection of the original sense of the objects of dogmatic theology is fortified. For it is on their basis that dogmatic theology attains the reality itself. It is often recalled to that reality by the "critical function"[10] of biblical theology, which this latter exercises because it is the theology of the source. Biblical theology can provide dogmatics with long-obscured or even forgotten data for its consideration. It did so by clarifying the central Pauline concept of the "Body of Christ". It can draw the attention to possible gaps and omissions in dogmatics. This is happening at the present, for example in regard to the lack of treatment of the word of God as a means of salvation in the dogmatic theology of the School. In certain circumstances it can also put new questions to dogmatics, including ones which concern its actual foundations, for example, the problem of the temporal, historical character of the world and of man, and consequently of being in general.[11] The more it clarifies its own

for dogmatics simply by discovering the dogmatic thesis explicitly in this or that passage of scripture. In that case, of course, it is forgetting the intrinsically historical factor in revelation. Out of fear of this danger, to which exegesis succumbed for centuries, the present momentary and objectively unjustified dislike of the practice of interpretation by dogmatic theology is, among other reasons, to be explained.

[10] Cf. K. Rahner in *LTK*, vol. II, col. 451.

[11] This question of temporality is not only put to dogmatics by biblical theology, but also, for example, by the philosophical thought of Martin Heidegger. Fortunately, even in dogmatic theology people are beginning to listen to this, as can be seen from the fact that it is only uninstructed persons now who speak of it with horror as "existentialism". It is true that biblical theology stands closer to dogmatics, to the extent that both have a living function in the interpretation of revelation. Moreover, biblical theology is in any case the preparatory stage of reflection for dogmatics whereas dogmatic theology is the decisive reflection on what is presented by biblical theology. Worthy of remark is Heidegger's pertinent statement that in his theological studies, from which the heading "hermeneutics" was familiar to him, he was "particularly intrigued by the question of the relation between the word of holy scripture and speculative theological thought". "It was, if

principles and content, the more clearly and forcibly it can do all this and more. That, however, is achieved in proportion to the conscientiousness and lack of inhibitions with which it performs and is permitted to perform its work.

There is no question of a conflict between biblical and dogmatic theology.[12] Both share in promoting the great process of interpreting revelation. Biblical theology interprets it as it has expressed itself in scripture, expounds the biblical belief and reflection in itself and presents it thus expounded to dogmatic theology. The latter thinks out the matter assigned to it, in certain cases thinks it out to a conclusion. But it does so within the domain and the limits of the open language of scripture, in perpetual discussion with the whole of tradition. The more carefully each partner here, intent on its own task, listens to the other, the more fruitful will be the theological knowledge obtained. For ultimately the two are interrelated by the character of revelation itself.

From experience gradually gained in laborious work carried out sometimes under opposition, biblical theology knows what inexhaustible riches of wisdom and knowledge, what powerful and unalloyed strength of thought, what great and living force of utterance is bestowed on the Church by the original believing thought of holy scripture. It knows that what Pius XII said applies precisely to it: *sacrorum fontium studio sacrae disciplinae semper iuvenescunt.* Freely and biblically translated that means: "By the study of holy scripture the theological sciences are renewed day by day."

you like, the same relation, namely between language and being, only veiled and inaccessible to me, so that I sought in vain a guiding thread by many detours and byways." "Without this theological origin I would never have struck the path of thought. Origin, however, never ceases to mean future." (M. Heidegger, *Unterwegs zur Sprache* [1959], p. 96).

[12] For that matter why should it surprise anyone that harsh conflicts can spring up between dogmatic and biblical theology, in view of the difficulty of the subject-matter, the difference of methods, the great estrangement between the two disciplines, the different degree of maturity reached by each and, not least, our human limitations and malice?

CHAPTER III

What is Meant by the Interpretation of Scripture?*

In what follows we shall be trying not so much to describe the procedure of scriptural exegesis as to discuss its significance from one or two points of view. Since the meaning, as well as the method, of any interpretation depends on the text which is being expounded, we must first and foremost make clear the special character of our text, sacred scripture. The interpretation of the legal source of a legal decision presupposes law as a reality that can be known. The exposition of a literary work opens out the pleasurable domain of the true in its beauty, and makes man "give praise that he is permitted to be".[1] If a statesman interprets an historic document, by the act of exposition itself our history becomes part of past history, though obscurely, as if it were a future possibility. What happens, then, when holy scripture is interpreted? That will become clear when we have determined what holy scripture is.

I

Holy scripture, as itself indicates, is in the widest sense historical testimony to historical events in which God revealed

---

* Dedicated to R. Bultmann on his eightieth birthday.
[1] Cf. Wilhelm Lehmann, *Die Kunst des Gedichts* (1961), p. 13.

himself in the actual world of history. In its text those events have found written expression in which God made himself and his will known to the world. They are the events, decisive for all history, involving the person of Jesus, in which the repeated promises of God to Israel were fulfilled. The apostle Paul says, at 2 Corinthians 1: 20 f., "All the promises of God find their Yes in him" (the Jesus Christ who is preached). This Yes, a concrete historical occurrence in which all God's promises to his people were realized, is preserved in holy scripture.

Those promises of God, which remained promises even in the face of the refusals of the disobedient nation, were accomplished in the course of actual history and, what is important, *as* actual concrete history. Israel's history, to which, as to all history, both deeds and words belong, conveyed God's promise to Israel. Just think of that course of events, o difficult to determine in terms of historical research, as it confronts us in the Old Testament from the times which, to express it in Greek concepts, had not yet any *logos* and were hidden in *muthos*, down to the days when Israel's history no longer found expression and fell silent. We read that a few nomadic Semitic tribes formed a settlement and, after taking over the land gradually in the midst of overwhelmingly powerful states, formed little oriental principalities with a holy city and a central sanctuary. Those principalities had scarcely arisen and united than they fell apart again. Those tribes and little states were led by charismatic heroes and kings and directed by priests, prophets, wise men and scribes who accompanied them throughout a long, sorrowful history, through deserts and exile, collapse and deliverance. And all that was not merely an historical setting; the actual events, great or small, together with the word that always accompanied them, constituted a divine intervention and revelation. The Old Testament was convinced that Israel's history and, in conjunction with it, all history, takes place in such a way that its course expresses God's will. And this expression is not simply something that supervenes on the event; it occurs in the very event itself. The Old Testament understands the occurrences concerning and in Israel and the world as an "event", if, as M. Heidegger has it, it is proper to an event that in it "saying" is found and "the saying" which is contained in the event, as manifestation, is the most authentic mode of the event.[2] For the Old Testament, history in its occurrence is God's summons, declaration and promise. That is why, though the connection was not always consciously realized, events are called *debarim*, "words". And that is why the great masters of words who to a considerable extent determined Israel's history, the prophets, who fixed, even in advance, the word of Yahweh comprised in his historic deeds and gave it expression, did not really add word to event. That is the basis on which the special relation between Yahweh's action and word is to be understood. The event in which Yahweh's deliverance or judgment takes place is only the utterance, and in that sense the fulfilment, of his word.[3] When Yahweh causes something to happen he utters his word, and he fulfils it when he pronounces it in the event.[4] If he utters it in the event, it occurs.[5] "Declaring the end from the beginning and from ancient times things not yet done, saying: 'My counsel shall stand, and I will accomplish all my purpose', calling a bird of prey from the east, the man of my counsel from a far country. I have spoken, and I will bring it to pass; I have purposed, and I will do it" (Is 46:10f. cf. also Ezek 12:21–8). As long as the word is not fulfilled, it stands threatening or promising before expectant

---

[2] M. Heidegger, *Unterwegs zur Sprache* (1959), pp. 262 f.

[3] G. v. Rad mentions that for the case in which Israel were to persist in disobedience, severe threats and curses had been expressed in Deuteronomy (Dt 32:47). Consequently in the terrible catastrophes, Israel was judged by Yahweh's word itself. *Theologie des AT*, vol. I (4ᵗʰ ed. 1962), p. 352 (E. T.: *Theology of the Old Testament*, vol. I, 1962). Cf. also vol. II, pp. 93 ff.

[4] Cf. for example 1 Sam 1:23; 15:11, 13; 2 Sam 7:25; 1 Kings 2:4, 27; 6:12; 8:15, 20, 24, 56; 12:15.

[5] Cf. for example, Josh 21:45; 23:13 f.

history.[6] If then Israel experiences Yahweh's action as a carrying out of his word—"I watch over my *dabar* (my word) to perform it" (Jer 1: 12)—this action comes as an utterance which aims at an answer from Israel. "'I gave you cleanness of teeth in all your cities, and lack of bread in all your places, yet you did not return to me ... I smote you with blight and mildew; I laid waste your gardens and your vineyards; your fig-trees and your olive trees the locust devoured; yet you did not return to me',—says the Lord" (Amos 4: 6 ff.).

Since the Old Testament regards historical events as a word spoken by Yahweh, it is implied that this word manifests Yahweh's summons to the people of Israel. As Yahweh's events, the historical happenings concern Israel from the first and do so by the very fact that they are addressed to Israel.[7] There is no "neutral" history which, as in our detached contemplation based on research, could be understood as an element in an historical picture. There is only one history, which makes a claim on Israel. History does not lose this character of being a claim even in the course of time and with increasing remoteness. Even when it has occurred, history remains a perpetual summons from Yahweh. "If you say in your heart, 'These nations are greater than I; how can I dispossess them?', you shall not be afraid of them, but you shall remember what the Lord your God did to Pharaoh and to all Egypt... You shall not be in dread of them, for the Lord your God is in the midst of you" (Deut 7: 17 f., 21). And in the sabbath commandment, the admonition to grant rest even to the slave is given as basis, "You shall remember that you were a servant in the land of

---

[6] Cf. *Handbuch Theologischer Grundbegriffe*, vol. II (1963), "Wort", II. Biblisch, pp. 845—67, especially 852 f.

[7] G. v. Rad, "Das AT ist ein Geschichtsbuch" in *Probleme alttestamentlicher Hermeneutik*, ed. by C. Westermann (1960), pp. 11—17. On p. 13 it is said: "God's judgment and redemption are now (with Genesis 12: 3 a) inserted into history; judgment and salvation are decided by the attitude to the historical fact of Israel."

Egypt, and the Lord your God brought you out thence with a mighty hand and an outstretched arm; therefore the Lord your God commanded you to keep the sabbath day" (Deut 5: 15). The act of deliverance remains a call here and now. "And you shall remember all the way which the Lord your God has led you ... to know what was in your heart..." (Deut 8:2; cf. Josh 24:1—18). In history which in its unfolding is simultaneously Yahweh's pronouncement, claim and promise, there is no indifferent happening, there are only significant events.[8]

If what happens is a significant event and, as such, a word spoken, it follows that it occurs with the whole ambiguity or multiplicity of meaning that words have. For words both reveal and conceal. History as speech is always history as a question requiring an answer. The deliverance from Egypt can be understood as follows: "Thou hast led in thy steadfast love the people whom thou hast redeemed, thou hast guided them by thy strength to thy holy abode" (Ex 15: 13). But it can also be understood as follows: "Would that we had died by the hand of the Lord in the land of Egypt, when we sat by the fleshpots and ate bread to the full" (Ex 16: 3). History as a summons keeps the truth which it expresses so open, that it can be heard or misheard, seen or overlooked. The truth of Israel's history is the fidelity of Yahweh, prevailing as hidden yet manifest, in events, in his commandment and in his promise, and known as such in the "quiet" and the "upward gaze" of faith.[9]

If in the Old Testament view God reveals himself in an event which is an intelligible utterance, it follows that this utterance in and by the event opens out a horizon of experience in which it finds a meaningful context. We are thinking here of the domain in which it finds expression, perhaps even before it is spoken about. The world is latent in language. Into this world

---

[8] Cf. H. W. Wolff, "Das AT und das Problem der existentiellen Interpretation" in *Evangelische Theologie* 23 (1963), pp. 10 f.

[9] Cf. for example Is 7:4; 22:11 b etc.; G. v. Rad, *Theologie des AT*, vol. II, pp. 169 ff.

the event is uttered, and in such a way that there is a response within a domain which it creates for itself. Thus God's revelation took place in such a way that its occurrence "chose" Israel and created its own effective domain in Israel.[10] It can also be said that as an event God's revelation opens out its own historical horizon within which it is historically preserved with the claim it makes, manifested again and again against repeated obscuration through contradiction.

The same structure of an historical event shown in God's revelation of promise in the Old Testament is also displayed in its fulfilment, which is attested in the New Testament. Of course there is a difference deriving from the realities themselves. The revelation-events of the New Testament do not all lie on the same plane. In fact they are only fulfilled and disclosed (and with them the promises of the Old Testament) in the light of a single event as revelation-utterance. This event is the resurrection of Jesus Christ from the dead in its manifestation to the witnesses. In it God's Yes is manifest, and this is no longer only God's promise but also his coming. In the light of this event, this advent of God in the risen Jesus Christ, the person and previous history of Jesus Christ, which culminated on the Cross, are manifested as being in their actual occurrence the word of salvation fulfilling all God's promises. That is noted several times in the gospels, in references of various kinds.[11]

This history of Jesus of Nazareth which in the perspective of the appearance of the risen Christ is significant as God's advent—it is often called "eschatological history"[12]—is, like Old Testament history, a concrete history. Seen from outside it is the out-of-the-way and rather striking, yet at the same time

---

[10] Cf. Ex 19: 3 ff.; Dt 4: 6 ff.; 14: 2; 32: 7 ff.; Is 41: 8 ff.; Ezek 20: 5 ff.; etc., and in general cf. H. Wildberger, *Jahwes Eigentumsvolk* (1959).
[11] Cf. for example Mk 8: 31; 9: 10, 32; Jn 2: 22; 12: 16.
[12] For example, G. Bornkamm, "Geschichte und Glaube im NT" in *Evangelische Theologie* 22 (1962), p. 13.

commonplace affair of a Jew who was more or less like a rabbi but also rather like a prophet and something more than a prophet,[13] and who caused a stir in a corner of the world in Galilee and Judaea and little Jerusalem, among an exhausted nation and a Roman garrison, and who did so by his strangely Jewish yet un-Jewish talk and charismatic deeds. Like many other prophets and teachers, he gathered disciples and pupils around him, became an object of suspicion to the secular and spiritual authorities, gave offence even to many pious people because he proclaimed God's reign here and now and also for a time soon to come, strictly and frankly, harshly yet humanely. Eventually he encountered bitter resistance, was brought to trial for alleged sedition and probably also for blasphemy, and with the help of the occupying power, was put to death on the Cross as a criminal. The story was soon forgotten in the official world and among historians, though various rumours were still in circulation about him, for example about some slave or other, Chrestus, who had caused disturbances among the Jews of Rome.[14] From the inside, in the eyes of those who had been with him and who in the context and the light of those events in Galilee and Jerusalem after his death which indicated that he was God's future advent understood things which had been quite unintelligible to them, the story looked rather different, very plain in fact, and almost simple, if only it had not always also given the impression of being an extreme case. Seen from the inside, it was the occurrence of a man's total obedience to God's will, complete fulfilment of God's will in mighty words and deeds, as against the disastrous and devastating devilry of men with their own man-made god and his inhuman law and satanic spirit destructive of body and mind. And seen from the inside, this story of Jesus of Nazareth, as the actual realization of unshakable obedience to God, was a total dedication to men,

[13] Cf. also R. Bultmann, *Jesus* (1951), pp. 181 f. "He is therefore bearer of the word . . ." E. T.: *Jesus* (1958).
[14] Suetonius, *Vita Claudii*, p. 25.

a total self-giving for those who were bowed in body and soul under the burden of self-seeking and fear, vanity and the loneliness of sin. Seen from within, the inflexible obedience of Jesus to God's will that he should be inflexibly present for men, culminated in the Passion and ended on the Cross.[15] The Cross, therefore, was at once understood and proclaimed, thanks also to the appearance of the risen Christ, as the decisive event in which this profoundly significant history was fulfilled and revealed. Here God definitively expressed his promise.

Jesus and his history, therefore, a history of real obedience and real love, of extreme obedience and extreme love, are the language of action in which God's last pronouncement is made. That is already implied in statements like Mark 8: 38: "For

---

[15] What R. Bultmann states ("Das Verhältnis der urchristlichen Christusbotschaft zum historischen Jesus" in *Sitzungsberichte der Heidelberger Akademie der Wissenschaften* 3 [1960], p. 11), seems to me implicitly to indicate why Jesus had to go to death. "With some hesitation ... the following may be said concerning Jesus' activity ... Characteristic of him are exorcisms, the breach of the Sabbath commandment, the transgression of prescriptions concerning ritual purity, the polemic against Jewish legalism, the company of social outcasts such as publicans and prostitutes, the affection for women and children; it can also be noted that Jesus was not an ascetic like John the Baptist ... Perhaps it may also be added that he summoned men to follow him and gathered around him ... a small band of adherents." And must he not also have seen this necessity of death himself—and willed it? Is it not likewise a "psychological construction" when, as against these facts and the first interpretation that the event received, it is alleged that Jesus was so to speak taken by surprise by his death? To my mind, James M. Robinson *New Quest of the Historical Jesus* (1959), is quite right and is not merely trying to evade the problem when he writes, "Consequently the Cross of Christ would be misunderstood if the chronological distinction between Christ's death and his preaching activity were to be evaluated as a fundamental theological separation ... On the contrary, Christ's Cross must be interpreted as the uttermost actualization of Jesus' message ... For that message called for a radical break with the 'present evil aeon', which for example includes the acceptance of one's own death from and in this world ... Jesus' exposure of himself to death probably cannot be limited to his death in Jerusalem. On the contrary, the concrete vital meaning of his own acceptance of the message of the divine *basileia*, and accordingly of his break with the present evil aeon, consisted in his perpetually taking death upon himself."

whoever is ashamed of me and of my words in this adulterous and sinful generation, of him will the Son of man also be a-shamed when he comes in the glory of his Father with the holy angels" (cf. Mt 11: 6 and Lk 12: 8 f.). The same fact is simi-larly referred to in the description of Jesus Christ as the Amen contained in God's promises and now uttered (2 Cor 1: 19 f.). In Acts 10: 36 f. we hear that God sent "the word" to the children of Israel. What word? The "event that had happened" (ῥῆμα)[16] throughout all Judaea. The Letter to the Hebrews makes even plainer the nature of the event that occurred in the person of Jesus Christ, in which God expresses himself, and at the same time links it with God's speaking to the fathers through the prophets. And it is God's last utterance "in these last days", his final word (Heb 1: 1 f.). In the Johannine writ-ings these facts found their appropriate terminology. Thus the opening of the first Letter of John proclaims "what we have seen and heard", namely, "concerning the word of life" (1: 1 f.). According to the prologue of John's gospel, however, "the Word became flesh", i. e. man, and in such a way that that man proved himself, by word and sign in his journey to God, to be the Word of God. He "made known" (ἐξηγήσατο) God whom no one has ever seen; one would almost like to translate it "inter-preted", "expounded" (1: 18).

Moreover, this historical self-expression of God in the historical man Jesus of Nazareth as the "Son", takes place in such a way that the whole significant event of this life and activity in its totality constitutes a claim to be heard. The disciples of John are to go and tell "what you hear and see" (Mt 11: 4; cf. 11: 13 ff.). That, of course, as the Baptist's question shows, is by no means unambiguous. Even Jesus' mighty deeds, and in fact precisely they, share the ambiguity of the language of events. The Jewish scribes, for example, said

---

[16] ʻPῆμα like *dabar* denotes an occurrence inasmuch as it is an historic event expressing a meaning for men.

that Jesus cast out demons by the most powerful demon (Mk 3: 22).

But the third characteristic of revelation as an historical event reappears here: when it happens, it creates for itself a domain to exist in, and a perspective within which to be effective, where it is preserved both as understood and yet not understood, and it adapts itself to a community and claims this as its own. In the present case it was the disciples whom Jesus called and the people which attached itself to him and to them.

We see, therefore, that the happenings in which, as the Old and New Testaments are convinced, God revealed himself in the destinies of Israel and, unveiling and fulfilling these, in Jesus and his way, forms an occurrence in the sense of a significant event which, by taking place, constitutes an utterance, and one which is a question and a summons adapted to a certain domain. God reveals himself in the action-language of this history of his, which was definitively accomplished in Jesus, in whom he finally expressed himself. But to express is itself to interpret,[17] or perhaps it would be better to say that it is already to be on the way to an interpretation. With such a significant event, in which God by revealing himself accommodated himself to the world, God already opened up and entered upon the road to interpretation.

II

Self-interpretation of this kind by God occurs in concrete experience and language. It takes shape in words in the oral

---

[17] Cf. H. G. Gadamer, *Wahrheit und Methode* (1960), p. 366: "Language is, rather, the universal medium in which understanding itself is accomplished. The way in which understanding is accomplished is interpretation... All understanding and all interpretation develops in the medium of a language which aims at making the object express itself in words and yet at the same time is the language of the interpreter himself."

tradition and writings of the early Church and in scripture. In the latter, fundamentally, it reaches its conclusion. We have said that in the significant event of the history of Jesus Christ, God expressed himself definitively. That is not a figure of speech, but denotes the very fact which that history states by occurring; occurrence and statement coincide. Nor do we mean it in a metaphorical sense, but are describing the course of this history, when we now assert that the language of this "statement" is the language of those who experience it. What this event says is articulated in the interpretative response of those who hear it. That holds good of all human history. It never occurs without occurring in men's understanding, whether this is expressed or not. That is also true of the history in which God speaks to the world. The New Testament is quite aware of this. What is meant by the history in which God reveals himself, becomes fully explicit in the tradition which interprets and states it, and which preserves it. If we may express the matter rather too briefly, the communication of God by Jesus Christ to the world merges into communication of him by the tradition of those who experienced it. God's self-disclosure to the world is disclosed precisely as such in history, in the explanatory speech of those who have opened themselves to it.

According to the New Testament, such speech, where it is an adequate response and so expresses the meaning of the divine event itself, is speech elucidated by the Spirit, and of course is expressed in the midst of all other speech. The Spirit as the revealing might of God, as his power of self-disclosure (cf. 1 Cor 2: 10 f.), the Spirit of the risen and glorified Christ, authentically unfolds the event constituted by the words, the deeds and the person of Jesus, in the corresponding speech and answer of those who thereby experience it in its truth despite all concealing and distorting untruth. In view of this, it can be said that by the power of the Spirit, God disclosed himself in the Jesus Christ-event which reached completion in the appearance of the risen Christ. But God now discloses by the power of the same Spirit the Jesus Christ-event in the interpretative word of those who experience it in the Spirit. That is to say, in Johannine terms, the event of the Word made man in Jesus, in virtue of his departure and ascent into the *doxa*, the radiance of God's power, is "brought to remembrance" by the Spirit and given expression in such a way that it is possible to perceive it in its truth.[18] That happens, however, in and in the midst of, all other words and human language.

Here too we must not overlook the fact that the event of God's revelation in Jesus Christ manifests itself in concrete human language within the horizon of man's experience. What is preached, as the apostle Paul writes to the Christians in Thessalonica (1 Thess 2: 13) is "the word of God". It is not "the word of men". But it is God's word as "the word of preaching from us which you have heard from us", that is, God's word spoken by men in human language. That must be taken with its full implications. For it means that the language of the event took concrete form not only in a particular human tongue, Hebrew, Aramaic, Greek, with its possibilities and limits, but also in the modes of speech and thought of the circle in which the event occurred. We are often naïvely convinced that the mode of statement of historical events to which we are accustomed, at least in theory—what we call an objective historical account—is the kind of report current at all times, and the one that was also preferred in those days. But that is not the case at all. Other forms were available for conveying history, and were not felt to be inadequate or untrustworthy. Not only popular narrative or rhetorical elaboration,[19] but

[18] Cf. Jn 14: 26; 16: 13 f.
[19] Cf. on the rôle of the "invented" speeches in Thucydides, A. Mirgeler, "Erfahrung in der Geschichte und Geschichtswissenschaft" in *Experiment und Erfahrung in Wissenschaft und Kunst*, ed. by W. Strolz (1963), p. 238: " By them, Thucydides indicates the turning point of events, the moments when the knot of fate is tied, or at least when light is thrown upon it. They are the indispensable 'subjective' contribution which turn the given situation

also the style of legend and of myth supplied a linguistic mould for events, or was authorized by the event to serve as its expression. If we may so phrase it, revelation as an event was not afraid that it might put obstacles to its own truth and certainty thereby. Obviously it considered that such a linguistic and thought-form suited it better in certain circumstances than an "historical" account. It is not only the latter, we might say, that was baptized, but also myth and legend. To deny this on principle as impossible by the very facts of the case, would amount to contesting the historicity and human character of God's revelation and, ultimately, the incarnation of the Logos.[20]

There is a further significance in the fact that the revelation-event expresses itself in the speech of the language area which it has determined for itself. It means that from the start it only finds expression in the interpretation of those whom it encounters. Even the most literal transmission of a saying of Jesus is interpreted by the context in which it comes to us. In other words—and this is one of the findings of historical research which will certainly be welcome to Catholic exegesis—from the start the voice of the Church is also heard. The original community in the broad sense of the term, interpreted what happened, inevitably but not arbitrarily, on the basis of the prior understanding it already had, and in the light of its own interest and its own questions. A. Vögtle has recently said, and

into a human one, or, more exactly, into one which makes demands on men. Thucydides succeeds in making this human contribution clear even for past situations by uncovering in speech and counter-speech the possibilities and consequences of the decision that had to be taken at that time."
[20] It is this fact which demands that the intention of the author, recognizable from form and content, must be discussed before the question of the factual character of the event. So, for example, the stories of the patriarchs in Genesis are to a large extent theological reflection in the form of saga and legend, which may not subsequently be historicized in contradiction to the author's intention. In them of course history too became and remained significant for Israel. Cf. D. Lerch, "Zur Frage nach dem Verstehen der Schrift" in *ZTK* 49 (1952), p. 358.

rightly,[21] "the transmission of elements contained in the story of Jesus, even in the stage before it was committed to writing, was a tradition with an eye on the present and, to a certain extent, varying from case to case, it linked factors of topical relevance with the transmitted account. Here and there, in other words, features serving to clarify, interpret and point out an application were introduced. These derived from the changing concrete vital necessities and questions of the early Church, its missionary, catechetical, liturgical, apologetic, disciplinary and other purposes." But the advance of the revelation-event into the corresponding speech of the early Church must certainly not be imagined as if in the first place a tradition was current which corresponded more or less to an historical report in our sense, composed with the detachment and impartiality necessary to anyone who intends to trace an historical picture, and that that account was subsequently corrected and supplemented on the basis of certain questions and interests of the early Church. There never was an historical account in that sense.[22] From the beginning, rather, there was only the manifold, dispersed and yet somehow single utterance made by the significant revelation-event of Jesus' history, an utterance expounded in the modes of statement proper to that age in answer to the questions of the community of disciples.

The forms in which the oldest oral tradition is met with, themselves indicate that it bore an interpretative character of that kind. Not only the gospels but their "sources" themselves were familiar, for example, with the story of Jesus told in the style of the miracle stories and with typical, or even charac-

---

[21] A. Vögtle, "Werden und Wesen der Evangelien" in *Diskussion über die Bibel*, ed. by. L. Klein (1963), p. 57.

[22] To have attempted to demonstrate that by a concrete example of the central tradition, namely the story of the Passion, seems to me the merit of G. Schille's essay on "Das Leiden des Herrn" in *ZTK* 52 (1955), pp. 161—205, Cf. also G. Bornkamm, "Geschichte und Glaube im NT", p. 7, "There never was any tradition which did not have its functional context in the life of the community of believers."

teristically adapted, features of the exorcisms, but told with no other purpose than the claim made by the Jesus-event as this was understood in the Church. That holds good even of the story of the healing of the Gerasene demoniac, told at length and, one might almost say, with relish. Mark in fact (5: 1—20) had rescued it for the kerygma when in the oral tradition it was already threatening to disappear. Matthew then vigorously condensed it, while Luke with more taste for an entertaining account, gave it the stamp of a short story. But even the short story has to serve God's summons in human language and must not be treated as of no account. Or we may think of the narrative of the Passion, which probably was told as a connected whole even in oral tradition, the oldest connected series of narratives of the story of Jesus that we possess. The decisive event of the Passion, in which the ground and meaning of Jesus' deeds, words and way were manifested and reached earthly fulfilment, perhaps first found linguistic expression in a eucharistic anamnesis of the worshipping community, perhaps also in a baptismal catechesis, [23] and there the events were immediately and almost as a matter of course understood and given form as the fulfilment of Old Testament prophecy. And was such anamnesis not right? Yet it did not, for all that, supply a systematic historical report, and was not in a position to give one, not through incapacity or lack of information, but because an historical report would never have been adequate to the significant event itself, in which, as clearly emerged in the light of Jesus Christ's resurrection, God's action "for us" crystallized in its most concrete reality. An historical report, in fact, would have had to disregard the decisive aim of stating the actual intention of the event, which was to be an utterance fulfilling and manifesting all God's promises and by its truth claiming nothing less than faith. The very earliest tradition, shaped by the event itself as its expression, did not wish

---

[23] Cf. G. Schille, "Das Leiden des Herrn", p. 175.

to, and could not, disregard that. After all, the tradition aimed simply at responding to and expounding the event.

Of course the oral tradition, of which in any case we have only an inadequate idea, was exposed to all the dangers of historical contingency, and so too as a consequence was the voice of the event. Not only could it have fallen into oblivion but it could have been drowned by talk in innumerable ways. The mythical or legendary form of speech might have unfolded its inherent linguistic tendency and so obscured or falsified the truth of the event's claim, or abandoned the truth of the claim to a mythical gnosis or an historicizing moralism. We can form some idea of such dangers if we consider the surviving apocryphal sayings and stories of Jesus, or the tradition, similar to the synoptic tradition, which John the evangelist saved in his gospel, by his and the Spirit's interpretation, from being deformed by talk. But it is characteristic that in the face of this threat, inherent in the historical nature of tradition, the pronouncement constituted by the revelation-event, endangered in a variety of ways but ultimately preserved, was maintained in the power of the Spirit in its language and interpretation, which were those of the primitive Church, through scripture and for scripture.

For this latter was what from the very nature of the case was required for saving, preserving and perfecting tradition. At the same time it represented the critical taking over of the latter by the Church. It is only in scripture that the utterance which the revelation-event constitutes, was fully unfolded in time and for time.[24] In scripture it was inscribed in history for

---

[24] That is true to a certain extent of the written word generally. Cf. H. G. Gadamer, *Wahrheit und Methode* (1960), p. 367: "In written form, everything handed down is contemporary with every present moment. In it there exists, therefore, a unique co-presence of past and present, to the extent that present consciousness has the possibility of free access to all that has been handed down in writing" and page 373: "What is fixed in writing, has detached itself from the contingence of its origin and author and is positively freed for new relationships."

history, reached its provisionally definitive form and so achieved its purpose. For the revelation-event was to be present everywhere and at all times. It was a significant event in the sense that while in itself it aimed at its immediate sphere of influence, it tended towards an unlimited horizon of experience. In scripture, however, it is kept close to the world.

Old Testament prophecy was already aware of this. "And now, go, write it before them on a tablet, and inscribe it in a book, that it may be for the time to come as a witness for ever" (Is 30:8).[25] The word pronounced and past can, when written, become God's call, by which the future of Israel itself is decided. This kind of conception lies behind the various literary versions of the history of Israel, which represent ever new interpretations made on the basis of the present for the present. Yet Israel's future is decided, as all future is, only at the end of the ages. This end has begun with Jesus Christ. And so the history of Israel, for example the journey through the desert, though it certainly happened at a definite time in the past, was written for today, when God's advent redeemed his promise. Paul expressly points this out in 1 Corinthians 10:1 ff. (cf. Rom 15:4). The New Testament views it in the same way. The fact that the apostle Paul wrote down his preaching, in which Jesus Christ speaks (Rom 15:8; 2 Cor 13:3), in letters, serves to bridge distances in place and time and so makes possible his, or rather our Lord Jesus Christ's, presence at all times in every place. When in Mark, in Jesus' apocalyptic discourse issuing a warning against Antichrist (Mk 13:14) we suddenly find, "let the reader understand", it is implied that Jesus' word is written for future readers too. The Revelation to John wants the prophecy of the book to be read aloud and kept as it is written (1:3; 22:7, 18 f.), because in it the entire future is regarded as evoked and manifested by the revelation that has taken place in Jesus Christ.

[25] Cf. Is 8:16 ff.; Jer 36:1 ff.; Hab 2:2. On this cf. G. v. Rad, *Theologie des AT*, vol. II, pp. 52 ff.

But holy scripture not only represents a consolidation in time and for time of the revelation-event and one appropriate to its purpose; in scripture that event attains its own definitive expression. To the extent that the writings which emerge from oral tradition later find a place in the Canon, the revelation-event expresses itself in a new, definitive interpretation and form. And in those writings, in critical confrontation with oral or even on occasion written tradition, the action-language of the revelation-event puts its definitive stamp on the authoritative written language of scripture. The preservation of tradition which we mentioned above, can be observed here in the form of discrimination.

The new interpretation, which such committing to writing of the meaning of the revelation-event represents, concerns the whole and also certain details. It concerns content and form. Just as the great narrators of the Old Testament or the prophets interpreted again and again and gave contemporary force to the ancient tradition and this process continued until a fixed form was attained in the scriptures, so the New Testament writings represent a last and authentic fundamental interpretation disclosing definitive aspects. In these writings, the Church's decisive realization grew through that of their authors belonging to the circle of the apostles. And so the summons of the revelation-event finally found expression in them as part of the whole body of scriptures. The various scriptures represent in this respect, of course, very different features. The saving-event is expressed in the Gospel according to Mark, for example, as the occurrence of the manifold *exousia* of the hidden Messiah, who after defeating the demons and overcoming the law, and after his revelation in word and deed before the world and before those who were his own, sets off, not understood, on the road to Jerusalem and the Cross. This saving-event is viewed differently from, though it is the same as, the one to which John and his *ecclesia* testify: the passing of God's *doxa*, in Jesus' words and signs, to its eternal manifestation, which occurs by his departure. And again it is expressed quite differently, for example, in the Letter to the Romans of the apostle Paul. Here, in confrontation with Jewish thought, it is expressed as the judicial rule of God's active fidelity to the Alliance, which had been shown in decisive saving deeds for Israel and has now been fulfilled in Jesus Christ, and opened to faith as that "righteousness of God" which is one with his "grace". It would be possible to continue characterizing one writing after another, and by doing so to show one past aspect after another in which the saving-event now presents itself in written form. In so many fundamental aspects, it is obvious that the individual details will be different and that they too arose through new questions being put, or were discovered through renewed attentive listening.

Moreover, by fixing in writing the tradition which had been discriminatingly accepted, the expression of the revelation-event attained its definitive form. If we consider the gospels, not only was tradition preserved from disintegration into talk, but Jesus' sayings, and narratives concerning him, and also the historical sources of the Acts of the Apostles, for example, were shaped, in accordance with the tendency inherent in them from the start, in relation to the claim which by their very nature they make. It is not difficult to recognize that in this process the forms springing from the life of the early Church, its worship, catechism, preaching, law, etc. also exercised formative influence. Thus, for example, the farewell discourses of St John's gospel are perhaps to be taken as agape-discourses. Some sections of Paul's letters are determined by hymns tacitly expounded in them, for example Philippians 2: 5 ff.; Colossians 2: 12 ff.; Ephesians 2:11 ff. But above all in this consolidation of the event-language of God's revelation into scripture, there took shape the general form which corresponded to that event and its language: the *evangelion* from which our gospels take their name, the *martyria,* the testimony of the so-called Acts of the Apostles, the *Logos parakleseos,* the word of exhortation as,

with Hebrews 13: 22, we might call the letters of the New
Testament, and prophecy, of which we have of course in the
New Testament the Revelation to John. Whatever distinctions
have to be made in detail, it is clear that through these general
forms which apply to the whole of the scriptures, the sense of
the claim involved in the revelation-event was definitively
brought out and fixed. That, however, also settled from the
start the sense of the truth which the revelation-event bears
within it and seeks to have acknowledged: its truth *is* God's summons uttered authoritatively in it and decisively open only to
attentive obedience. Only those come into the presence of this
truth who, drawn by it, approach it resolutely receptive, in
order to expose themselves to it.

These writings in which the historic event of God's revelation
in Jesus Christ finally expressed itself, now immediately cooper-
ated in consolidating and extending more and more the domain
of experience traced by the event, i.e. the Church, which had
also been vocal in the formation of tradition and scripture. But
as that happened, something occurred in regard to the various
individual writings also. They entered into dynamic relation
to one another. Their intrinsic unity, which is scarcely perceptible, or at least difficult to demonstrate from the writings
themselves, drew them together, separating them from others.
This occurred in the course of the experience of interpretation
which they imposed on the Church. In the midst of abundant
oral and written tradition and a long process, these writings
manifested themselves to the Church as the authoritative and
guiding expression of the revelation-event. In a long process
of clarification of its own mind, the Church decided that these
writings and no others, but just these as they stand, represent
the collection of writings in which the revelation-event, bearing witness to itself, is authenticated as norm and has finally
adapted itself to the Church. So brought fully into the domain
which the revelation-utterance itself assigned, the New Testament, and in conjunction with it the Old Testament, becomes,

as the counterpart of that utterance, its product in language and the mode of its continued existence in language. It becomes so with the whole contingent character of its historical nature which is now once again apparent in the peculiar disparate and fragmentary character of this "Canon" of belief. "The whole in the fragment" of which H. Urs von Balthasar[26] speaks in regard to the cosmos and the Church generally, is visible here also.

But did the revelation-event entirely enter scripture? Is there not outside scripture, though of course linked with it, also an authoritative and normative tradition which does not consist simply in the interpretation of scripture? And if it exists, what is its nature? This question cannot be answered here. But it must at least be raised and formulated so as to show its relevance. Is there not in the revelation-event, as according to M. Picard[27] there is in language (and therefore in history) generally "a surplus of truth in language which does not appear as spoken truth" but which is also a way in which truth is present? Or, to put it differently: is there not a domain of language in which scripture and its spoken language moves, in relation to which scripture is open, and which alone permits the word of scripture to live and prevail? Is there not, to put the question in yet another way, something unexpressed in the word that has been spoken, a silence in which that word dwells, which protects that word as word, but which that word itself takes under its protection too? Something unspoken which is preserved by silence but precisely as what is unspoken in the language of revelation, emerges as a question, and by questioning and being questioned gives answer through scripture and beyond it? We must leave this at this point. After this exhausting approach we must come to the very topic of our inquiry.

---

[26] Cf. H. U. v. Balthasar, *Das Ganze im Fragment* (1963).
[27] *Der Mensch und das Wort* (1955), p. 75.

III

We have in fact reached it, for we have laid bare the specific character of the text we are interpreting. We have thereby thrown light on the process in which we receive a share if we undertake to interpret this text—that of God's self-utterance in the Christ-event, set forth in the authentic, fundamental, final and authoritative tradition of scripture. The function of exegesis is actually to expound that from scripture for the sake of present understanding. If it does so, exegesis is simply fulfilling the intention of the event, of tradition and of scripture which, because they are all intelligible utterances, words, have themselves already made possible, and communicated, understanding.[28] Exegesis must, therefore, heed the guiding principles indicated by scripture itself.

In the first place these show that scripture is to be interpreted as a document of definite times, places, situations, persons, languages etc. The Bible shows itself to be such at first glance, and when more closely examined presents itself, as a whole and in its various writings, as historical testimony to a distant past. Its form and forms, its languages, ideas, terms, mode of thought and mental presuppositions show that. The problem is to trace these through methodical comparison with contemporary texts from the surrounding world and through careful regard for the context in the narrower and wider sense, and so to determine in the usual philological and historical manner what scripture primarily says. The more discriminatingly that is done, the more readily and altogether impartially what is strange and remote in sacred scripture is accepted, the more carefully the specific character of the particular affirmation there and then, and the manner of its affirmation, are ac-

---

[28] Cf. G. Ebeling, "Wort Gottes und Hermeneutik" in *ZTK* 56 (1959), p. 237: "...language, words, is what opens out and mediates understanding, and so brings about the comprehension of something. Language itself has a hermeneutical function."

cepted, the more readily the text will open itself to a first understanding. An approach of this kind to the text, taking due account of its historical distance and difference from us in the perspectives of historical investigation, does not imply an arbitrary or presumptuous attitude to it, but shows respect for God's having revealed himself into the course of history and tradition, and demonstrates the will to recognize his revelation for what it is.[29] By that, of course, the interpretation of sacred scripture which takes account of its withdrawal into the domain of what is past, is also involved in the risk which, if we may so express it, God himself incurred by deciding to meet man historically and in language. The interpretation of scripture as an historical document with historical methods inevitably shares all the uncertainty of the scientific historical approach to reality, its actual defectiveness, which can be kept within bounds, and its fundamentally questionable character which is inescapable and which is evident, for example, in the fact that the decisive personal or general experiences of history are met with quite apart from or beyond the way of learned research. But that does not relieve exegesis of its task of methodically presenting the "historic" i.e. universally significant text of holy scripture, which proves to be an historical one, as it is, with its specific historical character, and precisely by so doing to make it cast its first glance at us or address its first words to us. In fact, realization of the limitations of the methods of historical inquiry can only emphasize the conscientiousness with which they must be handled. Certainly the enthusiasm of the historian

---

[29] Cf. H. Kimmerle, "Hermeneutische Theorie oder ontologische Hermeneutik" in *ZTK* 59 (1962), p. 123: "Scientific understanding brings into clear focus the difference of past horizons, in order then expressly to bring them into communication with the horizon of the present. It integrates itself into the wider process of direct understanding which is that of tradition, by accomplishing this process consciously and by objectively taking account of the time-gap." Cf. also the quotation *ibid.*, p. 124 from R. Wittram, *Das Interesse an der Geschichte* (1958), p. 122: "It (history) gives our consciousness a new dimension and tests our conscience against a wider background."

must not count on a supposed omnicompetence of the historical method. Perhaps it will turn out on some not too distant day that that method was justified and necessary only in the time of what Heidegger called "subjectivity", and even then was not adequate for meeting actual reality. Historical enthusiasm can be of use because God has revealed himself in real and significant events and therefore (for our categories formed on the basis of the course of past events as we represent this to ourselves) in a way that can be the subject of historical investigation. Accordingly he meets us in the historical documents which are sacred scriptures, which we may not, therefore, treat as a mythical heavenly book but must acknowledge in their historicity. Holy scripture as the historical counterpart of an historical revelation-event intrinsically requires an effort of historical, philological comparison and reconstruction in accordance with its historical character, an effort capable of establishing contact with it over the interval of time, and of perceiving its specific character, which means its own mode of statement and its own proper content, persuading it as it were to spell out the alphabet in which its language is written.

But then the second guiding-principle which scripture lays down for exegesis emerges: scripture must fundamentally be understood as documenting a claim expressed in God's self-utterance in Jesus Christ, a claim now expressed in scripture. For when the formal and linguistic structure of scripture has been elucidated by conscientious historical work, as the conscience of the time requires, scripture turns out to be something quite different from a merely contingent historical document. Even the much-reviled form-history school, reviled chiefly by those who understand it least, contributed to this new clarification of scripture, by exhibiting the so-called kerygmatic nature and structure of all its strata. And the history of religions school itself, which was regarded with no less distrust, gradually led to an increased sense of the decisive difference of Christian preaching from any religion contemporary with it. Today exegesis is, generally speaking, aware that holy scripture contains the special call of God revealed in Jesus Christ, a claim which entered into the course of real events and thereby into the object of historical research. Scripture therefore indicates that it must be interpreted in relation to the truth of its claim. This involves two things. In the first place the interpretation of holy scripture cannot ultimately or from the start be guided by an endeavour to build up from it, as though it were an historical source book, a picture of those significant events, a picture which, by representing the orderly and coherent interconnection of causes, would "explain" the events in question and subject them, so to speak, to the scholar's "research"; such a picture would, of course, give him no assurance of salvation but only encourage his self-assurance. If scriptural exegesis is to follow the intention indicated by the form and content of its text, it must rather aim first and last at hearing the claim of the revelation-event of which the expression is fixed in scripture. For this purpose it has also to form ideas about the historical situations and persons and events, but that belongs to the fulfilling of the first requirement mentioned above, and in principle has only a subsidiary and transitional significance. The aim of exegesis must be to hear God's claim, expressed by and in scripture. For this and no other is the truth of scripture. To encounter it and no other, establishes truth. To unfold it from scripture for understanding, means to make truth take place.

The truth of scripture, to put it over-succinctly, is not the correctness of the information it gives on particular historical facts and dates. It does not consist in the fact that everything happened just as it says. For that would presuppose that it was written to guarantee men (of our age!) the course of facts presented, and to make men blessed by putting at their disposal a picture of events in agreement with history as it happened. But the truth of scripture is the peremptory claim of the promise and advent in history of God's fidelity historically fulfilled in the act of judgment and grace in Jesus Christ. And this truth, as we have already said, adopted even a mythical or legendary form of thought and speech, for example in the stories of the Flood or the narratives concerning Elijah and Elisha, or even in some miracle narratives of the New Testament. These have their truth in the purpose for which they address the reader or hearer. They too speak to him of the truth of God's fidelity realized in the history of Israel and its fulfilment in Jesus Christ. They too—viewed from the point of view of historical research—are effects (in the form of mythical or legendary or even deliberately stylized representation) of concrete experiences of God's action and then finally of the person of Jesus Christ and his history. For sufficient can be established about the latter even by historical research. Because they are effects of that history, which of itself demands the scope of myth or legend as a mode of verbal expression, those sections of scripture also are bearers and mediators of the truth of God's claim, which in that way too makes his fidelity heard. But exegesis has to grasp that truth. Its function is to expound it.

Besides, the fact that the truth of an occurrence also finds expression through fantasy—if mythical and legendary forms of verbal expression may be so described—and is not confined solely to historically exact report, is a universal historical phenomenon. Truth certainly does not always come home to us most in an historical report which sets great store by facts and dates and their correctness. That report may offer me a host of such facts and dates and guarantee the historical exactitude of what is narrated. Yet a single anecdote may make me better realize the truth about a human being, an event or a situation. That is not to say that the claim of truth when it is expressed in an historical report, could dispense with agreement with facts and dates, or, in the case of sacred scripture, to the extent that it aims at giving an historical report, that it did dispense with them. But the truth which according to its own intention is addressed to us as the truth of God's revelation, is of such a kind that it is not concerned only with such agreeement, but reduces it to merely relative importance and in fact makes it inoperative. If I attend to the truth, to the God who is revealing himself, in the narrative concerning Jesus in Gethsemane, the question of the precise sequence of events (and of course, most emphatically, the question of the source of the account) becomes as indifferent to me as it was to the evangelist John, who completely passes over the event from the chronological point of view and proclaims the truth of its tradition in quite a different context, in the light of his whole understanding of Jesus and in a decisive dialogue of Jesus with the Father (Jn 12:27 f.). Similarly, the very existence of John's gospel side by side with the synoptic gospels unmistakably shows that for the primitive Church the truth of the revelation-event is indeed connected with its historical reality but does not depend on the historiographical or purely factual character of what is reported. The truth lies in the claim of scripture as a document which in the most varied modes of statement preserves and testifies to the occurrence of God's revelation in Jesus Christ. The truth consists in the claim of this scripture as a manifold and multiple authentication of historical revelation. Perhaps in this connection the following must also be considered. What help would it be to man if, for example in the synoptic gospels, he only had historical reports, which in that case would of course harmonize with one another? He would only have an abstract of history. In itself, in the sense of the rational inference of historical inquiry, there is no fact more certain than the death of Jesus on the Cross on Golgotha. But what actually is that fact? What is the truth of that fact? Viewed simply on the basis of the fact itself, the question must remain an absolutely open one. But in that way the very fact as an historically significant fact evaporates. For it is an historic fact, in itself and in its historical influence, only when interpreted. Whose interpretation is to be considered valid? That of historical research, explaining the unknown on a mundane, causal basis, in terms of what can be verified, psychologically and sociologically, or the interpretation of the evangelists? The latter at all events were convinced that their interpretation alone brought out the truth of the event. They understood that event, the death of Jesus on the Cross, as—speaking generally—an earthly event and yet one which transcends everything earthly, produced by God for us men, a fulfilment and manifestation of all the suffering of God's Servant and of the just of the Old Testament. They were convinced that the "remembrance of Jesus' death", which is what the Passion narrative essentially is, could appropriately take place only in a form in which report and interpretation, reality and meaning are expressed together in mutual implication. And for that purpose even the legendary mode of expression was available among others. Exegesis today must of course bring to light this state of affairs by a systematic historical method, especially, for example, by that of form-history. But if exegesis is to give expression to the truth of Jesus' death in accordance with the intention of the gospels for the present time, it must cause this event to meet with understanding in its *truth*, that is to say, it must interpret the event as set forth in its truth by its interpretation.

That can only succeed, of course, if exegesis observes the other part of the second principle indicated by the special character of scripture. The claim of the truth can only be laid open to present-day understanding if the distance which separates us from scripture is bridged by philological and historical elucidation, and, in addition, if there is active attention to, and concern with, the truth which is making a claim on us through scripture. And it is simply appropriate if in the interpretation of scripture a kind of understanding is all the time at work which is derived from the subject-matter itself and which motivates the exegesis, an understanding which opens out into candid, living and obedient listening. Naturally that introduces into exegesis a risk which contradicts the ideal of a science safeguarding itself as far as possible against all imponderabilia. But it inescapably belongs to the elucidation of historic texts generally. Significiant historical texts, themselves fixed by historic events, seek to beget history. They tend to be texts in the history of the very person reading them. That is most certainly the case as regards sacred scripture, as itself testifies. The history of Jesus for example, as it is consigned in the Gospel according to John, is certainly non-historical in the sense of methodically verified and verifiable scientific history, yet it is certainly historical re-collection of the historical words and signs of the Word who came into history in Jesus, and is intended to awaken faith in response to the claim made by the truth of that history. But all the greater success will be had in interpreting intelligibly and bringing home to the understanding precisely that history and its texts if the methodical movement towards what the text meant at that time and place in the past, is accompanied and permeated by a kind of concern for, and indeed implication in, that history, which is non-methodical, imponderable but genuinely historical because duly attentive to the historical claim involved. The process of understanding at work in this kind of historically motivated exegesis, entirely corresponds to the general understanding of a human being and his history. I have not understood a person's life and history when I know many verifiable dates and facts, chronological, psychological about a human life, and set them in order for myself, perhaps with a certain power of sympathetic insight, to form a co-herent picture of his personality, but rather when, knowing perhaps little or only vaguely about him, I open myself to the appeal of his life, concern myself with it, abandon myself to it. Only in that way shall I learn to understand the substance and language of his history. Of course, such intangible sensitivity and receptivity to the claim of holy scripture is not a licence for a pious caprice convinced it can replace methodical inter-pretation by arbitrary fancy. Someone who really is attentive to the claim of the truth of God's revelation unfolded in scrip-ture and who meets it with understanding as he listens, will, because it is a question of the summons of scripture and not of his own heart, do his utmost to make contact by every possible means with scripture in the objectivity of its own specific nature. But he will do that in a way which also exposes him to the claim it makes.

Only because there is also, and in an ultimately decisive sense, this access to scripture through understanding of its historic significance, are three matters of common experience intelligible. There are in the first place the inadequate commentaries, inadequate not because they are lacking in learning or method—though there are of course those that are so lacking—but because they do not penetrate to, or bring out, the essential subject-matter at all, and ultimately do not wish to go as far as that, because that would be "unscientific". Anyone who reads them has the definite impression that he has been cheated of the essential. There is also the phenomenon, of which too little account is taken by what is called specialist exegesis, that for seventeen hundred years there was no question of understanding the text by its methods at all and, what is of even greater importance, that even today there is an exegesis which reaches the substance by a mysterious, abbreviated process of living historical understanding. It cannot be denied that the voice of revelation emphatically makes itself heard in its truth even to an unanalysed but in fact effective procedure of "naïve" interpretation.[30] Once again it must be repeated that the fact that this is possible does not mean any moratorium on methodical philological historical work which, respecting the contingent character of revelation, endeavours to elucidate what is actually stated by scripture, and exercises a critical function in regard to anyone interpreting it. But it does

[30] Cf. H. G. Gadamer, "Was ist Wahrheit?" in *Zeitwende* 28 (1957), p. 232, who draws attention to the fact that in moral sciences, "the scholar can sometimes learn more from the book of a dilettante than from the works of other scholars", which is a sign that "here a relation is revealed between recognition of truth and the possibility of expression which is not to be measured by the verificability of staments".

amount to a hint to the exegete not to neglect or forget the legitimate and proper process of interpretation. Finally, mention must be made of the phenomenon, notable even from the point of view of exact scholarship, that with the same method and equal ability in handling it, the results of interpretations are nevertheless often very different or, which is another aspect of the same thing, that exegesis is perpetually striving afresh to understand the biblical text. That is only to be explained by the fact that the situation of the interpreter, of his school and of his age, continually varies because it is determined by numerous factors and expresses itself in ever new questions put to the text which provoke ever new answers from the text. But that is precisely what points to the historical factor in the process of interpretation which, like all hermeneutical activity, in the last resort is refractory to regulation, however carefully the rules are observed.

A third guiding-principle of the interpretation of holy scripture follows from the specific nature of the text. We have seen that God's revelation as a significant event traces for itself a domain of experience which constitutes a mental perspective within which it is preserved, whether understood or not. The interpretation of that event from scripture also occurs within and under the influence of that domain. Not as though, to put it briefly, there is not exegesis outside the Church, or as though the text did not permit of interpretation on the basis of some general historical, aesthetic or ideological interest, often with a certain amount of success. Otherwise, of course, it would have to be denied that the text is generally intelligible and is itself capable of inspiring faith. But such interpretation is not the regular kind with most prospect of success. Leaving aside the fact that interest in this text was only kept alive through the centuries, and is emphatically so maintained at the present day, by the Church,[31] it is a feature of exegesis as an historical

---

[31] Cf. C. Westermann, "Was ist eine exegetische Aussage?" in *ZTK* 59 (1962), pp. 4 f.

process that it takes place in communication with other inter-pretation of every kind and in that way realizes the vital ur-gency of its questions and often receives its actual direction.

The Church, however, is the domain in which the claim of the revelation-event has always been already heard and is ever to be heard anew. Consequently the Church is the domain in which this event is perpetually the topic of mutual discussion, so that one understanding is offered to another and light is generated by mutual understanding. That does not mean that the interpre-tation which takes place within the Church as the domain where revelation is known, abolishes the rôle of the individual exegete as critical hearer—critical towards, in the sense of pass-ing judgment on, the interpretation produced by others and by himself, based on their attention to the language and voice of scripture. Exegesis as discussion and through discussion, is only possible if each partner is also and in the first place listening to the subject-matter itself and if he succeeds in making intellig-ible what he hears. But exegesis with mutual interchange of understanding always means that the question put by the individual, and therefore the answer which he receives, are con-stituted in part by the questions that precede and follow.[32] In this it must also be borne in mind that the discussion which interpretation pursues, not only with the subject-matter itself but also with the interpretation given to this within the domain in which it is experienced, need not necessarily take place ex-plicitly. That applies not only to the individual commentator but also to the interpretation current in the domain of ex-perience of scripture. The interpreter may refer to the sub-ject-matter all the more intensely by not expressing any argu-ment over such interpretation, although the latter in fact is vigorously enough pursued.[33] And the interpretation which as

---

[32] Cf. G. Ebeling, "Wort Gottes und Hermeneutik", p. 239; and also O. Pöggeler, *Der Denkweg M. Heideggers* (1963), p. 203.
[33] The commentaries of A. Schlatter may be recalled, which only aim at direct treatment of the subject-matter.

a matter of fact prevails at a particular time in the Church, is found not only in exegesis but also and often more influentially in worship, charism and law.[34] It takes place in the life of the Church as a whole. This establishes the general initial understanding, perpetually puts questions to the text and also in fact gives answers to exegesis, perhaps without the latter's being aware of what has happened. This can be dangerous, if the answer which perhaps once was directly relevant has become anachronistic and therefore distorts the text. It can be useful, however, if it has maintained its authenticity and so helps exegesis to inquire in the right direction. Here too, therefore, exegesis must be critical, not out of an itch for originality but in order to serve to elucidate the subject-matter, scripture and the mystery of revelation. This dialogue character of exegesis which ultimately derives from the character of God's revelation in Jesus Christ as a significant event and from the way in which it is encountered in experience, can only be overlooked or felt as a burden by an ideal exegesis which dreams of purely objective interpretation and is not willing to admit the historical character of the process of interpretation in this respect either.

The interpretation of sacred scripture takes place, as we have said, implicitly in the whole life of the Church, but there are, nevertheless, processes which in a certain way can be understood as a prolongation of interpretation actually and explicitly at work and with which exegesis is connected in a special way. For what holy scripture states also finds expression, linked explicitly with interpretation, in the liturgy, in doctrinal reflection and preaching.[35] It is not part of our subject to determine the relation of these activities to exegesis. But a few indications may be given.

The liturgy is permeated by sacred scripture and is therefore

---

[34] Cf. G. Ebeling, *Kirchengeschichte als Geschichte der Auslegung der Heiligen Schrift* (1947), p. 24.
[35] Attention has been drawn to this recently in his own particular way by C. Westermann in *ZTK* 59 (1962), pp. 6 ff.

determined by its interpretation. Every prayer is based on direct or indirect scriptural interpretation and on direct or indirect understanding of scripture. Liturgy is scripture transposed into prayer and action. But scripture itself figures in the liturgy and is quoted there on principle, so that its very words are present. What scripture states operates in this case as recapitulation. And this presupposes the conviction that the text of holy scripture itself gives expression, in a way that is effective for salvation, to the summons of God's revelation,[36] and does so within the order which, as an order of prayer, is directed towards the Eucharist, because by the nature of the case, and historically, it has its foundation in the Eucharist. But even scripture read aloud is present as interpreted. The interpretation is tacitly shown by the choice and arrangement of the passages of scripture, which everywhere exhibit some particular understanding of scripture, even if in the extreme case this amounts to no more than the implication that there is no question of understanding the particular passage from the context and in the context.

The relation of exegesis to dogmatic reflection is of course, of a different kind.[37] For even when in exegesis the revelation-event is brought out in all its aspects for present-day understanding in just the way it is viewed in the books of the Bible, it has not even then been thought out in its full meaning, but only as it was originally conceived. The reflective and inquiring elucidation[38] of the theological content, which has been

---

[36] Cf. H. U. v. Balthasar, *Das Ganze im Fragment*, p. 264: "The words of a great writer cannot be affected by philological criticism; they are what are and produce their effect as they are, regardless of the praise or blame of philologists. Praise and blame will pass, but Goethe's words will not. Similarly, but very much more so, the word of God is raised above all exegesis whether analytic or synthetic, helpful or impeding. It permits these endeavours, but they will pass, while the word endures."

[37] Cf. "Biblical and Dogmatic Theology", above, pp. 28—40.

[38] Cf. M. Heidegger, *Einführung in die Metaphysik* (1956), p. 6, E. T.: *Introduction to Metaphysics* (1959).

introduced by biblical theolgy as the goal of exegesis, must
be carried further. It must be drawn from the content itself
i.e. from actual reflection based on that content and directed
to it. This occurs in doctrinal reflection. Perpetually spurred
on by exegesis, this must above all enter into discussion with
what has already been thought in the Church on the basis
of scripture, and must think over what has been thought, so
that this may yield up what has not been thought[39] and disclose further the mystery of the subject-matter itself. In such
thinking directed towards the very reality that is in question,
the Church's reflection on the faith does not move away from
the truths of revelation but comes nearer to them, for they
mirror the one truth of the revelation-event. What exegesis
works out by a methodical process and attentive understanding as being what holy scripture proposes for our consideration,
is committed to the believing reflection of the Church, so that
this meditation may think over what has to be thought and penetrate the subject-matter itself. Perhaps at this or that point
success will be reached in thinking something out to a conclusion.
Such thinking out to a conclusion, which is shown by the consensus of the Church concerning its belief, may, if the hour
requires and permits, lead to its fixing in dogma. This, however,
does not mean the end of reflection, but signifies that what has
been thought, reflected on, thought over, and here and now
thought out to a conclusion, is raised to the rank of what is incontestably and permanently worthy of thought. For exegesis,
that does not mean the suspending of activity within the radius
of this or that text, but sends decided thought back to its beginning, to think it over afresh. Precisely by dogma (which of course
owes its truth to the revelation-event as such, through scripture
and through the surplus of truth recalled above which has
borne fruit), exegesis can learn that its very nature consists in

---

[39] Cf. M. Heidegger, *Was heisst Denken?* (1954), p. 110; *Unterwegs zur
Sprache* (1959), p. 134; O. Pöggeler, *Der Denkweg M. Heideggers* (1963),
pp. 284 ff.

an ever-new and endless activity within the course of history.

There is, however, a third prolongation of exegesis which is more direct than dogmatic theology and if one may so express it, more concrete and individual than the liturgy—preaching of all kinds. It does not always have to be scriptural preaching though, for a renewal of preaching, it would be well if it were so today. In preaching, the interpretation of the revelation-event from scripture is pursued here and now to the point of addressing the hearers in the particular, individual way appropriate to them in their particular individual situation. The concrete life of the individual in the first place and then that of the congregation, is brought by preaching into the light of the revelation-event and thereby disclosed in its truth. Scripture, therefore, speaks once again. But of course that is not the word which crystallized in scripture, so that every preacher would be more or less an apostle or prophet; it is language which expresses scripture. As such it is at best, and to the extent that it places no obstacle to the voice of scripture but allows its own discourse to be prompted by it, an approach to the word of revelation made possible by scripture. In that, of course, all the factor already mentioned as connected with scripture and its interpretation, play a part too. In *one* respect nevertheless, the intention proper to scripture is apparent in this word of preaching: that of bringing out the claim of God's truth, God's fidelity, in the concrete, here and now, and of making the hearer obedient to it. For, of course, biblically speaking, to preach is to bring to a hearer what the preacher has heard and continues to hear, in such a way that it is given an obedient hearing. In preaching, the arrow of the word reaches its target.

Viewed as a whole, exegesis of scripture undertaken specifically and responsibly in order to promote understanding, proves to be a laborious but important activity. The methodical elucidation and translation of the language of the revelation-event which has assumed written form is laborious in itself. For that language stands remote and alien in the far domain of distant history. No less laborious, and in fact even more laborious, is the attentive concern with the summons addressed by revelation, which the expositor must hear in and behind his methodical procedure, for such hearing is of decisive hermeneutical importance. The dialogue about interpretation which is always in progress within the horizon in which revelation is encountered, can be of general assistance to the particular interpretation, but can also on occasion be a powerful hindrance to understanding. Yet, despite the labour, there must be scriptural exegesis. For even if it represents nothing but a perpetual process of elucidation, a service which never ends, and which is ever new because of its ever-new questions and because of its constantly questioning the old answers, nevertheless precisely as such, if it has a right understanding of its own nature and does not waste time on useless matters, exegesis expounds the claim of God's truth which occurred as an event in history and is voiced in scripture for each successive present-day, and it holds open the rule of that truth in the world and for the world. In a world that does not know what it will be like tomorrow, who would not wish to live under that clear call of God which opens out all things and admits all that God's future holds?

CHAPTER IV

The New Testament and Myth

"We did not follow cleverly devised myths when we made known to you the power and coming of our Lord Jesus Christ, but we were eye-witnesses of his majesty." This sentence of the Second Letter of Peter shows that the question of the relation between the teaching of the New Testament and myth is a very old one indeed. From the beginning the objection was evidently raised that the original Christian message retailed myths. Equally from the beginning, however, that accusation was rebutted, and this was done with full awareness of the qualitative difference between myth and saving event. From the beginning too the Christian community was warned against myth. Its members, it is said in the pastoral epistles, were to be on their guard against "godless and silly myths", against the "profane", "empty", "intemperate", "impious", "diabolical" chatter of "what is falsely called knowledge" and are rather to hold fast to the "sound" and "good" doctrine of the apostolic legacy which contains "the truth": they are to hold fast to the "word". The New Testament recognized, therefore, as soon as its authors were obliged to reflect on the matter, that an abyss separated the *muthos* which they saw in the world around them from the *logos* of Christian preaching.

Yet it must be admitted that the scholarship of historians of religion and of exegetes is right in finding mythical ideas, not only in the Old Testament but also in the New. That is not at all surprising when we think of the intensity of the mythical element in ancient times. Just as the New Testament did not use a special kind of Greek but the common speech (*koine*) of that age, so also it could not express itself immediately in terms and ideas different from those which came from its Jewish and Hellenistic environment. And how, therefore, theologically speaking, could the Logos who was made flesh not by that very fact enter into the language and thought of that age, though of course without ceasing to be the Logos?

But if that is so, and if the apostolic message was also proclaimed in the terms and conceptions of myth, how can the New Testament so consciously and definitely deny that it is retailing myths, and issue a warning against myths? Are we to suppose that the scholarship and exegesis to which we have referred and which after all has become increasingly circumspect in its principles and methods, is simply in error, or that the biblical writers were deceived, as many people have asserted, since the time of the Gnostics and Celsus and Porphyry, throughout the centuries down to our own days?

Let us first consider more precisely what kind of myths could at that time have influenced at all the New Testament teaching. There was of course no longer any question of man's primitive myths, the earth and sky myths of the age of magical beliefs, nor of myths of gods and heroes of the so-called classical Greek period, the direct expression of Greek humanity. Nor was there any question of philosophical myths such as those to which Plato's rational discourse eventually led. All that was too remote. In the New Testament three kinds of myth are in question if we divide them schematically: the so-called mythology of Jewish apocalyptic, the primal-man-redeemer myth of a (Jewish) eastern Gnosticism, and perhaps also mythical ideas operative in connection with Hellenistic, eastern mystery-religions.

As regards the first kind of myth, we may think of the

copious and passionate descriptions of the first calamity breaking over the earth, the vision of the heavenly judge and saviour
and his arrival, the dreams of Sion's glory and the punishment
of the nations, in short, the themes which we find in the late
Jewish writings such as Henoch, Baruch or Esra.

But can the term myth be applied to such apocalyptic speculations at all? It is true that very ancient mythical themes are
often preserved in them, as in the prophecy of Gog and Magog
or in the representation of the power hostile to God in the
form of animals, or the dragon, rising from the sea—a detail
which retains its connection with an old creation myth telling
of God's struggle with the dragon of chaos, the sea-monster—
or in the mystery of Leviathan and Behemoth, which are there
to be consumed. But in general and by their very meaning the
apocalyptic speculations of later Judaism regarded themselves
at all events simply as further interpretation of Old Testament
prophecy by visionary "wisdom". And however different the
fundamental attitude of Old Testament prophecy may be from
Jewish apocalyptic writing (a fact which Martin Buber recently
recalled), not only the author of the Fourth Book of Esra
ranked the apocalypses of his circles side by side with, or even
above, the canonical writings of the Synagogue, but the Old
Testament itself recognized apocalyptic writing in principle, at
least with the Book of Daniel. Above all, the exegetical character of the apocalyptic speculations, and their connection with
Old Testament prophecy in regard to their main themes, can
be demonstrated in each particular case, even if arbitrary
visionary fantasy often separated apocalyptic exegesis very
widely from prophecy.

There is another variety of this apocalyptic myth to be considered. It had a long and varied history behind it by the time
it acquired the form in which it encountered the apostolic
preaching. And in the course of that history, by concentrating
on certain eschatological types, it had elaborated a sort of
apocalyptic symbol-language. Events which are narrated in

such mythological patterns, for instance in that of the description of the Flood, are not to be understood in the immediate sense which the description bears, but point to something which in fact is incomprehensible but which can be suggested and indicated by certain mythical symbols. After all, it is very significant, for example, that the central portions of the so-called Aethiopic Book of Henoch, one of the many apocalypses linked to the name of Henoch, are called *meshale*, "parables", and so bear the same name as the parables of Jesus.

The second kind of myth of which the New Testament shows traces, is the myth of the primal-man-redeemer which derives from extremely varied ancient sources, was current in the world of New Testament times and was later copiously developed in heretical Christian Gnosticism. This too probably entered Christian thought via Jewish circles who were not very far removed from the apocalyptic ones. The link was provided by speculations about Adam who, in Philo of Alexandria and occasionally among the rabbis, was regarded as an ideal and archetypal man, and by speculations about "wisdom", the latter even in later Judaism having become a sort of redeemer-figure. We find this primal-man-redeemer myth in the New Testament, for example in the background of the Gospel according to John or in what Paul has to say about the first man, Adam, with whom the "second" or "last" man Christ is contrasted, each of them in a different sense comprising humanity in himself. The same myth is even more clearly perceptible in the background of the Letter to the Colossians. There Christ is thought of in the categories of the pre-existent primal man whose body contains the elements of the universe, the "powers", but who at the same time, as the redeemed redeemer, establishes the new humanity in himself.

The formal characteristics of this myth also must be carefully noted. As far as the Testament environment is concerned, this myth too is linked to a certain degree with the Old Testament even though in the latter in actual fact no speculations about Adam are found; the myth is intended as exposition of the Old Testament and development of Jewish tradition concerning Adam. But the truth is that this myth too has already left its connecting link far behind and on its long journey has repeatedly been re-interpreted. It too in its immediately pre-Christian form often represents merely a symbolic myth. Its elements are frequently merely signs. So, for example, the five (six) vices which constitute the "old man" are called limbs and so distantly recall the primal man who consists of the five (six) fundamental elements of the cosmos and is the macrocosm of nature. In its totality the myth constitutes in many respects merely a mode of formal representation to assist comprehension of the connection between redeemer and what is redeemed.

In studies in comparative religion we often hear it said that the myths of the Hellenistic-oriental mystery-cults influenced the thought of the New Testament. It is difficult in fact to make out what concrete form these myths actually took. The original myth of chthonic vegetation gods changed in the early Hellenistic period into the salvation myth of the dying and in some cases reviving gods. Then about the beginning of the Christian era it was already frequently interpreted as a "Gnostic" myth of the redeemed redeemer and primal man who descends, establishes his self and ascends once again through the heavens. But what persisted through all these, was not only the idea of the god who succumbs to death and comes to life again, but also the conviction that the liturgical celebration and representation of the lot of the divinity gives the initiate a share in it. And this fundamental formal idea of the mystery-religions, which of course was linked to the myths, perhaps influenced one particular interpretation of early Christian baptism by the apostle Paul : when he affirms that it incorporates the baptized into the death and resurrection of Christ. Such a conception of baptism could not of course be expressed either in New Testament or in Jewish categories, which were guided by the baptism of proselytes or other purification baptisms. Perhaps, too, the Lord's Supper was placed by the apostle Paul in the light of certain mystery-religions in order to make it clearer in regard to the sacramental communion with the crucified and risen Lord. But our knowledge here is too slight.

Those, broadly speaking, are the myths which could have had some influence on the apostolic preaching. They are myths which were intended to unfold Old Testament revelation and expound and complete it as "wisdom", in many cases making the mythical element into pattens and so forming a sign language and on occasion stiffening into formal conceptual and imaginative categories designed to grasp and represent sacred events. The original Christian message in contradistinction to some strata of the Old Testament, was not uttered in the domain of spontaneous and living myth. The Jewish element, even outside Palestine, and the national element of the Hellenistic period, had already to a large extent diminished, though certainly not suppressed, the really mythical element in myth. Is the New Testament supposed to have revived it once more?

But are we not really rather too concerned with apologetics in this question? Did those myths even in the stage when they were the object of conscious reflection not possess sufficient mythical substance and force for them to contribute to form the content of the original Christian preaching? Is it not the case, to give a concrete, central and graphic example, that (as could be read once again in a recently published work on the intellectual history of early Christianity, just as it could be read 70 years ago in the time of the wildest hypotheses on religious origins), the proclamation of the resurrection by Jesus' disciples is only to be understood as deriving "from visionary experiences" and "from transference of the myth of the resurrected god"? Whether any such myth of a dying and risen god was generally current at that time was once again contested, we may note in passing, by M. P. Nilson in 1950. But we do not wish to enter into this point now.

Let us rather consider briefly, as is inevitable, what can be said on the basis of our oldest original Christian sources about the specific character of the original Christian kerygma in relation to our question as a whole. We have this oldest source in the tradition which the apostle Paul quotes at the beginning of the 15th chapter of the First Letter to the Corinthians and which he himself had received about the year A.D. 35. To this could be added other formularies of faith which occur on occasion in the New Testament, as well as the outlines of the original Christian missionary preaching which the evangelist Luke has preserved for us in the Acts of the Apostles as ancient summaries of the Christian faith. In these sources we have before us, speaking generally, the record of the testimony of certain competent eye-witnesses and actual hearers, who constituted such an exclusive circle that even the apostle Paul based himself on their testimony.

According to Acts chapter 10, these traditions testify, in Luke's mind, to historical events: Jesus' baptism in the Jordan, Jesus' activity in Judaea and Jerusalem, his crucifixion and death, his resurrection from the dead, his appearance to the witnesses and his return as judge of the living and the dead. The old community tradition quoted by the apostle Paul is shorter, but it too refers to actual events. It mentions Jesus' death, his tomb, his resurrection on the third day, the appearances of the risen Jesus to Cephas and the Twelve. Both traditions, therefore, testify to events of a history of Jesus. And among these events Jesus' resurrection from the dead and his appearing when risen is not only placed in a list with the others, but the latter have their goal in the former. At all events in the mind of the ancient tradition it is not an appendix to the crucifixion but the latter is the gateway to it. Sometimes old formularies of belief in the letters of the apostle Paul mention the resurrection of Jesus Christ by itself. For the ancient tradition, of course, however differently it may be interpreted in other respects, it is the transition to the manifest coming of the Lord. It is the dawn of the future revelation, inasmuch as it disclosed the unveiled reality of Jesus Christ to the witnesses, as a testimony. The crucified Jesus Christ, risen from the dead, displayed visibly in himself the reality ultimately hidden by death. By that, in an inconceivably concrete way, he committed provisionally to the testimony of witnesses what one day is to be manifest definitively to all. The faith of the Church assumes this testimony and in that way the "uttermost" which intervened in the world with Jesus Christ is preserved, so that it can be placed before the eyes of the world and kept there in the eschatological history which in this way has begun.

By the eschatological event of the resurrection of Jesus Christ from the dead, his death on the Cross and also his Passion and activity and even further back his birth, in short all the events of his life, were recognized and confirmed in their true character as events and placed in the light which was now thrown by the future. On the basis of that eschatological self-revelation of the risen Jesus Christ, however, the connection of the Messiah who had actually appeared with the events of the Old Testament was understood, and his person and deeds were seen as the continuation and fulfilment of those "mighty deeds" of God in the old "Alliance". The oldest sources themselves and the New Testament as a whole saw that the Old Testament had pointed to these events of Jesus' history. In the tradition quoted in 1 Corinthians 15 it is said that "Christ died for our sins in accordance with the scriptures, he was buried, he was raised on the third day in accordance with the scriptures". And in the ancient outline of preaching in Acts 10 it is said that "To him all the prophets bear witness".

The oldest kerygma, therefore, for its part was consciously proclaiming concrete historical events in the context of a concrete history of redemption by God. To these concrete events there also belongs the resurrection of Jesus Christ from the dead. Only through this does the redemptive meaning and interconnection of all other saving events become clear. For only in it was the ground of all other saving events disclosed. In that way, however, it is itself recognized to be the fundamental event of all history. The resurrection of Jesus Christ from the dead is no myth in the mind of the oldest kerygma. It is true of myth what Sallust said of the event announced in the myth of Attis and celebrated in the worship of Attis: "This never happened, but always is". Myth knows no historical events; it needs and wants none. For what it proclaims is not essentially characterized by having once happened *hic et nunc* but by its mirroring the eternally identical cosmic destiny of man. What myth announces is essentially, and merely, a symbolic event; it exists only to the extent that it has meaning and in virtue of what it means. "This never happened"—of course not. For what happened in Attis or the many-named primal-man of the Naasene sermon is only the exemplary reflection of the universal human condition. Man's profound cosmic destiny is comprised and projected in myth. The mythical event only *exists* in the mirror of myth. "But always is"—of course. What is significant is at all times. It only needs to be known. If talk of the resurrection of Jesus Christ from the dead were nothing but "the expression of the significance of the Cross", then that talk and the resurrection of Jesus Christ from the dead, the significance of the Cross, would in fact be a myth. But in that case,—this consequence is not to be avoided—the Cross as the Cross of the risen Christ and as saving event would also be a myth. In itself and without significance, however, it would be an incidental historical event like any other. That is how it was understood in the apocryphal *Acts of the Apostle John*. There the Lord is only "crucified ... for the mass of the people down there in Jerusalem, and struck with lances and reeds and given vinegar and gall to drink". The truth there, however, is the "cross of light" of gnosis, which appears to the Gnostic alone. In the "cross of light", the significance of that incidental historical event down there in Jerusalem shines forth and discloses the occurrence as "the piercing of the Logos, the Logos' blood, ... the suffering of the Logos, ... the Logos' death". But that it is only a question of the passion and death of the Logos and not of the Cross and death of the incarnate Logos, and that the real event is the "cross of light" of gnosis, the emergence of the significance of the real Cross by the emergence of gnosis,—that is precisely what the apostolic preaching emphatically denies. For that preaching, what is involved above all is history, the actual *occurrence* of what the Cross "signifies", and of what gives it its significance: the resurrection of Jesus Christ from the dead. For early Christian preaching, the resurrection of Jesus Christ crucified from the dead is not only the shining forth of the significance of the Cross and thereby the coming to rest of the Logos in the gnosis of the knower; it is that eschatological event of the real passage of the person of Jesus Christ through real death, the ascent of Jesus Christ into the real life which transcends and so overcomes death, a passage which at the same time constitutes his entry into the testimony of his witnesses. The resurrection of Jesus Christ from the dead completes as a real event the real occurrence of the Cross and in this way reveals it in its true and manifest nature. Only with such a conception of the resurrection of Jesus Christ from the dead is it possible to understand how the apostle Paul in his argument with the enthusiasts in Corinth who were inclined to mythologize the event, can say "If Christ has not been raised, then our preaching is in vain and your faith is in vain" (1 Cor 15 : 14).

Just as the resurrection of Jesus Christ, as an event, provided the grounds of the first apostolic preaching through his revealing himself to the competent witnesses, so also it soon shed its light on the entire tradition concerning Jesus' deeds, and shaped it by the illumination it brought. On the basis of that event all that had been handed down regarding Jesus was theologically illuminated. And just as in the light of that anticipatory eschatological event, Jesus' redemptive history stood out plainly as a continuation and fulfilment of God's saving deeds in the Old Testament, so also did the other decisive concern in the further development and reflective unfolding of the apostolic message, that of demonstrating that history as the accomplishment of the Old Testament promise. But if the original Christian preaching took shape under these two aspects which fundamentally are the same, myth cannot have been a constitutive principle either for the origin or for the development of the apostolic testimony. What part did it play then? This brings us back to the question we raised at the start, though not to the same starting-point.

Nowhere in the New Testament is an entire myth narrated. Neither the myth of the primal-man-redeemer nor the so-called apocalyptic myth appear anywhere in a continuous form, not even in the apocalyptic visions of the Revelation to John. And to the extent that fragments and elements of myth are employed in the New Testament, they draw upon myth-traditions of very different and even opposed kinds. We may recall for example, that the sacred names by which early Christian preaching expressed the person of Jesus, the name and title of "Messiah" and the name and title of "Son of man", derive from very different Jewish interpretations of Old Testament prophecy: national and cosmological eschatology. Or we might notice how in the Pauline letters, as a means of grasping more closely the phenomenon "world", fragments of very different views of the world, Jewish, Hellenistic and Gnostic, are found, which never provide a self-contained "picture" of the world that can be seen as a unity. It is true, of course, that early Christian preaching had no interest in doing that, even though it did aim at conveying a unified experience of the world. For that reason alone, it may be noted in passing, the thesis that the New Testament presents a mythical view of the world is not a very likely one. Furthermore, it may be emphasized that in the apostolic message on occasion mythical elements mingle with figurative features from the public life of antiquity. For example, when the apostle Paul wanted to elucidate a saying of our Lord about the fate at the Parousia of those who have already fallen asleep, about the coming of the Lord and about the Church's going out to meet him, he describes the event with apocalyptic symbols and at the same time gives it features taken from the reception of high Roman officials.

In the New Testament itself, mythical elements chiefly crop up when it is a matter of representing purely eschatological events, as for example in the description of Christ's descent into hell or his second coming. That does not mean that in these cases we are dealing with mythical events, but it does mean that they are scarcely susceptible of expression except by means of the traditional ideograms of human visions. It has always been noted that myth is met with least in the synoptic gospels. The reason is that in them the historical material of the story of Jesus' life in its individual elements had been, comparatively speaking, least subjected to reflection. Much more in fluence was exerted by mythical forms of representation in the more theological gospel of John and especially in the theological teaching of Paul's letters or of the Letter to the Hebrews. Naturally they mostly occur where, tacitly or explicitly, controversies are involved with circles of the early Christian community which had succumbed to heretical mythologization of the faith.

Such observations which could, of course, be further extended and refined, indicate in regard to our question that the apostolic preaching had only a very limited and incidental interest in myth. Consequently, it is not only reserved in regard to myth generally but it makes use of fragments and elements of myth only where the presentation of the subject demands it. A comparison of the New Testament with early Christian apocryphal works, for example, shows that at once. The gaze of the apostles was fixed on history and from the start conceded only a subsidiary role to myth.

We can perhaps make this role clear in the first place by two examples from the New Testament itself. One is taken from what with considerable lack of precision is called apocalyptic

myth. In this domain we find not only the gospels, but Jesus
himself. We have already mentioned the title "Son of man"
which Jesus, according to the synoptic tradition especially, very
often chooses to designate himself. What does this title mean,
by reason of its origin among apocalyptic circles in Judaism?
As they understood it, the Son of man dwells from eternity in
heaven. To the world he is a mystery. Only the elect and
righteous know of him. At the end of time he, who embodies in
himself God's rule, will be manifested as the Saviour of the last
days who leads the creation back to its original perfect condition. He will appear as the judge and ruler of the world,
destroying evil and saving the elect in order to be with them
for ever as ruler of all nations in the transfigured universe.
But what did Jesus and the traditions concerning him understand by that Son of man? That Son of man *is* Jesus. He
is so because he will appear in the clouds of heaven to judge
and save, and also because he has already appeared in a hidden way on earth. And he is so because his appearance in
this hidden way includes suffering and death in order to
rise again. The myth of the Son of man which had already
been obscurely adopted by prophecy, Daniel 7:13 f., has now
been brought right out of its apocalyptic wanderings into
concrete history. In the historical Jesus, the Son of man who
is before time and who belongs to the end of time is recognized. His future advent has already dawned in the present
even though it still constitutes the definitive end. And so his
hidden state in heaven has become an earthly one which shows
itself in his being unrecognized, persecuted, transient, in suffering and dying and in all this a servant. By its application in this
way to Jesus and by such a re-interpretation in the light of the
experience of Jesus, the prophetic myth of the Son of man is
not of course completely abandoned. It rather serves, together
with the mysterious sign, to speak in an appropriate way precisely concerning this Jesus: to point him out as the heavenly
eternally pre-existent figure, to bring about recognition of the

divine character of his hidden state even now on earth, his manifest rule in the future, his rule as being that of God and his relation to the eschatological community. The prophetic myth of the Son of man is, therefore, demythologized and critically interpreted, and so becomes a suggestive statement of truths acknowledged by faith in Jesus.

The other example is intended to direct attention to the use made by the apostle Paul of the myth of the primal-man-redeemer. In the second chapter of the Letter to the Ephesians the apostle wishes to make clear to the Christians who were once pagans, the saving event by which they, as well as Israel, have come "near" to God. In verses 13—16 we read: "But now in Jesus Christ you who once were far off have been brought near in the blood of Christ. For he is our peace, who has made both domains one, and has broken down the dividing wall between them; who abolished the hostility in his flesh, the law of commandments and ordinances, that he might create in himself one new man in place of the two (Jews and pagans), so making peace, and might reconcile both to God in one body through the Cross, and kill the hostility in himself." Here it is said that Christ Jesus unites the domains, the heavenly and the earthly, by coming down and destroying the wall which separates God from men and by ending the hostility between men and God and between Jews and pagans, which had its principle in the Jewish Law. For out of the two, both Jews and pagans, he makes a new man in himself and reconciles them, in his body on the Cross, with God. The apostle is therefore speaking of events which in themselves are also known from his other letters: Christ's death on the Cross, his abrogation of the (Jewish) Law, the reconciliation of mankind with God and of men with one another. But he is also speaking, if we listen carefully, of other things and in an unusual way. What is meant by the breaking down of the wall and the uniting of the two domains? What is the significance of the use of the term "hostility" without qualification? And the idea of the "new man" constituted by the Jews and pagans united in Christ is unusual. But we know of circles where such ideas were current. They were the ones which dreamt of the primal-man-redeemer. According to them,—their myth can be reconstructed from various sources— the primal-man-redeemer comes down from heaven, drives a cleft in the iron wall which surrounds the world, destroys the hostility of the angels (of the nations), gathers together his own, the souls scattered through the world, and leads them up in himself on his return to heaven. Clearly this myth, or particular fragments of some such myth, obscurely expressed for the apostle what actually took place in Christ's redemptive work. The apostle recognized that there is in fact a wall separating God and man, heaven and earth. It is that malediction which God's wrath had laid on men and their world, that impenetrable zone of death which of ourselves we cannot pierce. The hostility of the evil powers is a reality. It is mirrored in the archetypal pattern of hostility between Jews and pagans as well as in all enmity between men and God and among men themselves, which the Law, so sinister in the hands of the powers and of men, provokes and encourages. But the heavenly primal-man-redeemer who breaks through this malediction of death and flesh, and destroys, together with the Law, the hostility, who unites and reconciles to God Jews and pagans and in them humanity, is a reality. It is Jesus Christ who by his Incarnation drove a breach in the wall of the world and accomplished the whole work of salvation dreamt of and longed for by the myth, but he did so not in a mythical way but really and historically "by the Cross", through which he made his way to heaven. Here, too, therefore, the apostle applies the mythical occurrence to the concrete historical saving-event of Jesus Christ. In the latter, light is cast on the mythical event beause it is fulfilled. And so the redemptive event of Jesus Christ can now be expressed by means of the knowing yet unknowing categories of myth. But the apostle is not expressing it in the language of myth, as we often hear it asserted, simply in order to conform to the language of his surroundings. When something really has to be said, it is not possible to adopt simply any form of speech. The subject itself requires and seeks its appropriate language; it thinks itself in appropriate language. Now the language of the myth in question was clearly an appropriate one. It enabled the apostle simultaneously to express the saving-event and its profound redemptive significance. By interpreting the saving events in the light of myth and the myth in the light of the saving events, the apostle could make it clear, for example, that Christ's Cross is not only the historical event on Golgotha, the execution of a certain Jesus of Nazareth, pure and simple, but that as an historical event it is the foundation of a new humanity in the body of the Crucified bearing, uniting and reconciling it. And Paul can indicate that the Jewish Law is more than what it is from the historical point of view, the specifically national law of Israel, but that precisely as such it represents the deadly basic law of all hostility in the cosmos. And so the myth can serve the apostle to describe by suggestion the real dimension of these historical phenomena which of course has opened out with the resurrection of Jesus Christ and is now accessible through the testimony of the witnesses. The myth can, therefore, serve him appropriately to express what faith sees.

The New Testament, then, does not proclaim myth and a mythical redemptive event, but it expounds by a critical use of certain myths or fragments of myths, the revelation-event which has been made known to faith on the ground and in the light of the resurrection of Jesus Christ from the dead as the fulfilment of the saving events of the Old Testament. These myths contained, for those by whom the New Testament preaching was originally thought out and shaped, an adumbration of the redemptive event. The foreshadowing itself raised questions for the preaching, which answered them by reflecting on the redemptive event in relation to those questions and so critically transformed the antecedent adumbration into genuine understanding. In that way the preaching of the Gospel uses the "language" of myth.

It has rightly been remarked that myth in the New Testament has been "historiziced". But that in itself is a misleading expression. It cannot mean that myth has become history. If that were so, the New Testament would be relating a mythical history, a history which never happened and always is. Nor can it mean that from history there arose a myth, just as very soon after the death of Alexander the Great his history underwent a mythical development. Myth in the New Testament was "historicized", rather, in the sense that by being referred to Jesus Christ it was destroyed as myth but the understanding of God and world and man implied in it was taken up and clarified in order to lend the historical revelation of the crucified and risen Jesus Christ the symbols appropriate to the dimensions of that revelation.

Through being critically summoned in this way by history itself to assist in expounding revelation, myth came to an end which was at the same time its fulfilment. When apostolic preaching took the risk of incorporating myth into its "language", it demonstrated that Jesus Christ is not only the end of the Law, but also of myth. The law of the Jews, the prototype of all law, was not only purified in its requirements but also relieved of its legal character. And so it became once more God's Torah, God's instruction. But it must not be forgotten that myth too was stripped of its mythical character by Jesus Christ and purified in its affirmations in order to become a *logos* of revelation. That took place when Jesus Christ in truth fulfilled the Law and also myth. In that way he redeemed what was true in the mythical foreshadowings and intimations of human and divine possibilities, and gave it validity and expressive force. The incorporation of myth into the truth and language of apostolic preaching is itself a sign of the real fulfilment of time.

From this point of view there can be no "demythologization" of the New Testament. For neither its older form, the removal of what were alleged to be purely mythological statements, nor its modern form, the interpretation of myth in terms of a philosophy of the human person, does justice even to the fact that in the New Testament myth has already been demythologized in the way that has been shown. What alone remains to be done in view of this situation is the old task of translation. It is, to be sure, a question of penetrating through language to the subject-matter itself, and in our case this only succeeds if, supported and sustained by the living tradition of the Church, to which the New Testament is entrusted as a source on which to draw, we are open and receptive to both: on the one hand to the whole saving event as it finds expression in the apostolic preaching, on the other to the whole language in which apostolic preaching gives uterance to it. The saying of St Thomas Aquinas which is quoted in the encyclical *Divino Afflante Spiritu*, is also relevant here: "In holy scripture divine things are put before us in the way which men are accustomed to use." One of the many ways to present them is the language of myth. If with critical serenity even in its regard we are attentive to the full claim of holy scripture, we can have new knowledge of the old truth. For as the Father of the Church Hippolytus says in the last sentence of his *Refutation of All Heresies*, "God is not a beggar."

CHAPTER V

Man in Gnosticism

I

Gnosticism (or Gnosis), as is well-known, presents on the surface nothing like a unified pattern. The forms it assumed range from the mystery brotherhoods of antiquity to philosophical schools or to groups within the Christian community. The literary genres in which its writings were composed included apocalyptic books of the most varied kind, elaborate epistles, philosophical treatises etc. Even more varied were the traditions on which it drew and the imagery and concepts in which it thought. The colourful, confused world of oriental, hellenistic, philosophical and religious syncretism had to lend it its often threadbare symbols and allegorized myths in order to represent its "knowledge". But this confusing wealth of traditions and ideas which it drew upon and carried with it, cannot hide the fact that under the many-coloured surface formed by these different elements of gnostic thought and language, there was at work not only a single passionately intense disposition and a definite, coherent fundamental attitude, but also a unified basic conception, which was often dialectically a very elaborate one. What is true of Gnosticism as a whole also holds good of its doctrine of man. If, therefore, we wish to discover its view of man, we cannot, in view of the brevity inevitable here, consult all the various

texts of the various gnostic schools and groups, but must and
can be satisfied with indicating by a typical example who,
according to gnostic conviction, man is. The example is not
difficult to find, for though all gnostic "systems" are inspired
by the question of man, there is nevertheless one group in which
this anthropological tendency of Gnosis clearly emerged and man
became the explicit subject of reflection. This was the group of
Naassenes who probably belonged to the Syrian branch of
Gnosticism and are to be classified as christianized Gnostics
of the first half of the second century. Hippolytus has preserved, as well as a few other pieces of information, one of
their didactic discourses, a gnostic interpretation of a hymn
to Attis, which he himself perhaps took from an excerpt made
by an opponent.[1] This Naassene sermon, as it has been called,
is in itself an excellent example of the gnostic syncretism already mentioned. For the Christian preacher[2] of the former
Phrygian-Jewish sect very consciously and on principle expounds the hymn to Attis, which serves as his basic text and
which itself is typically syncretistic, not only with the help of

[1] Hippolytus, *Elenchos* V 6, I—V, II, ed. by Wendland, pp. 77—104. We
complete his observations only here and there by reference to other characteristic Gnostic texts. To the specialist, the parallels which might serve to
document the decisive unity of the Gnostic concept of man despite manifold
differences, will at once suggest themselves. Mere references mean little to
the non-specialist.

[2] W. Bousset, *Hauptprobleme der Gnosis* (1907), p. 184, already thought it
practically impossible to distinguish a pagan document as basis of the text
as we have it, as R. Reitzenstein in his *Poimandres* (1904) and in *Studien
zum antiken Synkretismus aus Iran und Griechenland* (1926) tried to do.
To my mind the Christian quotations seem to be on the same plane as those
from the Old Testament, that is, they belong to the original text of the
philosophical sermon represented by Hippolytus' excerpt. They are relatively
easy to "eliminate", not because they are glosses in a literary sense, but
because the author is unfolding without further elaboration his knowledge of
the myths, mystery-cults, poets and the Bible, and intends precisely by this
motley abundance of sacred words quoted one after the other to show that
everything essential published in the world is πνευματικά and refers to
"man". Cf. G. Quispel, "Der gnostische Anthropos und die jüdische Tradition" in *Eranosjahrbuch* 1953, vol. XXII (1954), p. 204, note 17.

the New Testament and Christian apocrypha as well as of the
Old Testament, but also with an abundant use of the poets—in
particular their prophet, Homer, as Hippolytus scornfully remarks (8:1)—and of mystery traditions and practices, in order
to bring to light the mystery of man which in his opinion is
expressed in all these texts.

This mystery is difficult to grasp. It is not simply open and
manifest who man is. That is frequently repeated, cf. e.g. 7:22;
7:27; 8:37 f. Insight into the mystery of man is not for the ignorant heathen (8:4) or for those who are earth-bound (the χοϊκοί
8:22), nor for those who only know the psyche (8:34), nor for
those who are blind by nature (9:20) but for those who have the
spirit, who are spirit (the πνευματικοί 9:6, 21) and can interpret
in the spirit (9:7), the initiates (the perfect, τέλειοι 8:9; cf. 8:28)
and who precisely are those who know, the Gnostics (6:4; 8:1;
11:1) who can sound the depths of being (8:29). These are the
rational living men (8:31), the elite of men, on whom rests the
hope of the world (8:29, 36), and in truth they are also the
sole Christians (9:22). Only the real human being can know
man. And the real human being is also the Christian.

That the mystery of man is grasped only by the few authentic
men, is connected with the fact that man cannot be understood
except by his becoming man. Man can only know man to the extent that man manifests himself to him, and he does this in man's
knowledge only when this knowledge is a mode of man's self-
disclosure. Gnosis is a concrete, individual existential knowledge
as we would say today. The mystery of man is profound, and of
such a kind that it only reveals itself to the man who is on the
way to man, to himself, to his essence. A sentence which Hippolytus twice quotes (6:6; 8:38) is characteristic: ἀρχὴ . . . τελειώ-
σεως γνῶσις ἀνθρώπου θεοῦ δὲ γνῶσις ἀπηρτισμένη τελείωσις
the knowledge of man is the beginning of perfection, the knowledge of God is complete perfection. What is the import of this?
Gnosis is a way to perfection, with a beginning and an end.
If one knows man, if one walks the way of knowledge which

manifests man, then ultimately the god discloses himself, but he is no other than man (7:38; 8:24), in fact he is precisely the knower himself, who in his cognition manifests man in himself as the god. The profound mystery of man discloses itself only to someone who is involved in becoming man—in cognition.

But who is man? He is—we might simply say with our text—the man (ὁ ἄνθρωπος 6:4). He is, as a hymn puts it, the man with the lofty name (6:5), Adam (8:9), Adamas (6:5; 7:30, 35, 36; 8:1, 2), the man Adamas (7:2), the great, blessed, higher man (7:7, 30; 8:1), the citizen of heaven (6:5), the perfect man (7:8; 8:20), the great, very beautiful, perfect man (7:7). This becomes clearer when we hear that he is designated by the symbol of a widespread myth,[3] the Primal Man (ὁ Ἀρχάνθρωπος 7, 30, 36; 8, 9, 10) and is therefore man in his origin, man in his original essence. As such, he is the transcendental essence of man ἡ αἰωνία ἄνω οὐσία (7, 15) and cannot be comprised in word, image, thought, form: ὁ ἄρρητος, ἀνεξεικόνιστος, ἀννενόητος, ἄμορφος (7:23) in every way prior to any "imprint" (ἀχαρακτήριστος 8:13, 14, 28, 32, 40); cf. ὁ Λόγος ἀχαρακτήριστος (7:33). Man is therefore primarily his perfect, transcendental and pure essence. To this "blessed" perfection belongs above all the fact that he is prior to all sexuality and the separation into man and woman, that he is ἀρσενόθηλυς (hermaphrodite), as is often stressed (6:5, 7, 15; 8:4). The essence of man lies beyond male and female. Man in his essence transcends sex.[4]

---

[3] On the historical origin of this idea, cf. as well as Bousset's account, which is still worth reading, op. cit., pp. 160—237; C. H. Kraeling, Anthropos and Son of Man (1927); G. Widengren, The Great Vohu Manah and the Apostle of God (1945); also Mesopotamian Elements in Manichaeism (King and Saviour II) (1946); G. Quispel, loc. cit., p. 195—234.

[4] On the hermaphrodite Anthropos, cf. for example, 14:3 (Peratans); Irenaeus, I 1:1 (Valentinians); I 14:1 (Marcosians); I, 18:2 (Gnostics generally); I 30:3 (Ophites); Corp. Herm. I 15, pp. 122, 9, ed. by Scott,

Man as Primal Man has at his side the "Son of Man". "They honour", we read in a sentence the text of which is not entirely certain (6: 4), "as the principle (ἀρχή) of the universe, the Man and the Son of Man." But this Son of man is not a second man in addition to the first, Primal Man, but is the latter in another mode of his essence. He is the Primal Man inasmuch as the latter, emanating from himself and begotten by himself, confronts himself in his own image. It is in him that the Primal Man represents himself to himself. He is the fruit of his nature, come forth from the Primal Man in whom he knows and possesses himself (cf. 9: 1 f.). When the Primal Man begot the Son of Man, the latter begot himself. Begetter and begotten are both one and two. The Son of Man is the Primal Man as the latter has himself present to himself. He who is ever prior (ὁ Προών 7: 9; 9: 1), has his being in the self-generated (ὁ Αὐτογενής 9: 1) present to him. The Son of Man is, therefore, the Primal Man in the image of his own conception.[5] He is, as it is said in a vivid objectivation, the brain in the head (cf. 7: 15; 8: 13; 9: 14).[6] To the nature of man there also belongs his image and the fact that he projects himself into his image. Further than this, to be sure, the relation between Primal Man and Son of Man is not worked out in our Gnosis.[7] Consequently the Son of Man plays only a small part in the whole system, though he is not forgotten at the decisive moment. He is in fact another mode of human nature. So Hippolytus in his summary account in the 10th book can also simply say that the Naassenes call the πρώτη ἀρχή

---

cf. I 9 *ibid.* p. 118, 10; Ps.-Clem. I 69; II 9; Philo, *De op. mundi* § 134 etc.

[5] Cf. Irenaeus, I 30: 1, where the Son of the Primal Man is *ennoia*.

[6] With the Peratans, the brain is the Father and the cerebellum is the Son, Hippolytus, V 17:11.

[7] Cf. the relation between ἀγέννητον, αὐτογενές, γεννητόν for the Peratans: Hippolytus, V 12:2, or between πατήρ, υἱός (= λόγος = ὄφις), ὕλη (17:1), and of the three ἀρχαὶ περιωρισμέναι whose οὐσίαι are φῶς — πνεῦμα ἀκέρειον — σκότος among the Sethians, Hippolytus, V 19; 1 ff.

of the universe "Man". They also use "Son of Man" with precisely the same reference (X 9: 1).

Man is, therefore, as Primal Man ἡ πρώτη τῶν ὅλων ἀρχή.[8] He is, as another formula puts it: ὁ πατὴρ τῶν ὅλων   (9: 1). And one of the hymns which is sung to him runs: "From you, Father, and through you, Mother, the two immortal names, parents of the aeons, citizen of heaven, illustrious Man" (6: 5). As at once father and mother, as begetter yet conceiving and giving birth, man is that by which and from which everything is. The universe and the aeons, the totality of the endless world epochs and expanses of time have their ground in the essence of man. For in him rest all powers and substances of the universe, τὸ νοηρόν, τὸ ψυχικόν, τὸ χοϊκόν (6: 6). His nature contains all essences within itself. Through him—and now it is the Son of Man, man aware of himself and in possession of himself— "everything came to be and without him not anything came to be", as the Naassene preacher says in the words of the prologue of the Gospel of John (9: 2).

Man has his being in a dual entity which ultimately is one: in the seed and in the word. In 7: 21 we read, "They place the original engendering nature (τὴν ἀρχέγονον φύσιν) of the universe in the original engendering seed (ἐν ἀρχεγόνῳ σπέρματι)".[9] In it is comprised the *physis* of all that has come to be, is coming to be and will come to be (7: 20). It is the principle of that creation which is changing and coming to be from man (7: 23). It is the origin of becoming and the ground of everything that comes to be (7: 25). The extent to which it is the principle of change is shown by the fact that the seed itself does not belong to what becomes and does not itself change. It "remains". It is the ἀκίνητον τὸ πάντα κινοῦν of Aristotle (7: 25). For this, which

[8] At V 6:4 also we should probably read τῶν ὅλων ἀρχή.
[9] On this "identification", from the point of view of the history of religions cf. Reitzenstein, *Die Hellenistischen Mysterienreligionen* (3ʳᵈ ed. 1927), p. 16, note 1.

is called the good, or even the good person (7: 28, 26) says, echoing the words of the God of the Old Testament: "I become what I will and I am what I am" (7:25). In that original seed—and this is important for our understanding—in the nature of the seed of all, a masterful will is operative which has its ground in its own unfathomable depths, a primal will, which is a will to becoming. The Primal Man, the essence of man, consequently appears as a radical will to becoming. From this primal will flows the universe and its epochs and all that comes in past, present and future. That is one aspect of the "great, hidden, unknown mystery of the cosmos" which as they, the Gnostics, know, is proclaimed not only in the manifold myths and mystery-cults but is also expressed in visible form in the innumerable images of the gods of the Egyptians and Greeks "in all the streets and lanes" and in the temples. That is why the statues of Hermes in particular are held in honour. For "Hermes is the Logos"; he is the ἑρμηνεὺς . . . καὶ δημιουργὸς τῶν γεγονότων ὁμοῦ καὶ γινομένων καὶ ἐσομένων: so runs the at first sight strange explanation (7:29), in which the interpretation and creation of the universe is attributed to him who is himself the image both of the seed and of the Logos. How can this be?

It is clear that the Gnostics arrived at the idea of this connection indirectly, by way of the pneuma. That man in whom the Primal Man is present to himself, is also called by them πνεῦμα ἐναρμόνιον (9: 3). Now another passage (9: 4) tells us that the spirit is there "where the Father too is; he is also called the Son who originates from this Father". The essence of man is therefore also conceived as spirit. And the latter, it is now said, is "of many names, many-eyed, incomprehensible, towards which every nature yearns, each in its own way" (9: 4). Nature therefore strives towards man as spirit, as the πνεῦμα φωτεινόν, the luminous and light-giving spirit as the Sethians, who were close to the Naassenes, said (19:17).[10] But why do they yearn

[10] There is also mention of ὀρέγεσαι, in regard to the ψυχή (7:10 f.) and the

for him? In order to be merged in intelligible life. The essence of man, in the radical will of the seed, causes the cosmos to become. The same essence (as spirit) causes it to enter into light. Man, unified in the primal will of the spirit, summons the cosmos to appear and be present. But now our philosophical discourse continues: "This is the word of God (τὸ ῥῆμα τοῦ θεοῦ). And this is the word of the *Declaration of the Great Power*. Consequently it will be sealed, hidden and veiled and lie in the house where the root of all worlds, powers, thoughts, gods, angels, spirits who are sent, of what is and of what is not, generated and ungenerated, incomprehensible and comprehensible, of the years, months, days, hours, and of the indivisible point from which the smallest thing begins gradually to grow. For the point which is nothing and consists of nothing and which is indivisible, becomes through self-knowledge an incomprehensible magnitude. This is the kingdom of heaven, the mustard seed, the indivisible point in the body which no one knows except the spirituals alone..." (9: 5 f.) The nature of man as spirit is the "word of God", "God's utterance". It may be noted in passing that this is stated in the gnostic apocalypse entitled "Revelation of the Great Power".[11] By essence he is Ἀπόφασις, revelation, illumination. This word of God, spirit as man's essence, lies hidden in the house where the roots of all things are found. But this house is itself, we read at VI 9, 4, man himself and his limitless capacity. The word, therefore, lies in man in such a way that he is it and consequently is the house of all things, in their very root. In the word which man is, the universe has its dwelling, all gods, worlds, times, and the indivisible, "point" from which everything grows, the seed,[12] the principle

water of life which flows from the Primal Man (9:19). Being in every form of being is fulfilled eros for the Gnostic.

[11] Cf. the Simonian "Book of the Revelation of the Voice and the Name from the Knowledge of the Great Infinite Power", Hippolytus, VI 9:4. It is also known simply as "The Book of Revelation", *ibid.* VI 11.

[12] He is ἡ ἐντὸς ἀνθρώπου βασιλεία οὐρανῶν ζητουμένη (7: 20) or the seed.

of the being who is liberated in self-knowledge.[13] Man as the
word of God, as the revelation which brings all things into the
openness of what is, is he who causes it to be as being; he is the
house which contains the root of what is. In him as the spirit
of revelation dwells what is generated by him into the light. He
is the illuminating ground of the illumination of all things.[14]

II

This Man, however, who contains within himself in his nature
the totality of gods, worlds and the ages, and who by the power
of the seed causes it to be merged into intelligible life in the
word, himself appears involved in a fate which has deprived
him of himself. It is the manner of this happening[15] which
forms the other interest of our Gnosis and of Gnosticism
generally. Two passages in the philosophical discourse with
which we are concerned may guide us to some knowledge of
this fate and of the situation in which man finds himself. At 7:30
we read: "They were brought down from the blessed Man on
high, the Primal Man, the Adamas, into the thing fashioned
of clay, so that they might serve the creator of this creation,

---

[13] On μέγεθος ἀκατάληπτον cf. 8:3.

[14] How decisive these thoughts are for these Gnostics can be seen from the
fact that when they are considering man's nature in the seed, they honour
him under the symbol of the "serpent" and take their name from the latter.
The same is said of it as of the original seed or of the Logos. Cf. 9:12—14.
Cf. however also the Peratans 16:7 ff.; 17:8. A different account is given
in the Baruch-Gnosis of Justin, Hippolytus, V 26. It may be conjectured
that the second name of the Naassenes, γνωστικοί was, in fact, as Hippolytus thinks, V 6:4, a later one. They perhaps assumed it when—in their
Christian period?—they had thought out more thoroughly the nature of
man as word, and therefore had a more consistent view of the character of
gnosis.

[15] Special interest is also devoted to it in H. Jonas, *Gnosis und spätantiker
Geist*, part I: "Die mythologische Gnosis" (2nd ed. 1954). His analyses of the
the conception the Gnostics held of themselves present frequent parallels to
our more limited inquiry.

Esaldaios the fiery god, fourth in number. For so they call the demiurge: father of the separated world." And the allegorical interpretation of a passage from the Psalms which has already been given a gnostic twist runs: "The inserted Adamas is the interior Man, the bulwarks of Sion are the teeth, as Homer says, fence of teeth, i.e. wall and fence inside which the interior man is enclosed who has fallen from there; from the Primal Man on high, from Adamas, he the circumcised Man without hands that cut, brought down into the vessel of oblivion, the earthly vessel of clay." (7:36) It can be seen that man as we find him is even now by essential origin, still the Man "from above", the Primal Man who essentially transcends sex (8:4), the "perfect Man" (8:5). But he is so as the "inner" or "interior" Man, the "inserted Adamas", who as such does not emerge outwardly. He is so as "the one who has been brought down" (10:5, 6), who has "flowed down" (8:41), "fallen", "been thrown" (8:32), "scattered" (8:28), "robbed" (7:23), "over-powered" (7:7). Existence for man means decline, flux, fall, throw, dispersion, despoliation, defeat. Existence includes a fall in essence and to a depth the calamitousness of which is shown by the fact that it is created and ruled by a god who stands outside all divine possibilities, a supernumerary demiurge smouldering in the fire of passion,[16] and that this depth itself represents a separate, special world (ὁ ἰδικὸς κόσμος) lying outside all possible worlds, and which is the outpouring of limitless, bitter chaos, nothingness (cf. 7:9; 8:5; 10:2; X 32:1). Man, that primal will which calls forth all things, lies fallen or rather thrown down and dispersed in the alien remoteness of the chaotic world of a supernumerary god who, enigmatically, is not his god. He finds himself and his world and even his god without foundation. And in this world he finds himself in his body, in that earthen structure of clay of the "carnal", "corruptible"

---

[16] Cf. on fire 8:16, on the fiery god as the demiurge Hippolytus, VIII 9:7; 10:1; X 16:5 (Docetists); cf. also VII 38:1; X 20:1; VI 9:2.

man of dust, as is often said with fear and contempt (cf. 7:30, 35; 8:19, 32; 7:36; 8:14, 18, 23, 31, 36). He finds himself in the statue of which the Gnostics frequently speak,[17] which produced by many evil powers lies motionless, without breath (7:6), but to which then—no one really knows from where—a psyche is given which makes it come to life (7:7f.). But his soul, which constitutes his life, does not break through the fatal wall of his body, but is precisely what binds him to that scene of the perpetual conflict of mutually contending elements (8:19), makes of him in life a dead man who lies buried in the body as in a grave and tomb, to which the saying about the whited sepulchres full of dead men's bones aptly applies (8:22f.). The psyche, whose essence and manifestation is hard to grasp, is the principle of life desired by every physis; it is the principle of the manifold vital impulse, of generation but also of death, for this latter is also an urge impelling man. Persephone—Kore also loves Adonis, it is said in the mythological language of these Gnostics. But the psyche is also the impulse towards what is higher. Yet this does not set man free, either. Imprisoned man will only succeed in rising above himself, escape from himself and his world, when the higher, blessed nature divides the life-principle and the ἀρρενικὴ δύναμις τῆς ψυχῆς follows its call, the male, i.e. spiritual power of human nature. The Gnostic is no Vitalist. Vital instinct, "desire" and "eros" in any form, does not deliver man from his imprisonment but merely enslaves him, punishes him and causes him to suffer (7:7). His soul, his vital power, simply drives him along in the "transitory creation" (8:37), in the "mingling in the depths", in the ceaseless river, the ocean of generation and corruption (7:38ff.). The vital principle causes him here below to accomplish the "lesser my-

---

[17] Cf. Irenaeus, I 24:1 (Satornilus); 30:6 (Ophites); Tertullian, *De anima* 23; *De praescr. haer.* 47; *Ginza,* ed. by Lidzbarski (1925) 108, pp. 4ff.; *ibid.* 454, pp. 18ff. For Judaism cf. E. Preuschen, *Die apokryphen gnostischen Adamsschriften, Festgruß für B. Stade* (1900), pp. 226f. Cf. also H. Söderberg, *La religion des Cathares* (1949), p. 116.

stery" of "carnal birth" (8: 44), so that he, like Saul, "lives with the evil demon of carnal desire" (9: 22) and yet remains sterile (8: 31). The soul, which in the gnostic hymn appended to this discourse (10:2) is man himself thrown into existence, drives him restlessly and ineluctably like a fugitive deer astray in the labyrinth of life. Tied as a living man by his lower and higher eros to this existence of generation and corruption, he finally loses himself. For in this dark body of the world he forgets his way and sinks unconscious into sleep (7: 30, 32, 36).[18] This human existence is forgetfulness of self and a sleep of prisoners. In this alien, hostile land, men dream themselves and their dream.

III

Nevertheless there is an escape. Man can recover himself. But who is man? Only the rational and living men, the Gnostic replies, only the pearls which man has cast (8: 31 ff.), only the seeds scattered into the world by men, only the ineffable race of perfect men (8: 5), or whatever other names the Gnostics use to denote themselves. Who these are can only be recognized subsequently as it were, by whether a man enters into gnosis and from being a man attached to the flesh and the soul, becomes a man determined by the pneuma (8: 44, 45). At all events they are few. What does the number matter, after all? (8: 36). But at any rate there is the human man, the man who bears man within him, that radiance of man's essence (8: 40) which can shine forth once again. Man is not extinguished in his human elements, the humanum. Therefore he can be saved (8: 41). In

---

[18] Cf. the well-known passage from the Hymn of the Pearl, *Acts of Thomas* 109 (in A. A. Bevan, *Texts and Studies* V, pp. 10—31, Cambridge 1897): ". . . Moreover they gave me their food to eat, I forgot that I was the son of kings, and I served their king; And I forgot the pearl for which my parents had sent me, and by reason of the burden of their foods, I lay down in a deep sleep."

him the stream of becoming can once more flow upwards
(7: 38, 41; 8: 4), and the great "turn" and "change" can take
place (8: 34). Through whom? Through man himself. In what
way? By knowledge of himself. For prior to the inner man in
man, there is always also the inner man who is already saved,
who is the archetype and exemplar of salvation and of man who
is to be saved. From him, whose sole identity is that of archetype and exemplar, self-knowledge is kindled. When has man
come as such an archetype and exemplar? On the one hand he
was always there, in myth and in many shapes and forms
(πολύμορφος   9: 9), the names of which do not matter
(πολυώνυμος 9: 4); by the ignorant he is called Attis, Adonis,
Osiris, Hermes and so on. Nevertheless for the man who knows,
he is always one and the same: the saved saviour. On the other
hand, however, the saving nature of man is found as archetype
and exemplar wherever it is recognized as present (cf. 8: 3).
His coming, therefore, occurs always yet never, [19] every time
there are those who discover it in the ambiguity of the world
and every time he, man, becomes his own epiphany. The Saviour
who, being himself saved, saves, is in process of coming in each
mysterious voice of gnosis which, once it has spoken, can ring
out again and again, provided it is heard. For it is nothing but
the voice of the gnosis by which man comes to himself, in the
double sense that in the call of gnosis the archetype of man presents itself to man and that man finds himself in it. This is
given particularly clear expression in our text in the passage
where, with the help of the myth of the Primal Man's descent
and ascent, an interpretation is given of the manifestation of
gnosis in regard to its archetype and model (8: 13 ff.). What is
the exemplary occurrence in which man once more returns to

---

[19] Cf. the passage in Sallust, Περὶ θεῶν καὶ κόσμου (c. 4), which runs: "All
this never happened at all, but always is. The Nous sees everything at once,
but the Logos says one thing first, and another second." On this translation,
see H. Jonas in the second part of the book quoted above (note 15). Cf.
also his observations on myth as gnosis, pp. 13—16.

his nature? That process is an incomprehensible descent and mysterious coming down of the pure nature of man, breaking through all powers (they are at the same time principles) of "what is present" i.e. the foundations or substances, a condensing of the essence into a voice (φωνή) of an unknown and unrecognizable *eidos*. There is in the world, our Gnosis affirms, a mysterious voice of deliverance, inconceivably originating in and descending from man's pure essence and incomprehensibly breaking through all the world's principles and substances. This voice of the "God who dwells in the flood[20] and cries out from many waters", from among men, is—in the second place—a pleading appeal to the pure essence of man for deliverance, and at the same time a consoling encouragement to man, the assurance that he is unharmed and not forgotten. The voice of the Saviour, of gnosis, which is the voice coming down from the pure essence of man, rings out around man as a lament which is at the same time a consolation, because the very lament implies and proclaims who man is, and that he is in the world. The call of fear, which itself implies confidence, dwells in the flood of chaos. This voice, however,—and this is the third point in this connection—which resounds among men, is fulfilled, one might say becomes spirit and word, in the emergence of gnosis, which is a return of man to himself. Deliverance takes place, the Saviour, that voice of salvation, is saved in the knowledge of himself, which in fact is nothing else than a conversion, a turning to himself in the spirit, the return, the bending back upon himself, the re-flection in which man receives himself, receives himself as man, conceives his essence. In this sense the salvation of the now saved Saviour is called ἀναγέννησις, rebirth. Similarly, gnosis as salvation is an ἄνοδος, a path and movement upwards, an ascent (to himself, or rather, of himself), which leads through the "gate", the "gate of heaven", that is,

---

[20] κατακλυσμός for the Gnostics also bore the meaning of "destruction", "oblivion".

through the incomprehensible and indefinable occurrence of gnosis. And in gnosis, in the conception, in reflection, of his essence, man has in fact escaped from the world and his body and, once a reproach and rejected by his people, man enters, as it is written, like a king into the essence which awaits him. That is the "wonder of wonders" (8: 18).

Among the many saving voices in the world, there is also, for the Gnostics we are concerned with here, the voice of Jesus. For most Gnostics his is only one voice among many, and not even a very important one. This Jesus too is the Primal Man (7: 2), the bearer of all possibilities of human nature (6: 7; cf. 8: 17). He descends in the call of the gnosis which is evoked by his words and signs (7: 33; 8: 7; 10: 2), and he is hidden, as interior man, as Christ in us, as "imprinted as Son of Man by the unimprinted Logos in all who are born" (7: 33), to return in gnosis and as the "gate" through which men enter the king-dom of heaven of their own true nature (8: 21; 9: 21). He too can dam and cause to flow upwards the great Jordan in the depths, the lower river of change leading to corruption (7: 41).

Now what happened and continues to happen in the nature of Man as archetype and exemplar, also happens in his image. What took place in the saved Saviour is accomplished in the corresponding occurrence in each one who is to be saved and who is, of course, in essence none other than the saved Saviour. Man lies captive in the sordid pit of this world, buried in the tomb of his corruptible body. But with him and in fact in him, is his saving archetype, whose lament and consolation breaks the spell of intoxication and oblivion of self. "Adamas says to *his* men : even if a woman forgets it, I shall not forget you" (8: 17). And Hermes the Logos wakens the true suitors from the sleep of the world and summons the awakened to remembrance (7: 30; cf. 7: 32). Man, his saving nature, calls silently from silence and like Anacreon's beaker, makes known in wordless speech to man who he is to become if he listens to the mystery hidden in the silence (8:7). If he hears his voice from the silence, then in his self-knowledge the gate to his own self opens and, by knowing, he becomes what he is. But what does the cry which rings out from the silence, call to the man sleeping in the world of Lethe? Nothing but himself, his own nature. And what does the hearer, the man in man, come to know? Nothing but himself, his own nature. And what does the man become who is summoned to himself in this way and who comes to himself in knowledge? Nothing but himself, his own nature. But what is he himself in his own nature? We have already heard: he is the one in whom all that exists has its protective dwelling and in which it is present as in its domain.

This way of gnosis, the "holy way" (10: 2) of man to himself, which is the tracing out of his own track, the track of his archetype, is described in our discourse with the full force of mythological visions and terminology. What is gnosis? Flight from Egypt over the Red Sea into the desert (7: 39), an escape from the misery of what belongs to the body and from the "lower mingling", an escape from self by crossing the stream of being (8:16),[21] an escape "upwards", an ascent (8: 41; cf. 8: 18), a rise, a coming forth from the grave, a resurrection from the dead (8: 23 f.). Gnosis is entry through the gate; it is the gate itself, for it unlocks (8: 31; 9: 21). It is the "higher" birth, re-birth, the pneumatic, heavenly birth (7: 40; 8: 2, 21, 23, 30, 37, 41). In gnosis man comes into his own proper nature (8: 12); he comes to his οἰκεῖον, what is his own and proper to him

---

[21] Cf. the instructive cognate passage from the Peratan Gnosis, Hippolytus, V 16:5 f.: "The exodus from Egypt means exodus from the body ... and to cross the Red Sea which means the water of corruption, that is, to cross Kronos and get over the Red Sea which means to transcend becoming and to come into the desert which means to get out of becoming, where all the gods of corruption and the god of salvation gather. The gods of corruption are the stars which impose the necessary law (τὴν ἀνάγκην) of change on what is in process of becoming. Moses called them the serpents of the desert which bite and destroy those who think they have crossed the Red Sea." Here the connection between body, becoming, stars and time are clearly expressed as what can be transcended in gnosis.

(9:19, 21). Through gnosis he becomes of identical essence with himself (ὁμοούσιος 8: 10). He becomes a πνευματικός (8: 7), who worships in spirit (9: 3). He becomes "strong" (8: 41), "living" (8: 32), "immortal" (7: 40), he who "remains" (7: 36). He is taken into the circle of the perfect (8: 2), in the Jerusalem on high (7: 39), enters the house of God where the good God alone dwells (8: 44). He becomes "independent" (ἀβασίλευτος 8: 2), and shares in the pleroma and its power of generation and fulfilment (8: 30). In gnosis he plunges into the ocean which, "flowing up against the wall and the rampart and the Leucadian rock, is the birth of the gods" (7: 38). In gnosis man becomes God (7: 38; 8: 24). He becomes "the blessed aeon of aeons".

Such gnosis, in which man returns from the disorder of the world to the home of his own nature, is for the Gnostic a life's task and dynamism. It affects his mode of life. It gives him the central principle of his conduct. It demands of him the perversion of sex, in the kind of Gnosticism we are dealing with, by rejection of heterosexual intercourse, in order to interrupt the fatal circle of birth and to maintain the breach of existence which has taken place in gnosis. One must do the will of the Father and not merely listen, says the Naassene preacher, giving a gnostic interpretation to a saying of our Lord (2:28), and as the context shows, he is conscious of the eschatological character of gnosis and the Gnostic. He knows that here an extreme human possibility is operative. This asceticism, which however can hardly be called such, is the practical accomplishment of gnosis, in which the Gnostic flees the world.[22] In it he with-

---

[22] It cannot be called asceticism because, if I have rightly understood the context of 7:17 ff., homosexual intercourse is not only permitted, but is regarded as a mystery. In their "asceticism" the Gnostics are only concerned for the ἀνάγκη γενέσεως to be ended. The Naassenes combine Gnostic Encratism with libertinism. The relation between gnosis and praxis is not examined in our text. Nevertheless we may gather from the text as a whole that it regards practice as an important aspect of redemptive gnosis. That was no

draws, in a way appropriate to the disorder of the body, from the disorder of cosmic birth into death. And in it he releases himself for the perfect supra-sexual essence of man, for his spiritual existence, which gnosis discloses. The lesser mysteries of carnal birth, our preacher says in his gnostic interpretation of the Eleusian mysteries, must be abandoned in order to be initiated into the great and heavenly ones. Through the virginal spirit, all must become emasculated bridegrooms (8:44; cf. 8:31, 40ff.; 9:10f.). Ultimately only through gnosis and "asceticism" can the perfect man be "characterized", "imprinted" (9:18; cf. 8:14, 21; 7:33).

That this happens is, however, not only a matter of life and death for the individual human being in question, but also for the world as a whole. For only through the individual Gnostic, in whom man comes to himself again, is, on the basis of man's essence, everything in the cosmos brought to a stop which is failing to attain itself in perpetual change (8:28). Only through him will the world reach perfection (8:28). In the light of this concern for the world, which, it is true, is not often expressed, concern for a world which in the depths and abandoned by being pursues its course in the ocean of becoming and passing away, it can also be understood why the Gnostics impelled by missionary zeal considered their preaching necessary. "It is necessary", they write (8:3), "that the 'great ones' i.e. the natures of man, the blessed nature above, the mortal nature in the depth, the nature reborn into the height, should be said ... For if they were not said, the world could not endure." It only subsists through the increase of gnosis in the elite (8:3).

No one will fail to recognize the magnitude and profundity

doubt the situation as regards baptism among the Naassenes; as in gnosis generally, it had an initiatory meaning (8:19) and as regards that technical saving knowledge which for the Naassenes was condensed in the efficacious salutary ideograms of the "three mighty words" Καυλακαῦ, Σαυλασαῦ, Ζεησάρ (8:4). Perhaps they are the σφραγῖδες the seals, which the descending Saviour brings with him (10:2).

of the gnostic conception expressed in the philosophical sermon we have been examining. Here in a strange place in the world, in an apocryphal Phrygian Jewish-Christian Gnostic sect, something strange happened. Under the veils of very odd language, man clearly and decisively addressed himself as God. That happened in conjunction with the acceptance and rejection of a number of tendencies which were operative elsewhere in the mind of later Antiquity. It also happened in contact and conflict with the powerful movement of Christian preaching. But it occurred because of a fundamentally gnostic experience. For what is characteristic in this apotheiosis of man, which is almost without parallel even in Antiquity, is that here man has and attains his divinity in his self-consciousness. As we have heard, the "wonder of wonders" is that he has his essence, and thereby essence universally, the essence of all, in the form of his representation of himself. We have seen how this involves a monstrous depreciation of the reality of reality. It is true that in this way man now contains all the possibilities of man and world in himself. But all the reality of the world and of man is despised, and is merely a hindrance to be overcome in the way of the god who is coming to be. In Gnosis there is an inhuman abstraction from reality. Here there is no longer either God or man. There is only god as a way of being man and man as a way of being god. In this rigorous Idealism, every real datum whatsoever, God, man, history and historical redemption evaporates. The Church realized that. Consequently in face of Gnosticism it affirmed above all the reality of God as Creator and the reality of man as creature, and thereby the reality of the redeemer and the redemption, in a way that to Gnostics often seemed naïvely simple. Only in that way could the Church preserve, down to the present day, the humanity of man.

CHAPTER VI

Man in the Light
of the Earliest Christian Preaching

According to the earliest Christian preaching, the voice of which on our present theme can most clearly be heard in the writings of the apostles John and Paul taken as a whole, the question of man, in a certain ultimate sense, belongs intrinsically to man himself. For according to that preaching, it is part of man's historical nature that he *is* questioned and therefore questionable, worthy of question. What does this mean?

I

We may begin with what in itself is a simple matter of fact. According to the New Testament, man has from all eternity a fixed goal. That goal is his salvation, which is eternally to fulfil him. It is the basis of his nature and his historical existence. It is not one of the human possibilities chosen and laid down by himself, yet it is *the* possibility of his life. It is always the source from which and towards which man moves.

With this goal, man's way is also determined from all eternity. This way is already the goal, in the sense that anyone who takes it can reach the goal. The goal is God himself as salvation as such, purely and simply. And the way is Jesus Christ as the way of ways. "He destined us in love to be his sons through

Jesus Christ for himself" (Eph 1:5; cf. Rom 8: 29), says the apostle Paul. Man's nature and existence have received their stamp from the fact that before all else God has given himself, as salvation, to man as man's goal, and by the fact that he has sent man from the start on the way to this goal. Man always carries this destiny with him and is never released from it. The nature of man is no random thing and his existence no chance incident of history; man is certainly not a capricious idea of his own, or an accident; he is determined by God's loving care from which he comes and towards which he goes. He is eternally defined by that love. His definition is: to belong to God through Jesus Christ.

With every human being, therefore, an unfathomable promise has been expressed. His divine definition gives him indescribable dignity. Consequently he bears an immeasurable responsibility for himself. According to the New Testament, and, in fact, to the Old, his life is of limitless importance and great splendour. We only need to take seriously for a moment this conviction of man's eternal destiny deriving from and directed towards God, to realize how remote it is from the degrading view of themselves in which people in many respects live at the present time. But of course they are largely unaware of the fundamental domain into which the early Christian preaching knew that man is admitted.

According to the New Testament, however, man is not only defined by God in such a way that man is for him through Jesus Christ; by that definition man is created with God as his goal. More precisely, through the Word which is God himself (and then became man in Jesus Christ), man is called to the life which is open to God. "In him—the Word—was life, and the life was the light of men", we read in the prologue of the Gospel of John. Man as creature lives a life addressed by the Word which is God, a life summoned to God as goal, a life which in that way, therefore, is an enlightened one. Because he is such a creature, man understands himself and his world as a gift and lives his life as a gift of himself to God. Because he is such a creature he interprets himself and his world to himself and to other men in relation to God. Because he is such a creature he makes of his own life a gift to his fellow-man. The German language says there "gives" (not there "are") such and such things, clearly preserving some recollection of the original and genuine nature of the world. It is also possible to say with the apostle Paul that man has God to thank for his existence (cf. Rom 1: 21). To be a creature is to have God to thank for oneself, it is to be thanks to God in thanksgiving, on the grounds that God is mindful of man, even as creator, in fact, precisely as creator, and in his act of creating.

According to the New Testament, the very condition of being created or called forth by God through the Word for himself, already bears the stamp of the eternal destiny of man : to be for God through Jesus Christ. In man's very condition as a creature the glory of his allotted destiny already appears and even on that account the New Testament can agree with the psalmist's words: "What is man that thou (God) art mindful of him ... Thou hast made him only a little less than a god; crowning him with glory and splendour" (Ps 8: 5). To be sure man's destiny is not exhausted by his condition as a creature. But it is already contained in man as a creature to the extent that it is decisive for his created condition; as creature he is called forth and summoned for that purpose and therefore orientated towards it.

Even this dimension of man is largely alien to one modern conception. I need simply recall that for this, the principle of man's life is not giving, but achievement; that man's reality is not called forth, summoned, spoken to, so that it has its nature in the Word, but man lends informative language to the reality he himself has achieved, a language which to a large extent, therefore, can be conveyed to a language-machine. According to such a conception, man's possibilities end with what lies within his control. He therefore does not know the immeasurable dimension of the light of life established and granted by God, but only the measurable one of a world which can be imagined and manufactured and planned. This conception of man is of course not the only one even today, though it is an extremely characteristic one. Nor, of course, did it suddenly appear, for it has roots reaching far back beyond Nietzsche and German Idealism. Ultimately in fact, it arises from a view and attitude that characterizes real men generally in the concrete world of history. This however brings us to a second point in our reflections.

II

The question of man is not in fact settled for the earliest Christian preaching, when his destiny and created character have been dealt with. Man as he appears and is met with in history no longer corresponds at all to his original destiny nor does he preserve his true character as a creature.

According to the New Testament, man as he exists in the world appears in puzzling disobedience to God. He displays this disobedience as a member of humanity, as a human being, that is, but in such a way that he gives proof of it in his personal decision. The apostle Paul indicates something of the character of this disobedience, to which man is always in the position of having consented, when he speaks of the gentiles before the time of Christ. In Romans 1: 21 for example we read: "although they knew God they did not honour him as a God or give thanks to him". Man as he appears in history, therefore, no longer gives God the honour due to him as God and refuses him the thanks of a creature. The disobedience of man as shown in history is primarily a thanklessness which is no longer willing to admit that man himself exists thanks to God as God and as Creator. With man's aversion in thanklessness, the light in which the creature and his world were illuminated is extinguished, the apostle tells us. His "heart", the centre of his life, is "darkened". This darkness of heart affects thought and action. Man's thought becomes "futile" or "senseless". He is no longer mindful of reality in its truth. In his thanklessness reality has closed itself to him as God's summons and claim, and it presents itself to him with a call and claim of its own to be the ultimate ground and goal, final promise and threat, ultimate security and fulfilment. To the heart darkened in thanklessness it appears from the start in the apotheosis of an independent world and an independent life. How utterly futile man's thinking then becomes, is shown by the fact that instead of realizing his futility, he takes his foolish thought for "wisdom", "claiming to be wise, they became fools" (Rom 1: 22).

Such prejudiced thought, which in thanklessness has lost candour in face of reality, produces behaviour to suit. The loss of light through man's thankless aversion from God and his turning to himself and his world as if to gods, affects the way he leads his life. The thought of his heart which in the deepest sense is futile, ultimately finds expression in self-willed and self-seeking action. All men, gentiles and Jews, prove this. The gentiles are characterized, according to the apostle Paul, by licentiousness and anxiety. Ingratitude to the Creator robs man of his fulfilment. Influenced by futile thoughts, he seeks refuge in himself and his world. But the latter does not keep its promise. Unsatisfied, man indulges in what he takes to be all the possibilities of living, all the good things of life, and greedily strives to draw life for himself out of their vacuity. In the concrete, the profligacy of such an unsatisfied, because permanently empty, existence consists for example in insatiable itch for something new, aimless chatter, restlessness and inconstancy of decision and abode as well as in unbridled licence of desire and dissipation of feeling. The other fundamental feature of pagan life is anxious concern. The world which by man's thanklessness has gained ascendancy over him, seems alien to him in its ambiguity. He has the feeling that in aversion from God, it is tending towards nothingness. And so man knows that the world makes no provision for him. This gives rise to his anxious determination to provide for himself. As he has no success in this, anxiety persists all through life as uneasy concern about himself, and makes him go about perpetually seeking provision for himself.

The apostle Paul considered the basic feature of the mode of life represented by the Jews to be "performance" and "taking pride in". In this, thankless aversion from God found expression in a vehement and at the same time more hidden way. Taken as a whole, the Jews knew more about the Creator and his commandment in the fulfilment of which alone there is life. But they too succumbed to that selfishly preoccupied thankless mentality. And so they no longer saw in the commandment the Creator's instruction for living but regarded it as the law of self-centred salvation. They were not only zealous in fulfilling the commandment but they were over-eager for achievement in its regard. The self-centredness of such zeal is displayed in "boasting" and that means, according to Paul: self-righteous building up life by their own efforts.

That very briefly is the Pauline view of the fundamental tendencies of human life when by that strange prior misjudgment of reality it is no longer willing to thank the Creator. The Johannine view is in essential agreement. According to it too the existence of the world and man, the historical world as it exists, is dominated by darkness, which obscures the way and the goal. The historical life of man is an inescapable self-imposed obscuration. This finds expression in the domination of a strange illusion, the semblance of being a world and a life which exist of themselves and for themselves. John's Gospel calls it the world's "lie". Untruth here is not primarily a moral but an ontological phenomenon. The source and force of the lie or untruth or unreality of a world which wants to make out that it exists of itself although it does not, is a lying being. This being is called the devil or the evil one, and is, we are told, the "ruler of this world" (Jn 12:31; 14:30; 16:11). "There is no truth in him" (Jn 8:44); he stands outside the reality vouched for by God, and is not fulfilled by it. His nature is nothingness which pretends to exist and this pretence is his being. But he permeates the reality which owes its reality to the Word, which is God, with the appearance of an independence indebted for nothing. And so he has the illusory appearance of being able to live of himself and for himself. But the power of sinister self-condemnation of the world is even greater. The falsehood of the world: to be of itself for itself, dominates not only its view of itself, but also its behaviour. The world has a desire. To the extent that this means it is "intent on", and is a mode of going above and beyond itself, this is something that belongs to the creation. But the desire of the self-willed world of men as in fact they are, is a self-seeking urge. Its accomplishment is sin. This presents itself as the "unrighteousness" or "lawlessness" of "evildoing" and, as opposed to God revealing himself once again in Jesus, as unbelief. But in essence it is different. It is an attachment to the world of illusion and the unreality of the arbitrary. "Every one who commits sin"—and this can also be expressed: who "does not do the truth" (cf. Jn 3: 21), who therefore accepts, not the claim of the reality of a life granted by God, but the command of a self-seeking and self-willed life, "is a slave" (Jn 8: 34). Sin, which thinks itself an expression of freedom, is the accomplishment of unfreedom. For in it what is not real binds man to itself. And in such domination by arbitrariness the self-condemnation of the world is made more profound and the reality of the darkness is intensified.

This shows itself in death. There the power of nothingness appears, which already dominates in falsehood and sin. It decomposes the reality of the life originally enlightened by the Word which is God, but which is dominated by falsehood and sin. "You will die in your sin" (Jn 8: 21, 24). For that reason those who perpetually engage in a self-willed life in an independent world are called "the dead" (Jn 5: 25). And they are "dead" who cause others to experience their death. Their exemplar is Cain (1 Jn 3: 11 f.). But in all men who hate—that is, those who do not love—death glows as the last reflection of the self-willed being, but in reality gives the latter the lie.

Thus we see that according to the New Testament, licentiousness, anxiety, the building up of self in zealous self-righteousness and achievement, self-obscuration through indulgence of the self-willed nature which finally seals itself off in death, are the decisive fundamental tendencies of the human being who is not willing to accept having to thank the Creator for himself, and whose heart in aversion from God and attachment to himself has entered into equivocal darkness. By such tendencies he contests his own condition as creature. For in the disobedience which dominates them he threatens the eternal definition which God's love in advance bestowed.

But however many deadly defeats the creature inflicts on himself through his mysterious thanklessness, however alien and sinister his actual historical life becomes thereby, the creation and its destiny cannot be destroyed by man. Even the will which in a conscious divinization of the world and of man imposes its despotic rule on the earth, will not destroy the gift of life either mentally or physically. As long as the world and human life are supported by the patience of God withholding the breath of his anger, the creation rises up again and again against man's self-darkening. So the New Testament sees that the inquiry and desire for God is not extinguished even in the darkness and ambiguity of a self-ensnared world. When the pagans worship gods, they are not simply denying God but show at the same time that they still know about God and need him. Their gods in fact are supposed to be God and even the worship of the "unknown God" simply hides the quest for the true God. In their conscience, which of course can become completely formalized and which can err, they nevertheless hear again and again obscurely or even clearly, a summons of the Creator instructing them to listen to one another. And so even in a world blindly intent on gaining and preserving its life by unjust or self-righteous self-affirmation, here and there there is found selfless fulfilment of the claim of the neighbour and, consequently, protection of life.

That is Paul's view and that of John's Gospel is not different. According to John, too, men still somehow know about true life and the true light, desire the water which can slake the thirst for life and the bread of life which satisfies all hunger for life, and they demand the bread from heaven of which they dream in the desert of their existence. They are also on the look-out for the "good shepherd" i.e. for the guardian who will give them protection and pasture. For all their perversity and dissimulation they are still orientated towards truth and not abandoned by the summons of reality. When it comes they at least become restless. Even Pilate, who rejected the truth which in Jesus stood before him, and did so with the apparent superiority of a person who ostensibly, thanks to his office, has nothing to do with it, could only with difficulty avoid its claim and as a consequence failed even politically. And even when they have killed the truth, they will, it is written (Jn 7: 34; 8: 21), "seek" it. The question about truth is not ended by evading it, nor by expunging it.

But of course all this presentiment, questioning, knowledge, longing and restlessness about truth, all this feeling for what is genuine and authentic, and the occasional acceptance of reality, all the pious honouring of the gods, the altar to the unknown god, the quiet or loud summons of conscience and the occasional fulfilling of a commandment of created existence,—all that cannot save man. The bent of aversion from God in ingratitude is too strong and the darkness of self-obscuration is too deep for man to be able to lift himself simply by good will and clear understanding out of his failure, collapse and corruption.

It is scarcely necessary to stress that the spirit of the present age is very alien to these convictions of the New Testament. For those who see man in the light of a self-determined goal, and regard human life as fundamentally under man's control and therefore as constituting not a gift but an achievement, know nothing either of the thanklessness of fundamental self-will or of the self-obscuration which it involves. Nor do they know anything of the consequent ceaseless contestation of man's character as creature, of his eternal destiny, and the concrete forms they assume. Starting from an autonomous world as self-evident and an independent existence as perfectly justified, they interpret as long as possible every form of the conflict of man in history with his created character and destiny, as historical, physiological, psychological or, at most, moral phenomena. The aimless and restless profligacy, the hatred, boasting, the many forms of illusion, and what fundamentally is angry revolt, all this is given an interpretation in terms of this world on the assumption of human sovereignty. The limits of such interpretations are mostly only felt where such features of life become pathological, or in the enigma of the immediate onset of death. And of course in an historical world, which fundamentally is coherent, because it is in agreement with itself, all questions and all transcendent longing, all existential restlessness are at once banished and as far as possible excluded, perhaps also by historical, physiological, psychological or moral interpretations. In this way a world which regards itself as a closed system increasingly closes in on itself in its thought and behaviour. The man who follows the interpretation it gives of itself levels out all the depths of undisguised reality and covers over the abyss to which of itself it inclines, supported as it still is solely by the tirelessly merciful creator. And so self-willed human existence stretches out in history into a calculable surface, a desert of tedium, broken only by catastrophes.

III

Early Christian preaching, however, said that man who by his fundamental thanklessness prepares for himself an obscuration of authentic personal life, must be envisaged under a third aspect. This is the most decisive one. Man as he exists in the world is also confronted with the proffered action of God who himself wills to save him. We cannot expound in detail from the New Testament this offer of God which he made in Jesus Christ and his history. But the following can be indicated.

In Pauline terms it can be said that God, who maintains the vocation he gave to man and will not abandon his creature, expressed his offer in the Cross and resurrection of Jesus Christ from the dead. That was the formula even in the days of the apostles. For most people nowadays it is a worn and even incomprehensible formula. But it indicates briefly and pregnantly the event by which the sinister closed world of men who have fallen victims to their own self-seeking is penetrated by God. It means that in the midst of human history, in what historically speaking was an accidental place, God, through a man, Jesus Christ, causes his eternal saving will to find effect in a new beginning for each of us men. His eternal salvific will which of course is his eternally merciful will, was what was intended "for us" and displayed in every word and action of Jesus' forgiving, healing and instructing and was perfected in his Passion and death on the Cross. For on the Cross of Jesus Christ whom God from all eternity foreordained for that purpose, two things take place in one. In him in the midst of a self-willed humanity shut in on itself in selfishness, there is realized the selfless obedience of a life open to God and his summons. And in him there is realized at the same time in the midst of men ceaselessly attentive and devoted to themselves, the selfless love of a life open to them. On the Cross Jesus Christ, in obedience to God's command which men fail to hear or falsify, took upon himself and exhausted in his death the deadly self-will of man's fear and desire, but made no claim on life for himself. What is said in the First Letter of Peter 2:24 is to be taken concretely and literally: "He carried up our sins in his body to the tree that we rid of sin might live to righteousness; by his stripes you have been healed". For now he on whose body man's self-seeking lay and was carried even to the grave, is "raised from the dead". That means that God makes this obedient love of Jesus Christ, in which all our disobedient pretensions sank away, to be more powerful than the power of all powers, more powerful than death. It means that the Jesus Christ who endured self-seeking men even to death, is now there for them in unshakable, eternal divine power and that in *his* life *for* them a new life has been opened. Now men who, as they are, perpetually fail life, can receive the life again and again which he holds out to them in his sacrificed life, if they seek it from him and allow it to be given to them by him. God holds it ready for them in him who acquired it for them in obedience and self-sacrifice. He, who was crucified and raised from the dead for them is the place where men can once more have life given to them. He is the gift of life, offered once more to man, through his presence in the Holy Spirit, in his abiding domain, the Church.

The evangelist John says the same thing only in a different way. He proclaims that that Word which gives the light of life to every man as a creature, and whom man as he is perpetually fails, in Jesus Christ has become "flesh", that is, a man in human history. This Word on which the life of man depends, has found utterance in the Son of God made man, expressed itself in Jesus Christ in such a way that Jesus as the Son has done the "work" appointed to him by the Father. That work included two things: giving up his life and bearing testimony to such sacrifice in word and sign. God sent him for this self-giving into the world and into "the hour" of his self-sacrificing death, which became the hour of his ascent to his original glory, that is, the radiance of the eternal Word who gives the light of life. God sent him so that the world once more, and now for ever, may have with it the Word of the life that was given for them. The Son, however, Jesus of Nazareth, obediently accepted this being given by the Father and himself also gave his life to men as gift. He died, by his free will, as the grain of wheat which falls into the earth and bears fruit. The Good Shepherd gives his life for the sheep.

In this event of Jesus' self-giving to God for men, the eternal Word expressed itself historically. In him, the Word which gives light to life, thanks to which world and man exist and to which they owe thanks, but which they failed in their self-darkening, has once again spoken and this time in the midst of history. And then he himself gave explicit expression to this event that involved his person and his sacrifice. That is the other side of his "work". In his words and signs and in his self-giving he bore witness to himself as the Word made flesh. In his words and signs he spoke to men on behalf of himself and his work, making known to them the life sprung from his death as life for them. And so according to John too, in the midst of a world which is dominated by a despotic being and has therefore become untrue, and which suppresses life and deprives itself of life, the true i.e. the genuine life from God open towards God, has appeared for men and has offered itself as a gift. It continues to offer itself to men in the power of the Holy Spirit in the word and signs of the Church until the end of the world. And so man, who every day contests so blindly and self-righteously his authentic life, is confronted, whether he wills it or not, with this merciful offer of life. It therefore belongs to the nature of man as he appears in history, as he is now, and whether he knows it or not, that by this offer a new ground of his life is open to him. Man is not only destined for God by the eternal disposition of God's love, not only created by God for that destiny, not only one who fails God again and again in history in thanklessness, perpetually contesting his creation and destiny, but he is also—and that is what is really incomprehensible to him—summoned by the reality of true life in Jesus Christ which has appeared once again in the midst of man's history of falsehood, sin and death.

Consequently everything depends on man's answering this call and giving himself up to this life granted him once again in Jesus Christ. We cannot further discuss here what surrender to this summoning truth consists in. At all events it means that man amidst the almost impenetrable din of innumerable threatening and flattering invitations, listens to this voice and, among the great and powerful signs of these days, pays heed to the plain and simple gestures of the incarnate Word. At all events it consists in his not declaring, like the Pharisees of the Gospel according to John, in regard to this light that has come into the world: *"we* see" (Jn 9: 41). It also consists in his not affirming, like the Jews, that he is free (cf. Jn 8: 33), but in allowing himself to be measured and "exposed" by the truth which has appeared in Jesus. Finally it also involves that having been "exposed" by the truth, he will give himself up to the truth and decide, in faith, as someone who has been questioned once again, and finally, by God, to accept and preserve God's question which is itself God's answer to man, the failure.

CHAPTER VII

Christian Existence*

The Christian does not regard his life as a Christian simply as one of the many modes of human conduct. Of course it can be looked at in that way from outside. But the Christian knows that it is authentic human life precisely as such, the true and authentic realization of man's possibilities. That does not prevent its appearing a rather strange phenomenon to the ordinary idealist or materialist conception of man. Christians themselves are not always really aware of the precise character of their life. Consequently it is no harm to be reminded of it sometimes and to reflect on its basis, practice and character as authentic personal life.

The basis of Christian existence

Every authentic life has a ground of its own from which it springs and from which it is never severed but which belongs to its very constitution, giving it a basis and a stamp. The foundation on which the Christian knows himself to be grounded as a Christian is ultimately, or first of all, God's revelation. The

* Dedicated to Dr. Paul Schütz on his 70th birthday (23. 1. 1961) in memory of Schwabendorf.

existence of the Christian is rooted in the fact that God has revealed himself and that he has encountered that revelation. Such a statement itself, the intrinsic importance of which is not to be overlooked, distinguishes Christian life from all others.

God's revelation on which Christian life is based, took place in human history and was itself concrete and historical. It consisted of God's appearing in Jesus Christ. Christian existence has its basis in Jesus Christ. If we wanted to translate the term "Christian existence" into the language of the New Testament, the best choice would be the Pauline phrase ἐν Χριστῷ 'Ιησοῦ εἶναι or ζῆν : "to be", or "to live" "in Christ Jesus". Christian existence is an existence in Christ Jesus in whom God has manifested himself in history and remains accessible. This itself indicates more clearly the specific character of Christian existence. For the Jesus Christ in whom God revealed himself, is the ground of Christian existence inasmuch as he sacrificed, his own human existence for men and for that was raised by God from the dead and exalted to the right hand of God. His sacrifice, victorious over death, laid the foundation of authentic Christian life. Presupposed as an antecedent to the life of all men is this self-sacrifice of God in Jesus Christ for them. All men can, through this self-sacrifice of God for them, once again find the firm basis of their life. The Christian accepts this condition bestowed on the world through Jesus Christ, and accepts the basis of life bestowed by that sacrifice. For, of course, the Christian knows that man must be saved. He also knows that man is never saved by force and mendacity. Similarly he knows that he is not saved by good sentiments or good will or by good words and deeds. Not that he does not strive for them and acknowledge them. But he knows that they are not sufficient in this world and soon reach their limit. The Christian is not so naïve as to expect salvation from force or from appeal to the goodness of man's nature. He knows that only sacrifice saves, the sacrifice of God himself.

What does God's sacrifice mean ? "When he was reviled, he

did not revile in return; when he suffered, he did not threaten; but he trusted to him who judges justly. He himself bore our sins in his body on the tree, that we might die to sin and live to righteousness. By his wounds you have been healed" (1 Pet 2:23 f.). God's sacrifice means that God has endured men and Christians and that Jesus Christ has taken from them all their weaknesses, injustices, self-righteousness, malice and depravity and taken them upon himself, and took them down into his grave. His sacrifice means that to the deadly sins, which are certainly no illusion, but secretly or openly, brutally or unnoticed, lay waste the goodness of creation daily and hourly, he offered his body and soul in order to bear them and to give us his life thereby. His sacrifice means that at last once in this world no claim was raised in reply to opposing claims but Jesus Christ offered his life in unconditional love as the indestructible and unconquerable foundation, as a foundation superior to death, as the resurrection of Jesus Christ from the dead proves.

This sacrifice which lays a new foundation for all men, has been offered. And this sacrifice of Jesus Christ's self-giving is victorious in the resurrection of the victim from the dead. The victim who is raised in power to the right hand of God, holds out his sacrificed life to men so that they may find their ground in it and be saved. He exists for us. A third condition of Christian existence is here apparent, for the crucified Jesus Christ who is raised to the right hand of God, in whom God has revealed himself, is always present in the Holy Spirit. Christian existence has its ground, therefore, in the fact that he in whom it has its being, Jesus Christ, makes himself known in the present by the Holy Spirit. Christians are not Christians because they still stand under the historical influences of Jesus Christ and share in the civilization which bears his stamp—and which is now in fact in dissolution. That is how Christianity may appear viewed from outside in analogy with adherence to other historically important men such as Goethe, Hegel or Marx. But Goethe is dead and Hegel and Marx have gone and their spirit is the spirit of dead men which one day will die after them. But of Jesus Christ it is written "the same yesterday and today and for ever" (Heb 13: 8). That statement is not intended to emphasize his historical greatness, but to bring out his perpetual presence as the identical Jesus Christ crucified and raised from the dead for us, who makes himself known through the Spirit who reveals him.

The Spirit himself, in virtue of whom the sacrificed life of Jesus Christ is manifested as the ground of our life, is a concrete one. Certainly he blows where he wills. But he blows in the concrete domain which Jesus Christ forms for himself through him i.e. in the Church. In this the Spirit makes known Jesus Christ through the concrete means entrusted to it, word, sacraments and the gifts and powers conferred on it. By many kinds of call the summons of life is uttered in it by the Spirit. The same Spirit incorporates those called, through baptism, into the Body of Jesus Christ and prepares them for all the crosses and new splendour of their newly acquired existence in Christ and in the Body of Christ. If they have shut this off again through mortal sin, he judges and cleanses them by the words of absolution. Every day they render present, by the proclamation of the Lord's Supper, his sacrifice on the Cross and receive under efficacious signs his Body given for them which in the power of the Spirit confirms and strengthens them in their Christian existence. In all these ways Jesus Christ by virtue of the Spirit gathers his people to himself, causes his Body on earth, the Church, to grow, builds it up as his temple under the protection of the Spirit.

Christian existence would, of course, have no need of all this if it were merely one of the many philosophies and ways of life which are open to men's choice according to their convictions. But it can be recognized by all that the Spirit makes use of in order laboriously to produce and preserve Christian existence, that it is precisely not of that kind. But just as it has its ground in God's concrete revelation and owes its being to the actual concrete Cross of Jesus Christ raised from the dead and now present at all times in the power of God, so it also attains its identity and endures through the Holy Spirit ruling in the concrete abiding domain of Jesus Christ, the Church, by concrete means and in concrete ways. All that, which appears so remarkable to an outsider and even proves repugnant to a modern conception of authentic personal life, belongs to the reality of Christian existence. In short, that life precisely as Christian, is a Church life. Of course an individual can move far away from the actual mind of the Church and yet still be a Christian in his behaviour and—why should we not admit?—perhaps a better one than someone who remains within the concrete operation of the Spirit in the Church. But leaving out of account the fact that even he personally exists only through the influence of the operation of the actual Spirit of Jesus Christ in his domain, the danger with him is particularly acute that Christian existence will be reduced to a purely moral or even Christian aesthetic level. Cut off from the Church's life, Christian existence loses its simple everyday concrete form and, above all, its depth. For the latter opens out through the Spirit who has chosen human means of that kind, founded on Jesus Christ and his actual death on the Cross, according to the will of God who has stooped to reveal himself concretely, in a human way.

The realization of authentic personal Christian life

If it is true that Christian life has its ground in Jesus Christ in the sense explained, the question arises in what way this is so, and we shall now deal with this. In quite general terms the answer might be that the Christian lives with Christ as his source, in a Christ-like way, with Christ as his goal. How does this take place? In faith, hope and love.

What is faith as a function of personal life? Faith begins with hearing, and hearing means listening, the attention focussed, with the sensitive receptivity which we have to God through Jesus Christ, to God's offer that has been made through the sacrifice of Jesus Christ. Christ himself addresses us in the domain of his presence, the Church, in the power of the Holy Spirit. It comes to us as the offer of his good news, the Gospel, in the midst of the world's messages of victory and catastrophe. Faith begins with a man's collecting his scattered self in order to attend to this message. This in itself means a turning-point. And so conversion is already taking place in such listening. In it man turns away from all suggestions of himself or of others and turns to this one voice. Such turning aside and turning towards, means that the listening is more than just listening and hearing. It is a continued hearing involving decision, and decision means free consent and assent. The believer who in his listening is already converted, consents to what he hears, adheres to it and fixes his conversion in it. What is heard, however, is the offer of the life opened to us by Jesus Christ, the offer of his life and so of the righteousness and truth which *he* holds out to us. As he listens, in such a conversion of faith, man becomes obedient to God and accepts Jesus Christ's offer of life through belonging to him. To hear—to obey—to belong: thereby conversion is complete, the decision decided upon, the self-giving accomplished. The believer by faith has committed himself to or rather, entered into the new foundation which God gave to man in Jesus Christ.

The accomplishment of conversion in faith cannot be grasped in psychological terms. It is impenetrable like all ultimate human decisions. For the person who accomplishes the conversion in faith, its necessity is clear and its truth incontestable. For him as he hears, the decision of obedience in faith is a consent to saving freedom that is incumbent on him and accepted by him. Before he believed—he now realizes—he was fettered: to the world, to its power and opinion, and above all to himself, in bonds of selfishness, self-assertion, selfish independence, arrogance, and consequently fettered to the injustices, self-righteousness and self-centred prejudices that spring from dread and craving, and to building for himself his own human reality. In faith the fetters fell away because the believer goes out from these pseudo-festivities, climbs out of the ship and takes to the sea, to walk on the waves towards the voice of Jesus calling from the storms "Come!" It is written of Peter that he "walked on the water and came to Jesus" (Mt 14: 29). Faith is not a change of standpoint in the same plane, not a move from one ideology, as people like, misleadingly, to call it, to another. Faith is the venture of settling in a new dimension which to unbelief appears dubious and even absurd, although it is simply the old dimension of a created being in a new way: that of life conferred and received.

Faith is the beginning of Christian personal life, and one which is never left behind, but endures as its continual source. But personal Christian life is not exhausted by faith. For when man by faith enters into the sacrifice of Jesus Christ as the new ground of life provided for him, he does not open himself only to God, but also to his fellowman. And so love becomes the other mark of Christian life. It is the voluntary realization of faith for one's neighbour. In it, as the apostle Paul says, faith is at work.

We have already noted that in the faith which accepts the life granted by God in Jesus Christ, freedom is gained from the preoccupation with and enslavement to self of a human being filled with anxiety and self-centred craving. In faith a man knows he is provided for and fulfilled. Precisely for that reason he is now as a believer set free for others and can devote himself to them. That means in the first place that he can actually see his neighbour. He sees him as the person God has assigned to him and to whom he is assigned. He sees him in his real need and as a help to himself. Knowing in faith that God himself is there for him, he has the freedom himself to exist for others. Believing in the Yes which God has addressed to him and which, he has been assured, God has addressed to all, he can say Yes to his fellowman, even, in certain circumstances, to the extent of sacrificing himself. It will, of course, be a Yes to others which comes from God's Yes to him. Consequently it will always be a discerning Yes. That is to say, if occasion demands, it will also include a refusal of the other's claims. Not a refusal for the sake of self-assertion, but one for the other's sake. For however limitless the devotion of love may be, it will not serve another's selfishness but his salvation and truth and freedom. And so, love precisely as such must meet, not the fellowman but his egoistical claims with refusal if the sanctity of God's commandments and their accomplishment in regard to the community as a whole demand this.

This has to be stressed in contrast to a romantic and idealistic love which mistakes itself for Christian love. Certainly Christians have often refused the world and men their love. Who is not found wanting in this every day, out of the weakness of his faith? But such failure is not compensated by pretending it is love to satisfy someone's every wish, for example of a child or even of the citizens of a state. Nor is the failure of genuine love made good by applying the term Christian love to an incessant talk with a "partner", the name under which the neighbour is disguised. What is called a "social" attitude, and that kind of endless discussion, are not themselves Christian love at all and may be exactly the opposite. For love owes the neighbour truth, the unvarnished salutary truth, which often emerges precisely at the point where the neighbour is made to feel a due limit, and where one is deliberately silent and ends discussion. A Christian knows how much man is in need of love, for after all he knows this from his own case, and knows how little he gives to his neighbour. But he also knows that love is the sacrifice which gives the neighbour the truth which is often hard for him, but through which alone this world is saved.

Of course criticism of such false conceptions of the nature of Christian love, made in order to assist correct understanding of Christian personal life, is only possible if it is not forgotten how much patience and long-suffering, humility and magnanimity, meekness and gentleness, what acceptance of weakness, what forgiveness, but also how much sharing and giving in word and deed, in small things and large, in short, how much openness, willingness and devotion love involves. Such love is the salt of Christian personal life and consequently the salt of the earth. It is one of the eschatological signs when "wickedness is so multiplied" that "most men's love will grow cold" (Mt 24: 12). Love of that kind has overwhelming force. But precisely such love will also provoke contradiction, and nowhere is there any promise of its visible triumph on earth. After all, it was such love that was nailed to the Cross. For man as he is prefers, at least imagines he prefers, to live by achievement rather than by gift, by his own righteousness rather than by forgiveness, by prestige duly earned rather than under the gaze of love. "Grace" has become an unusable word and "alms" a despicable thing. Only those condemned to death ask for grace and only a beggar is grateful for alms. And who admits to being condemned to death or even to being a beggar? Yet love even accepts being unloved, and is tested and becomes stronger and deeper thereby. For it is not only the driving force of a faith that has ventured over the abyss; it is suffused with indomitable hope.

Hope is also a way in which authentic Christian life is realized. Jesus Christ, whose offer of life faith enters into so fully that it conveys it to others by mirroring it in love, also gives hope to the Christian. Christ himself is the hope of the Christians, for he is their future. He is the future absolutely: "from whence he shall come to judge the living and the dead". Hope is an essential feature of human existence generally. Even when it is still vague and naïve, hope is perhaps the most human thing about humanity. For in all hope man testifies to the insufficiency of the transitory, and demonstrates his trust in what is to come. It is, of course, true that human hope generally is based on human possibilities and draws hope by reading the future in them. Human hopes ultimately derive from what man's world and life promise. But the future for which Christian existence hopes in faith, and to which it holds fast in love, is that of God made manifest, that in which Jesus Christ crucified raised from the dead to the right hand of God is already present. Its actual coming, beyond all utopias, beyond all realizable or imaginable possibilities, is left in God's hands. To hope, in the sense it bears in Christian life, means to entrust oneself to Jesus Christ present and future and to live for him.

If faith is attentive obedience to Jesus Christ's express offer of life, if love is the holding open to the neighbour of this offer which has been accepted, hope is a looking forward to, and advance towards this offer and its fulfilment. In hope the Christian goes beyond faith and love, though without abandoning them, into the prospect which has been opened out by Jesus Christ. It is true that no one except one who hopes, trusting in the God who awakens the dead, sees any prospect there. No one and nothing can take from the man of hope the risk which his hope represents. On the contrary, in this world there is so much that contradicts it, and what the world does to faith and love does not make life seem more hopeful. At all events illness, old age and death represent very definite objections to hope, and so does the confused history of mankind. To hope means to hope against death. It does not mean to hope as if death presented no difficulty. Hoping is not dreaming. Hope presupposes undistorted insight into earthly possibilities and destinies and the human situation. The Christian who hopes unaffectedly, accepts and soberly observes the reality which confronts him. To be sure he does not ultimately trust it. For it always brings its own interpretation with it. And hope mistrusts this on principle. Hope mistrusts the appearance of things not really out of mistrust, but out of the unfathomable and unlimited trust in God which the overwhelming summons in Jesus Christ has awakened for faith, and which is continually strengthened by putting love into practice. Nothing and no one preserves those who hope from the apparent disappointment of death. But even in death, or rather precisely by death, those who hope break through the darkness of this deceptive world through the perspective opened towards God who awakens the dead.

Hope hurries expectantly towards what is hoped for. Christian life, because one of hope, is also one of waiting eagerly and of hastening expectantly. It hurries ahead of all time, whilst hopelessness lags behind time, because it seeks to be up-to-date. Hope is not in search of lost or vanished time. It has no care for time because in hope it has already found the future which comprises all time. So it can wait in patience. It does not anticipate anything presumptuously and timidly, not even the end, whereas the man without hope, through impatience, gets lost in sheer illusions even in regard to the end. And so Christian existence in hope proves to be both subject to fear and yet calm; characterized, as it might be expressed, by sober enthusiasm. It is sober and watchful and also sharp-sighted and farseeing, with what is to come in the future already present before its eyes.

Faith, love and hope describe the fundamental features of the accomplishment of Christian life according to its formulation by the apostle Paul. These fundamental elements can be developed in many ways. For faith, love and hope involve many different things: wisdom, justice, truth, purity, humility, friendliness and much else. But we do not wish to go further into that here. In this connection we shall simply indicate one thing, namely that faith, love and hope have something in common which in, and under, all that has been said, characterizes Christian existence. Christian life in its faith, hope and love is gratitude and joy. It can always in the last resort be recognized by these, however obscured by weakness and sins it may be. The Christian is a human being who has God to thank for himself in faith, love and hope. And the term "to thank" must be taken here in its active sense. His life is to be thankful (again) for himself. In faith, that mindfulness of gratitude occurs. Faith is remembrance of thanks. In love, gratitude is preserved in memory. Hope, however, is what it is directed to. Because Christian life exists as such thankfulness, it is also impossible without thanks*giving*. In this the gratitude for Christian life, as something received, is expressed. And as an existence which has itself to be thankful for, it is disposed to joy, attuned to joy and permeated with joy. This is the very resonance, and in more than a figurative sense, of an existence that returns thanks for itself to God. Its joy echoes the closeness of the Lord who is given to it.

The authentic and personal character of Christian existence

Having tried briefly to describe the basis of authentic Christian life and its realization, we must now turn our attention to two characteristics which alone make it meaningful to speak of the Christian conduct of life as authentic Christian personal existence. It is in fact a characteristic of Christian life that being a Christian is something which must perpetually be preserved, that is to say, perpetually achieved afresh. In Christ Jesus man *exists* by *abiding* in him, and he abides in him by continuing perpetually to come to him afresh. Certainly the foundation of Christian existence was laid once and for all by God in Christ's death and resurrection. And certainly the Christian is stamped once and for all as a Christian by baptism, and his life is given its pattern with Christ Jesus as its basis and its end. God does not retract what he has done and given the world, and the seal that is impressed by baptism is indelible. There are decisions of God which are antecedent to the world and on which its opinion was not asked. And there are decisions regarding the individual which fix the basis of his life without his being consulted. But they are decisions for which he himself must then decide. For this decision, in which he lays hold of the new foundation of his life by the sacrifice of Jesus Christ, is made in opposition to the still living resistance of the world and himself. Both the world and the "flesh", as the apostle Paul calls the self-seeking nature of historical man, exert all their power to defeat a person whose life in Jesus Christ has at last been realized. The means and ways to this are as indescribably various as life itself. But they subserve two tendencies: they threaten and attract.

What makes faith so difficult? Certainly not learning, science or technology, with which people often evade the issue. As if faith were easier in Domitian's time than today! Authentic Christian personal life is endangered in a way which, if we may so express it, is entirely pre-scientific and pre-technological. It is in danger from man's own heart. Faith, hope and love are perpetually contested by the fact that the world expresses itself to man directly as the force which has ultimate power over him. It presents itself as deadly destruction and at the same time as the only safe refuge. As the all-powerful, everlasting aeon, by destruction and annihilation of life and of the soul, by unintelligible turns of fate and the sorrow of farewells, through terrible evils and impenetrable obscurities, it demands the believer's fear and anxiety. But at the same time by its greatness and splendour, its gifts and promises, by its comforting and perpetual presence, it awakens the believer's longing for it. Christian existence is perpetually threatened by such an onset, which fills everyday life but which also concentrates in theoretical systems. At all times the Christian has to ward off threatening and enticing appeals and is exposed to them again and again in fear and desire.

Yet the world, the totality of nature and history in which we find ourselves, would not have such power if it did not find in us human beings and believers ourselves an ally which accepts such a pretentious self-interpretation from it. The aeon of this world would have no power over us if it did not, so to speak, rise up against us in ourselves, if we ourselves were not afraid for ourselves, and self-seeking. By desiring ourselves we desire the world, and by being anxious about ourselves we concur in the ostensible truth of its threat. Finally the Christian life is a perpetual conflict between the spirit and the flesh, as the apostle Paul calls it. We ourselves are the flesh, inasmuch as we are exposed, even as believers, to self-seeking and arbitrary self-will. The spirit, however, is the spirit of Jesus Christ, which cannot any longer be driven out of this world and is infused into our hearts from the Church, his abiding domain on earth, in order to help us in our struggle. In this struggle, faith often becomes weak, if indeed it does not founder entirely; love often becomes cold, if indeed it is not entirely extinguished, and hope often falters, if indeed it does not collapse altogether. The apostle Paul had that struggle in mind when he wrote: "Let anyone who thinks that he stands take heed lest he fall" (1 Cor 10: 12). It gives Christian life that fundamental characteristic which is described as "putting off the old man and putting on the new man". It means expressing faith only as the father of the possessed boy did to Jesus: "I believe; help my unbelief" (Mk 9:24).

If Christian life, then, is in fact a concrete individual accomplishment of faith, love and hope, in other words an abiding in Jesus Christ which is an ever-renewed decision for him by believing, hoping and loving, its other aspect must also be considered. It is only an authentic personal existence as a unity of faith, love and hope. In view of the intrinsic connection between faith and the works of love, hearing and doing, that is at once evident. Too many sayings of Jesus and his apostles emphasize that unity for there to be any doubt. The connection of faith and love with hope is also recognized, though less readily. For the life of the Christian is after all in many cases described simply as hope, but faith and love are not thereby forgotten. Faith and love are in fact filled to the brim with hope. But Christian existence calls for an accord of love and hope, and all that derives from them, with faith. The latter is not only their source, which they never abandon, but also the measure of their truth.

Genuine, true Christian existence is only found where it maintains the measure of faith and does not overstep this in self-willed and therefore only apparent piety. Authentic Christian personal life is also in this sense humble and discrete. The Christian well knows that faith is always called upon to fulfil its measure in love and hope but also in knowledge. He remembers the parable of the talents which he is not to bury but to use to good purpose. But the Christian also knows that the gift of faith is given to each in a different measure and that each has to observe his measure. It may perhaps not be very great. Let him not question it but fulfil it. Then he will bear fruit and certainly more faith also will be given to him for him to be able to bear more fruit. If, however, he presumptuously exceeds the measure of his faith, he will bear no fruit and his faith itself will run into danger. His faith is, as we say, "overdone" in inauthentic love, imaginary hope and especially in pseudo-pious talk. Faith which is "overdone", "puffs up" as the apostle Paul expresses it, does not build up, does not edify. But that is precisely what shows its dishonesty and inauthenticity. Christian life is authentic existence as a person, only according to the measure of the faith granted, and does not reach out in self-will beyond this. Only faith knows the measure, which it receives humbly and thankfully, in order to fulfil it.

We have seen that Christian life rises from the vital foundation newly established for man by God in Jesus Christ through the Holy Spirit. Thanks to this it gives thanks for itself in faith, love and hope. It must be preserved ever anew against external and interior temptations, as a coherent personal life with the modesty that corresponds to the measure of faith received. Who could fail to see that as such it is a fulfilment of man's authentic personal life? For to exist as a human being means to accomplish one's life on an foundation that is offered, in open gratitude and in the joy of what is allotted.

CHAPTER VIII

On Hope

I

We are accustomed to describe the life of the Christian as a life of faith. Christians are "the faithful". We also firmly hold that the life of Christians must be a life of love. We cannot conceive of being a Christian without love. But that being a Christian is essentially characterized by the fact that Christians hope, is something far remoter from us and in many ways alien to us. Yet that is the case. At all events according to the New Testament the life of the Christian precisely as such can be described as a life of hope. The pagans are those who "have no hope", the apostle Paul says on two occasions (Eph 2:12; 1 Thess 4:13). It follows that the Christians are those who have hope. It is God who has begotten Christians to "living hope". If they give an account of their faith, they are "prepared to make a defence to anyone that calls [them] to account for the hope that is in [them]" says the First Letter of Peter (1:3; 3:15; cf. 1:21). To continue steadfast in the Christian faith amounts in Colossians to "not shifting from the hope of the gospel" (1:23). According to Hebrews it means to "hold fast the confession of our hope without wavering" (10:23; cf. 6:11, 18). There is no doubt, then, that hope is an essential feature of authentic Christian life.

This hope that Christians have is of a special kind. Clearly it has nothing in common with the other hopes that men have, except that it is in fact hope. For of course the pagans, whom the apostle describes as without hope, had all kinds of hopes, as he was well aware. They had gods, and gods are questions and promises. But hope, *the* hope, they did not have. The hope which in the New Testament sense alone is hope, comes to man with and by a gracious summons from God. It is, as the various phrases put it, "the hope to which he has called you" i.e. the hope disclosed as result of (God's) call (Eph 1:18; cf. 1 Pet 2:9; Tit 1:2 f.), and it is the "hope that belongs to your call" i.e. the hope that opens out by the fact that you are called (Eph 4:4). It comes in that call and belongs to those who are called. It raises its voice in that call and in it, "in the word of the truth", which it contains, it is "heard" (Col 1:5; cf. 1:23). If men look out for it, wish to be certain of it, are willing to hope, it rises for them in that call and word, in the "Gospel".

There the Spirit of God infuses them with it. "May the God of hope fill you with all joy and peace in believing, so that by the power of the Holy Spirit you may abound in hope" (Rom 15:13),—such was the prayer of the apostle for the Roman Church. It is the Holy Spirit who proclaims this hope, who infuses it into our hearts in the gospel with the love of God (cf. Rom 5:5) and calls us to it. He who is the Spirit in whom God reveals himself, the Spirit in whom Christ Jesus manifests himself, also opens hope to us and makes us open to hope. "The spirit of the world", the spirit in which the world discloses itself and its possibilities to us, cannot unlock such hope to us. Hope consists in none of the prospects which the world can grant us. It transcends the world. It comes in from "outside" or "above", from God, in virtue of his life and light-giving Spirit.

The Spirit opens an entirely unexpected and astonishing possibility, namely, the possibility, as we can say with the New Testament, of being able to live once more with our world "in

Christ", from God. This Pauline phrase "in Christ" cannot be taken in too real and concrete a sense. We cannot enlarge here on what it involves in detail. But at all events it means this, which is readily intelligible: Jesus Christ in his self-sacrifice for men, has taken their life upon himself, has taken it from those who refuse it to God, to their neighbour and themselves, and has borne it even to death on the Cross; and, raised from the dead and taken up to God, he carries it to God as a life reconciled and saved in him, in his body (cf. 1 Pet 2:24; Eph 2:15 f.; Rom 8:34). This is the fact: "None of us lives to himself and none of us dies to himself. If we live, we live to the Lord, and if we die, we die to the Lord; so then, whether we live or whether we die, we are the Lord's. For to this end Christ died and lived again, that he might be Lord of the dead and of the living" (Rom 14:7—9). No one can alter this fact any more. It is a fact that is still hidden with God in and with Christ Jesus on high. But even this, precisely this, above all this, will come to light in due time, when all that is hidden is manifest. ". . . you have died, and your life is hid with Christ in God. When Christ who is our life appears, then you also will appear with him in glory", says the apostle Paul (Col 3:3 f.). The fact that Christ has taken upon himself and bears the world and men, and that the world and men, without foothold because of their sins i.e. through their refusal of themselves to God, find their ground once more in him, in his boundless love, that fact is the hidden reality of life, which one day will be made manifest. Even now, however, the Spirit discloses it to us by placing us by word and sign within it as our hidden reality and hope. In the power of the Spirit who calls us into it and seals us for it, it reveals God to us as the prospect before us. "In Jesus Christ", in his person, within the domain of his person, who died and was raised from the dead for us, firmly grounded in him, we have a prospect before us. He is our prospect, a prospect already disclosed but which will eventually open fully: we will eventually "inherit" this hidden wealth of our life, that of being borne in Jesus Christ by his love, by God's love in him. He is the hope of the "sons" who at the same time are "heirs". "Blessed be the God and Father of our Lord Jesus Christ! By his great mercy we have been born anew to a living hope through the resurrection of Jesus Christ from the dead, and to an inheritance which is imperishable, undefiled, and unfading, kept in heaven for you, who by God's power are guarded through faith for a salvation ready to be revealed in the last time" (1 Pet 1:3—5). Here we have a summary of all that has to be said about hope as the New Testament understands it: we owe it to God's great mercy. It came about through the resurrection of Jesus Christ crucified for us. We baptized believers have been begotten into a life of hope of that kind. It is our hidden inheritance preserved for us in heaven. It is the salvation which eventually—in that "last moment"—will be revealed. For it we are preserved in faith by God's power.

It is impossible here to develop in detail all that is comprised by this hope of a life "in Christ Jesus". But in fact when the New Testament itself expressly deals with hope, it uses only a few fundamental terms to comprise it. In general we must first recall that what is bestowed in Christ Jesus is described as: "What no eye has seen, nor ear heard, nor the heart of man conceived" (1 Cor 2:9), and that this therefore also holds good of hope. Those who hope are hoping for salvation and redemption absolutely. That is what we already heard in 1 Peter 1:5. We also hear the same, for example, in Thessalonians 5:9: "For God has not destined us for wrath, but to obtain salvation through our Lord Jesus Christ, who died for us so that ... we might live with him." "The Lord will rescue me for his heavenly kingdom", the apostle Paul writes in 2 Timothy 4:18. This rescue applies to the whole world and to all men (Jn 4:42; 1 Jn 4:14; 1 Tim 2:4 etc.). Nothing is past help. No man is beyond salvation. God in Christ has reconciled the world to himself (2 Cor 5:19). "If while we were enemies we were reconciled to God by the death of his Son, much more, now that we are reconciled, shall we be saved by his life" (Rom 5:10). And so those who are "in Christ" can say: "in this hope we were saved" (Rom 8:24).

This saving redemption is "life". In Christ our existence has a prospect of life before it. And as this prospect is not only what "in Christ" we are orientated towards, but also our origin and our abode, our existence in Christ is itself already life. It is life because, if it maintains itself in Christ, it will in the future be life. For in Christ there awaits us resurrection from the dead with him, in the power of the same Spirit who raised Jesus from the dead (Rom 8:11). We still sigh, and with us not only all who have the Spirit, but the creation also in secret, for "what is mortal to be swallowed up by life" (2 Cor 5:4; cf. Rom 8:18ff.). In Christ, in whom death is already swallowed up in victory, those longings are fulfilled and "the perishable" will put on "the imperishable", and the "mortal" will put on "immortality" (1 Cor 15:54). The prospect of life is a prospect of "freedom". "The creation itself will be set free from its bondage to decay and obtain the glorious liberty of the children of God" (Rom 8:21). "Christ has set us free for freedom" (Gal 5:1). "You were called to freedom" (Gal 5:13). "The Jerusalem above is free" (Gal 4:26) and we are its children. We can live in view of that freedom and we do so if we preserve and express it in love. As our future, but in which is our origin and in which we already are, that freedom will reveal itself in us, and through us in the whole of creation. The hope which is held out in regard to life in Christ is that of a free life, a life set free. "Set free" in the full sense of the term: loosed from deadly attachment to self, redeemed, released from self. Released, therefore, into the movement of giving and receiving, set free like those who simply receive and no longer work, in the Sabbath rest of which Hebrews 4:1ff. speaks, and also the Revelation to John: the Spirit who hears the voice from heaven saying "Write this: Blessed are the dead who die in the Lord henceforth", says "Blessed indeed, that they may rest from their labours, for their deeds follow them" (Rev 14:13). Set free also, however, in the sense that this life has found its solution, the fulfilment for which it was designed and to which it was directed.

As a prospect of such saving redemption, of life and of freedom, hope is also a prospect of glory. Life in Christ is open to this; distant yet proximate, it already irradiates this life. "Glory" is an inadequate translation of *doxa*, and so is splendour or transfiguration. The "transfiguration" which awaits us in Christ is not at all a sort of covering over and veiling of our present life with an appearance which is alien to it. The transfigured life, life in *doxa*, is the one which has begun with the radiance intrinsic and proper to it and which is bestowed on it in Christ, because he already in a hidden way permeates it (cf. Rom 8:30) and in a hidden way is already changing it (2 Cor 3:18). Glory as what is in prospect for life in Christ might in view of 1 Corinthians 15:42 ff., be described with the apostle Paul as strength, honour, permanence, spirit, which are the contraries of the "weakness", insignificant appearance and corruptibility of the psychosomatic nature of our earthly life averted from God and therefore lustreless and powerless. Clearer still is what the Gospel according to John indicates about it. In the 17th chapter, Jesus says of the *doxa* which the Father has given him and which he has given to his disciples: "Father, I desire that they also, whom thou has given me, may be with me where I am, to behold my glory which thou hast given me in thy love for me before the foundation of the world" (17:24; cf. 17:5). The glory which Jesus' disciples are to see is the power and radiance of the eternal loving gaze of the Father on the Son. It is the life-giving light of the glance which the Father gives his Son. It bestows honour and renders glorious. And so what already falls even now on our life as the radiance of our future and comfortingly, but at the same time terrifyingly, is addressed to us from that source, from "outside", is the splendour of God's love with which the Son is radiant, and we in him. That is our hope. The glory before which our life in Christ stands open, so that even as future it illumines our life, is the powerful radiance of the freedom of eternal life in the sphere of salvation: in the splendour of God's loving gaze.

It can be seen that the hope spoken of by the New Testament comes to us from the Gospel in which the Holy Spirit causes it to shine forth and be experienced. It is hope "in Christ Jesus" in whom as dead and risen for us we are grounded anew, established and preserved so that the saving redemption secretly bestowed by him, life, freedom and glory, may stand open for us as our "inheritance", in prospect for us. But the way in which we keep open this hope and maintain ourselves open to it, is by hoping. We shall now turn to this, i.e. to hope as an activity.

II

Hope is accomplished in faith. It has faith as foundation from which it cannot be separated because it grows from it. For the sake of emphasis we might even go as far as to say that hope is a mode of faith. By faith man obediently accepts the message of the Gospel, gives himself up to it and to the hope that prevails within it. In faith man turns away from the hopes which the *eidola*, the gods, offer him, in order "to serve the living and true God", fixing his eyes on the future appointed by him: "to wait for his Son from heaven, whom he raised from the dead, Jesus who delivers us from the wrath to come", as Paul writes in the oldest of his letters (1 Thess 1:9f.). In faith the believer abandons himself, for example, to Christ's righteousness, refusing to base any hopes on his own self-righteous achievements. Justified in faith by Christ's justice, not by his own, nor by that of the world, he looks forward in faith. "By faith we wait"—says the apostle Paul— "for the hope of righteousness" (Gal 5:5). In faith the believer discovers the basis on which his hope rests. In this sense faith, as the Letter to the Hebrews says, is the foundation (*hypostasis*) of what is hoped for, the "proof", demonstration (*elenchos*) "of things not seen" (11: 1).

Hope is not the same as faith. It goes as it were beyond faith without, however, leaving it behind. It outstrips faith by establishing itself in hopeful trust. That can be seen, according to Paul, in the father of belief, Abraham, of whom it is said: "He believed in the God who gives life to the dead and calls into existence the things that do not exist. In hope he believed against hope, that he should become the father of many nations; as he had been told, 'So shall your descendants be'. He did not weaken in faith when he considered his own body, which was as good as dead because he was about a hundred years old, or when he considered the barrenness of Sarah's womb. No distrust made him waver concerning the promise of God, but he grew strong in his faith as he gave glory to God, fully convinced that God was able to do what he had promised" (Rom 4: 17 ff.). We see that hope, as the New Testament understands it, is hoping without hope, and even against all hope. There is so much that contradicts this hope and enters a protest against it; there is above all the objection of old age and death. To hope really means to hope against death. We can see that hope in the New Testament sense does not mean to ignore such an obstacle to hope. To hope is not to dream. (Only when hope is fulfilled shall we be like men in a dream: Psalm 125:1). Hope in the New Testament sense, presupposes a clear and undistorted insight into the particular situation and earthly and human possibilities and powers. It candidly accepts the reality standing before our eyes, and soberly observes it: "In perfect sobriety hope for the grace that is coming to you at the revelation of Jesus Christ" (1 Pet 1:13; cf. 4:7; 5:8; 1 Thess 5:8). But we also see that hope as the New Testament understands it does not ultimately trust the perceptible, calculable reality before our eyes. It profoundly mistrusts it. Yet it mistrusts not out of mistrust, but out of trust, out of an unfathomable and unlimited trust in God, turning with simplicity to his promise, abiding with him contrary to all doubts and thereby becoming greater and firmer. In that way hope establishes itself in trust. We can also say, perhaps more appropriately, that in that way it builds itself up in trust. Hope is trust established and built up under the steady gaze of God.

The inner structure of hope clearly appears in another passage of Paul's letters where, however, the word "hope" is not used. In 2 Corinthians 1: 8 ff., the apostle speaks of a grave affliction experienced in Asia: "We were so utterly, unbearably crushed that we despaired of life itself. Why, we felt that we had received the sentence of death (through the circumstance in question), but that was to make us rely not on ourselves but on God who raises the dead; he delivered us from so deadly a peril . . ." Precisely in the situation of extreme helplessness and of not knowing where to turn, hope springs up. It springs up in acceptance of the situation clearly recognized for what it is, in acceptance of the sentence of death which that situation expresses. And it springs up as humble trust in the God who raises the dead. It arises as bold self-abandonment to the God in whom death is life, and as consent, because it is life, to the death which he sends as our lot. And so in general in the New Testament the abandonment of all anxiety and fear through attention to the encouraging voice of the Spirit calling us to boldness, appears as a mark of hope (cf. Rom 8: 15; Phil 4: 6; 1 Pet 5: 6 ff.; Heb 10: 34; 11: 27 etc.). In trust and precisely by trust, hope shows itself to be an entering into a life that is open and full of prospect in Christ Jesus. Here everything is open. Except by hope and trust no one can see that there is any prospect there. Nothing and no one relieves those who hope and trust of the risk involved in their hope, or guarantees what is in prospect. Nothing and no one preserves them from the fact that hope is only fulfilled in death. Everything remains open. But trust knows and hope dares that with entry into that open attitude, with the trusting hopeful consent to the attraction of that open attitude, a perspective opens out which leaves everything free and open for what is in prospect from the God who raises the dead. The hope which rests on faith and springs from it, not only springs up in trust but also hastens in expectation towards what is hoped for. And one might say that this eager expectation is the essential thing in hope. Anyone who is waiting is alert. And so hope means a consciously vigilant existence. "So then let us not sleep, as others do (the pagans who have no hope) but let us keep awake and be sober" (1 Thess 5: 6). This call to vigilance, to the clear-sighted carefulness of a tirelessly attentive and listening, ready and watchful life rings through the whole New Testament (cf. for example Mk 13:35, 37 par.; 14:38, 34 par.; Lk 12:37; 1 Cor 16:13; 1 Pet 5:8; Acts 3:2; 16:15). But vigilant hope is not only on the alert; it strains forward towards what is to come. The apostle Paul uses a very expressive and unusual word: *apokarodokia* (Phil 1: 20; Rom 8: 19). It means the tense, eager but also confident raising of the head to gaze at what is approaching in order to see it fully. Paul sees this *apokarodokia* operative even in the creation in bondage which is waiting for the revelation of the children of God. It also represents, however, the very pitch of hope, which is that Christ in any event will be honoured in his body whether he lives or dies (Phil 1:20). It is what is meant too when Jesus says to his disciples: "Now when these things begin to take place, look up and raise your heads, because your redemption is drawing near" (Lk 21: 28). But hope does not simply stand gazing towards what is hoped for; it moves towards it. In hope man sets off into the darkness of what is hoped for, which in faith is light—"For darkness is not dark with thee and night shines like day; the darkness is like light" (Ps 139:12). He leaves behind everything visible and temporal in order to stride forward and advance into the invisible that is to come. As it is said of Abraham in the Letter to the Hebrews: "By faith" (which of course already demonstrates the invisible things to him) "Abraham obeyed (the command) when he was called to go out to a place which he was to receive as an inheritance; and he went out, not knowing where he was to go" (11:8). Hope departs into what is promised without knowing the goal. As the same chapter of Hebrews indicates, it implies a realization of the alien character of this earth, which prompts it to set off to seek the homeland, greeting the latter already from afar (Heb 11: 13 f.). Trust and pleasure in the here and now, and indolent sleepy-eyed hanging of the head does not stimulate hope, and stifles what hope there is.

But of course this eagerness of hope is also patient in waiting. It does not anticipate what is hoped for. It is not presumptuous. So it does not misjudge itself. If it looks forward and leaps ahead, it does not overlook our inevitable lot, what is laid upon us. The stronger hope becomes, the surer its vision and the firmer its advance to establish itself in the invisible which is security, the more patient it becomes. It hears the promise and lives with it: "Be patient, therefore, brethren, until the coming of the Lord. Behold, the farmer waits for the precious fruit of the earth, being patient over it until it receives the early and the late rain. You also be patient. Establish your hearts, for the coming of the Lord is at hand" (Jas 5:7 f.). Hope is so much a waiting in patience that what appears from outside to impede its fulfilment becomes a stimulus to even greater steadfastness. It is made firm in patience which endures the test of suffering. Hope put to the test is hope increased (cf. Rom 5:1 ff.). Listening with the heart to the "comfort of the scriptures", which promise us the patience of Jesus Christ as our support, we obtain hope "by way of patience" (Rom 15: 4). This characteristic of hope, which urges it on towards what is hoped for and at the same time receives this calmly, finds explicit expression at one point in the New Testament. In 2 Peter 3: 12 the Christians are addressed as those who are "waiting for and hastening (earnestly desiring) the coming of the day of God". Even in this dual attitude everything is left open; what is open is left open and so is oneself.

III

We have seen that hope springs from the firm ground of faith in the form of trust and eager expectation. How, we may ask, does it take effect? How does it show itself?

According to the New Testament, hope shows itself first of all in holiness of life. "Every one who thus hopes in him purifies himself as he is pure", we read for example in 1 John 3:3 (cf. 1 Pet 1:13 ff.; 2 Pet 3:11 ff. etc.). A being that is not holy is always hopeless too. Behind all impurity is hopelessness, which clings to apparent and momentary pleasure. Where human existence is no longer eagerly directed towards God in hope and maintained in this tension, it becomes dissipated, not only sexually but in covetousness, desire for possessions of all kinds, and also and especially in the *evagatio mentis*, dissoluteness of mind, the symptoms of which are the verbal abundance of empty chatter, insatiable curiosity, unregulated dissipation into indiscriminate multiplicity, inner restlessness and agitation and finally inconstancy of purpose, capricious moodiness and perpetual movement, the homeless departures of the rootless. It is not meant in a moral sense but as evidence of the effect of hope, when it is said in 1 Peter 3:3 f., that "the holy women who hoped in God" wore no other ornaments than that "of the hidden person of the heart with the imperishable jewel of a gentle and quiet spirit, which in God's sight is very precious". By not wanting to shine, they shone before God. But they did not want to shine because they hoped in God and in hope consecrated themselves to him. Directed to him in hope, they were averse to any human esteem and committed to God's approval.

Hope prevails in love. Love however is supported and fulfilled by hope. Love is hope. "Love hopes all things", says the apostle (1 Cor 13:7). It is the reflection of hope. Consequently it is unending in hope. Conversely, however, hope is the reflection of love. God's love shown for us in Christ makes us hope. And so hope is simply love in action and is itself carried further by love. The apostle Paul says to the Christians at Colossae: "I have heard of your faith in Christ Jesus and of the love which you have for all the saints, because of the hope laid up for you in heaven" (1: 4 f.). The prospect set before their life bids and causes those who hope generously to open themselves to the claim of their neighbour and, in fulfilling this, that prospect is renewed while remaining the same. In love man comes into the light of hope. Hopelessness works itself out in hate. Absence of any prospect is mirrored in its darkness.

The New Testament sees hope at work in many other things: in humility and patience (Eph 4: 1 ff.), in gentleness or for-bearance (Phil 4: 5 f.), in peace (Rom 15: 13). It recognizes the language of hope in prayer of whatever kind (cf. Rom 12: 12; Phil 4: 6; 1 Thess 5: 16 f.; 1 Tim 5: 5; Lk 18: 1 etc.). Hope shines forth in *parrhesia*, the freedom and frankness before God and men, that makes it possible to say anything to them (2 Cor 3: 12; Phil 1: 20; Heb 3: 6; 10: 35). We should like to note another connection. Hope is inseparably linked with joy. Where there is no hope there is sadness (1 Thess 4: 13). But of Christians it is said that they love Jesus Christ without having seen him, and now believe in him without seeing him, "and re-joice with unutterable and exalted joy, because as the outcome of your faith you obtain the salvation of your souls" (1 Pet 1: 8 f.). They are exhorted, "Rejoice in the Lord always; again I will say, Rejoice ... The Lord is at hand" (Phil 4: 4 f.). Hope, to whose eager expectation the Lord's close presence reveals itself—the more hope, the closer the presence—is per-meated with joy. Hope breathes afresh in joy. We may recall once again Romans 15: 13: "May the God of hope ... fill you with all joy and peace in believing, so that by the power of the Holy Spirit you may abound in hope." Joy of that kind cannot be destroyed by any suffering or any parting: "Even if I am to be poured as a libation upon the sacrificial offering of your faith, I am glad and rejoice with you all" the apostle Paul writes to the Christians in Philippi, "Likewise you also should be glad and rejoice with me" (2:17 f.; cf. 1 Pet 4:12 f.). In joy, which after all is a total attitude to life, there is a spontaneous power to reveal; what it reveals is the same as hope reveals: the prospect of security in Christ Jesus. This outlook chimes in with joy. And so it is the first and direct message conveyed to us by the open quality of our life which is hidden in Christ Jesus. Joy is the reflection of the glow of dawn which has risen and will rise with Christ the morning star. It heralds in our hearts the day in which hope is fulfilled (cf. 2 Pet 1: 19).

Since hope in the upsurge of its holiness, love and joy is in harmony with the frank enthusiasm of a life now secure, it is clear that with it faintheartedness and despondency and weariness of life disappear (cf. for example, 1 Tim 4: 10; Heb 10: 38 f.; Rev 2: 3). In hope we become young again. The apostle Paul expresses this on one occasion as follows: "So we do not lose heart. Though our outer nature is wasting away, our inner nature is being renewed every day. For this slight momentary affliction" (which constitutes the whole of life!) "is preparing for us an eternal weight of glory beyond all comparison, because we look not to the things that are seen but to the things that are unseen" (2 Cor 4: 16 f.). Disregarding the temporal and what is immediately at hand, and considering the eternal and invisible, the loving light of God's gaze already penetrates our open hearts. Thereby we revive from day to day afresh among our defeats. Day by day we who hope become young, even when we are tired and old. How does hope speak? "Introibo ad altare Dei: ad Deum qui laetificat iuventutem meam." "I come to God's altar: to God who gives me joy, so that I may become young."

CHAPTER IX

The World and Man
according to St John's Gospel

I

Before we turn to the actual question with which we shall be concerned, namely, how St John's Gospel views the world and man, we must make it clear what this gospel means by the term "world", with which man has to deal.

In the first place, world is "all things", *panta*, everything that has come to be and exists. What is stated at 1:3: "all things were made through him" (the Logos), is expressed at 1:10 as "the world was made through him". This term "all things" is not emphasized, but the evangelist in speaking of the world spontaneously refers to "all things" which man finds (as having come to be) before his eyes. The world is also the world or "all things" in which man finds himself and dwells. When we are born, we "come" into the world, 1:9; 16:21; 18:37; etc.; at death we separate from it, we "depart out" of it or "leave" it, 13:1; 16:28 etc. As long as we are alive we "abide" in it, 17:11; 1:10; 9:5 etc. The world is the time and space in which man dwells, the domain and stage of his life. There is scarcely any reflection on this. Such reflection is only found when there is mention of man belonging or not belonging to the world, that is to say, formally speaking—and for the moment we are concerned with such formal considerations—when it is a case not only of a man's living in the world but also of his standing in a certain relation to it and of its having a special relation to him. According to 15: 19, the world loves "its own", and "its own" are those men who are "of the world" or from the world. The world is, therefore, also the source and basis of life for those who belong to it, 8: 23; 15: 19; 17: 14, 16. And the possibility of man's belonging to the world, and conversely the possibility of the world's being man's principle, are not simply externally but intrinsically connected. The world is what can determine the existence of man and his "speech" and what in fact determines both, in man as we actually find him in the world. At John 3: 31, Jesus says, "He who is of the earth belongs to the earth and of the earth he speaks". The world of man as it is, the earth, provides his basis and his speech. That is the world which can give him his mode of existence and the language he speaks. The world is such that the man who dwells in it can apprehend and understand himself on its basis, in other words, the world can be the source from which he exists. The more it is so, the more intensively man uses and understands the world as a principle of his life, the more apparently familiar but in reality, of course, the stranger it becomes. For it then appears with the alien character of a power which disposes over man and as a power which is not free but has itself already been brought under the disposal of another. With this we formally envisage the phenomenon of the "ruler of this world"; we shall also have to speak of this, of course. Formally speaking it characterizes the world as man's utterly alienated source. But the world is not only man's abode and source: conversely, man is also the basis and source of the existence of the world. That is a misleading way of putting it. What is meant is that the world only exists intelligibly in man. The world is the world only by encountering man, which means, by being accessible to him. It is man who hears, sees and understands it; the world only sees, hears and understands itself in him. When man, as we heard above, bases his speech on the earth, he does so by experiencing its appeal and giving expression to this. That is the formal consequence of 1:4: "And the life was the light of men". The world has access to itself only through man's understanding. The world *is* in the light and speech of man.

Consequently—and this is the second aspect of our preliminary formal reflections—St John's Gospel uses the term "cosmos" in particular for the totality and unity of man's world. For the evangelist, the world is in the first place what we call the world of history. "He was in the world and . . . the world knew him not" stands next to the statement that "he came into his own and his own (i.e. mankind) received him not" (1: 10 ff.). "This is the judgment, that the light has come into the world, and men loved darkness rather than light" (3: 19; cf. 7: 3, 4; 12: 18, 19; 16: 8, 9 etc.). Of this world everything is then asserted which can be asserted of man. In its totality it "sees" (14:17), "knows" (14:31; 1:10; 17:23, 25), "receives" (14:17), has "evil works" (7: 7), "hates" (7: 7; 15: 18 f. etc.), "persecutes" (15: 20), "gives peace" (14: 27). Mention is made of the "sin" of this world, the world of men (1: 29; 16: 8), of its "dying" (8: 21, 24), its "salvation" (3: 17; 4: 42), its "judgment" (3: 17; 12: 31, 47 etc.), its "joy" (16: 20), of God's love for it (3: 16 etc.). The world in which and on the basis of which man lives, yet which only exists as world to the extent that it becomes intelligible in human reality, is primarily met with, according to St John's Gospel, in the thinking and understanding, desiring and willing, acting and suffering world of man as a whole.

The extent to which it is the world of history that is meant, however, is clear from the fact that for John this human cosmos is represented by the world nearest to him, the concrete cosmos of the Jewish world. Certainly that Jewish world always stands merely as representative of the world generally and is therefore depicted with features that make it serve as a type. This gospel frequently speaks quite generally of "men": "The life was the light of men" (1: 4). "The true light that enlightens every man was coming into the world" (1: 9). "He knew what was in man" (2: 25). "I have manifested thy name to (the) men" (17: 6 etc.). The evangelist knows other nations as well as the Jews: Samaritans (ch. 4), Romans (11: 48), Greeks (7: 35; 12: 20). But his interest is engaged almost entirely by "the Jews". They are not only his world and the world of the events he relates, but "the world" generally. They stand as a paradigm of the world of men. When John relates that "the crowd" of the Jews was following Jesus, he describes the Pharisees as commenting, "Look, the world has gone after him" (12: 18 f.). Or Jesus can say at 18: 20, "I have spoken openly to the world; I have always taught in synagogues and in the temple where all Jews come together ..." (cf. also 7: 4, 11 ff.). "The Jews" are consequently only incidentally and approximately described in their empirical historical circumstances. This gospel envisages them as typifying men and the world. So, for example, no interest is shown in the historical features of the Pharisees and their relations with the "chief priests" and "authorities". All these without distinction are the authorities and as such the decided representatives of the "cosmos", while the "crowd" represent its less definite agents or the wavering, divided and ignorant world which does not know where it belongs. It is also characteristic that "the Jews" on occasion figure almost as a unified and redoubtable tribunal of the world (1: 19) and, for example, in chapter 5 they act almost like an official authority in regard to the blind man whom Jesus had healed. Moreover, they are viewed to such an extent as typical representatives of the world, that those who have dissociated themselves from the world by faith, no longer appear as Jews at all, even though by origin they are. So, for example, John the Baptist is singled out from the "Jews" and contrasted with them (1: 19 ff.; 1: 31, 32 etc.). And Jesus, who is explicitly said to be a Jew (4: 9, 22) is so far removed and alien from them that when he speaks of the Jewish law, he speaks to the Jews of "your" law, not, for example, of "ours" (8: 17; 10: 34; cf. 7: 19, 22; on the other hand cf. 7: 51).

And the narrator, too, dissociates himself in principle to such an extent from "the Jews" that he not only refers to them in general with perceptible distance, but speaks, for example, of the purification rites "of the Jews" (2: 6), of the "Passover of the Jews", and the "feast of the Jews" and so on (2: 13; 5: 1; 6: 4; 19: 40, 42). Jesus and those who are his are not "Jews" although they naturally belong to the Jewish people. But "the Jews" in this gospel are viewed precisely as the world as it is manifested through Jesus' coming.

II

This world, the totality of human life which the evangelist sees as the world of history represented by the Jews, is, to speak quite generally, by origin a gift of the Logos. It owes its being not to itself but to "the Word". "All things were made through him" (the Word), "and without him was not any thing made" (1 : 3 f.). This "Word" is God, God with God, or as we can also say, the Son in the glory of the Father's love (1 : 1 f.; 17 : 5, 23 etc.). At the same time it is "the Word" as such, the Word "in the beginning", eternal and prior to all. "Logos" has not lost its conceptual content in this context. The world *is* through this Word, which is its ground; it receives its being through this Word. The world is also *in* this Word. This Word is, as we read, "the life" of what was made and at the same time its "light" (1 : 4). This Word is the vital force of all that has come to be and that comes to be. The Word gives it its life, and does so by causing the world, which owes its existence to the Word, to emerge into intelligibility in man. "That which was made was life in him (the Word) and the life was the light of men" (1 : 4). In the Word as such life is given, life in light, manifest, translucent life. We can therefore also say that the world which has been called into being by the Word which was in the beginning, which is God with God, the world which stands in that primordial Word which is God with God, as in a life which is translucent, intelligible, is now for ever the revelation and exposition of that Word. And we can go on to say that as such a presentation of the Word which is the light of life to the world, the latter allows the Word in itself and through itself to be heard by men. Its existence and specific character makes known the Word through which and in which it has its light of life.

This fundamental structure of the world as a world given in the Word and manifest in the Word, is only explicitly noticeable in the prologue of this gospel. But it is a presupposition of the entire conception of the world (and of salvation) by the evangelist. His theme is indeed a different one, even in regard to the world and to men. But precisely his main theme is developed step by step against the background of the conception of the world we are examining.

The evangelist who proclaims the coming of life and light into this world in the person of Jesus, sees that the reality of the world which originally was manifest and open through the primordial Word, has shut itself in, and continues to shut itself in, in a terrible way. The world as it appears in history has become for the evangelist a very unreal world through this continual occlusion of the original Word to which it owes its being. It is no longer found in the luminous and living essence which it had in the primordial Word, but as "darkness". The presence of Jesus, the Word made flesh, is described by the expression, "The light shines in the darkness" (1 : 5). Men who do not allow their life to be enlightened anew by this light "walk in darkness" (8 : 12; 12 : 35, 46; 1 Jn 2 : 6, 9, 11). And the term "darkness" (σκότος or σκοτία) is not simply a rather exaggerated biblical periphrasis signifying that the world and human life are not completely transparent, but states the very real present condition of the world. This historical world, the human cosmos, in which life unfolds and from which it takes its direction, and this life itself, *is* darkness. Anyone who does not believe in him who has come as light "remains in darkness" (12 : 46). The world as it now exists, is darkness. And so "darkness" shares in the formal structure of the world. It is in the first place a "space" which surrounds and comprises man, a "dimension" in which he abides. That is shown by the statements we have quoted. As such, however, it is a "power" which spreads, oppresses, overcomes, binds. Those who once more have light, must beware of its clutches. They must defend themselves against its power (cf. 12 : 35, 46). For it blinds (cf. 8 : 12; 1 Jn 2 : 11). It darkens human life in the world.

The fundamental characteristic of this power of the darkness of this world which overpowers men and fills them with itself, is obscuration. The term is not employed in the gospel itself, but it denotes very well what in general is meant. Light discloses; that is what it is to be light. It "convinces", transfers from the state of being hidden to that of being manifest. Darkness conceals and covers over. It obscures (cf. 3 : 19, 20; 12 : 35; 1 Jn 2 : 11). It obscures goal and path. "He who walks in the darkness does not know where he goes." That is meant in a fundamental sense. Thomas says, "How can we know the way?" since we do not know the goal (14 : 4 f.). Darkness as the dimension of the world which is perpetually taking hold of man, obscures all paths and purposes and by its aggressive shutting out of light, banishes man into its gloom. But this obscuration (in the active sense of the word) takes place in man. He accepts it and enters it and abides in it. Those who believe in it have fallen into the darkness. Consequently, one should now "believe in the light" which has come in Jesus (12 : 36). The man who "loves" the domain of darkness remains attached to it. "Men loved darkness more than light" (3 : 19). Their "evil deeds" which they owe to their faith in darkness, seek to remain hidden in it (3 : 20). Just as in man's hatred, according to 1 John 2 : 9 ff. and 3 : 14 f., the supposed and deliberately willed opacity of human existence appears and at the same time takes effect through the medium of those who hate, so the darkness

which is accepted by those who give themselves over to it produces new darkness. The darkness of human existence confronts
the individual human being from the start in the world of man's
history, and is intensified by the man who acknowledges it and
succumbs to it. In what is for him the overwhelming power of
the fundamental obscuration, the world appears as darkness.
In God there is no darkness (1 Jn 1 : 5). God is in light and is
light (1 Jn 1 : 5, 7). His creation intelligibly translucent in his
primordial Word, is alive, open and full of light. But the world
as we find it now appears as darkness. It brings down again and
again on itself that factual and active obscuration (which cannot
be traced back further here) through those human beings whose
inclination is for darkness and who adhere to it.

But how does the world show itself to be such a self-
condemnation to darkness? According to St John's Gospel it
is falsehood, sin and death which permeate and dominate the
world and men, and represent forms of darkness. They are the
fundamental modes of the self-darkening in which the world
is found. They are spoken of chiefly in the eighth chapter of the
gospel.

The world as we find it is dominated by an enigmatical kind
of semblance which is the deliberate outward show it makes of
being a world mighty in itself and of itself. It is this wilful and
resolute show of being in itself a powerful and independent
world which the evangelist calls the world's "lie". In 8 : 30–47,
we find a sinister discussion about it. There it is said that the
Jews, as the representatives of the world, allow what they are
to be instilled into them, not by God whom they nevertheless
call their father, but by the devil (8 : 44, 47). But what they
allow to be instilled into them corresponds to their will and
action. What they seek and what they do corresponds to the
person whom they allow to disclose it. So they have his "desires"
and do his "works" (8 : 38, 40, 44). He is "the ruler of this
world" who has his dominion in the world and exercises it
through the world. But at the same time this is the one who

"does not stand in the truth", because "there is no truth in him" (8:44). But truth, according to St John's Gospel, is the reality of an open and manifest life bestowed by the primordial Word. It then appears again in the Word which became flesh in Jesus. Into that dimension of life bestowed by the Word and therefore open and manifest, the devil did not enter; he left no room for it in himself. It does not fill and determine his being. He is, rather, utterly alien and hostile to it. His being is the un-truth of self-will or autocratic pride, of radical which is based on itself and not bestowed by the Word, and arbitrariness and self-seeking. His being is the "lie" of a reality therefore set on itself and closed in on itself and no longer open. His being, we can also say, is nothingness which pretends to be, and in this pretence appears to be (Bultmann). It is precisely this distortion of being he communicates to the cosmos and causes to prevail there as the domain which he rules. In that way he gives the world the appearance of the unreal world of his own unreal being. From out of the world, he addresses to man the falsehood of an apparent autonomy, the lie of seeming independence. And so the world and human existence appear in the mendacity of him who in himself is the "liar" in person, whose own characteristic property (τὸ ἴδιον) is lying, who is the "father of lies", because he is perpetually engendering them by perpetually "speaking" them (λαλεῖ τὸ ψεῦδος). By listening to the call of the mendacious being of an autonomous and self-seeking world, men desire to be independent and self-centred and so shut themselves off from the true being of an unobscured life bestowed by the Word. By listening to the claim of an apparently autonomous world, men bring to nothing the original truth of their life which was given them by the Word who is God with God in order to bring them into his open light and to preserve the translucence of the life he bestowed. The world which is nevertheless indebted for its being to the Word, rises up in ostensible autonomy, as though indebted for nothing, in the

power and splendour of a self-originated and self-centred will
which pretends to a capacity to exist of itself and to an ob-
ligation to be itself. Men acquiesce in this semblance, put themselves at the service of this falsehood and, consequently, of
their own alienation from themselves. They thereby serve self-
condemnation to darkness. The deliberate semblance of an
autonomous world and an autonomous life, which in history
is always in fact the basis of the world and human existence
and to which they again and again succumb, is one of the
fundamental modes of the "darkness" of this world.

The darkness in which the world and men remain is, however, something different from, and in a certain sense even
more than, "falsehood". The lie which dominates the world:
to be itself of itself for itself, concerns not only what it says
and therefore its mental outlook, but also its activity and
behaviour. Darkness also shows itself, according to St John's
Gospel, in "sin". When that gospel speaks of sin (1:29; 8:21,
34, 46; 9:41; 15:22, 24; 6:8, 9) or of sins (8:24; 9:34; cf.
19:11), it has concretely in mind the "wrong", the "injustice"
ἀδικία   7:18) or, with 1 John 3:4, the "lawlessness", the
"wicked transgression" (ἀνομία 1 Jn 3:4). That is the form of
sin. The nature of sin is described in another way. It is already
named by implication at 15:19 when it is said that "the world
loves its own", cf. 1 John 4:5. Sin is men's self-seeking attachment to themselves as their own possession, and thereby
it is their attachment to untruth and unreality. At 8:34 it is
stated what the nature of sin is: "Every one who commits
sin is a slave." Sin is slavery or the contrary of freedom. Such
unfreedom is of course convinced that it is freedom (8:33)
just as the "blind" think they "see" (9:41). But in reality,
since it is the opposite of "doing what is true" (3:21), it is
an enslaving consent to the untruth and unreality of autonomy
and its world, an acquiescence in its "desire" and consequently
a succumbing to its "evil deeds", its "evil-doing" (3:19, 20),
the acceptance of a servitude from which only the appearance

of a new reality in Jesus, the historical "Word", can set free. "The truth will make you free" (8:32). "If the Son makes you free, you will be free indeed" (8:36). By fettering man to the lie of an autonomous self-willed life and to the unreal world it involves, darkness establishes itself even more. Such enslavement becomes particularly explicit in the unbelief or disobedience of man in regard to the truth which has appeared once again and definitively in Jesus. Consequently for our evangelist the unbelief of the Jews is sin in its intensest form, sin in which man in face of truth will not abandon his attachment to the arbitrary (cf. 8:24; 9:40f.; 16:8 etc.).

Darkness discloses itself in death. This already prevails in falsehood and sin. The devil, the liar, is also a "murderer from the beginning" (8:44). "And you know", we read in 1 John 3:15, "that no murderer has eternal life abiding in him." Jesus says to the Jews, "The slave does not continue in the house for ever" (8:35); "you will die in your sins" (8:24; cf. 8:21). Death is already at work in the opacity of falsehood and sin. The pretence of the unreal and the accomplishment of the counterfeit are themselves modes of reducing to nothing. To enter on an autonomous, self-willed existence drags down into its empty futility. It draws men away from the reality of the life bestowed by the primordial Word. For that precise reason those human beings who give themselves over to the sham power of the apparently self-sufficient world, are called by Jesus "the dead". "The dead will hear the voice of the Son of God" (5:25). The dead, as the sign of the resurrection of Lazarus (c. 12) shows, must be awakened from death. The death of the world attached to and succumbing to death is not mere words, inauthentic talk, but is the consequence of the falsehood and sin of this world and the revelation of its secret. Death is the sheer power of darkness. The ostensibly so "realistic" world likes to hide death from itself in a variety of ways, but it already makes its appearance in this world symbolically, in the significant event of bodily

death. In murder, however, of which according to 1 John
3:11 f. Cain is the archetype, the murderer causes another
human being to experience his own dead state, and consequently death itself. The fact of killing a brother is only
the culmination of the hatred in which the darkness of
autocratic life reveals itself. In St John's Gospel, the Jews as
the representative of humanity manifest their determination
to have the darkness of autonomous life by the rejection and
persecution of Jesus and finally by their will to kill him. That
determination results from their impermeability to the reality
of a life bestowed by God and accepted as a gift (which has
now appeared again in Jesus), and which by its very nature
is open to God and to man (cf. 8:40; 11:53), The dead do
not tolerate a living man among them. In the world and
among men as they are, death gleams as the last reflection
of the falsehood and sin of a self-willed being. Death is the
sombre *doxa* of the autocratic self-willed being which rules,
dominates and decomposes the creation.

We see that the world as it is manifested in world history,
in fact appears as "darkness". This darkness is the real self-
obscuration (in the active sense of the word) of the autocratic
being which governs the world. This is shown in the perpetual
refusal of the authentic life given to the world by the primordial Word, through the falsehood of the world of self-suf-
ficiency; secondly in the perpetual failure of its life by sin
or the servitude of self-seeking action; thirdly in the perpetual
corruption of its life, through the eruption of the innermost
force of such falsehood and sin in the death which reduces all
to nothing.

III

We must now consider a third general view which is not, it
is true, dealt with directly but does nevertheless turn up
repeatedly in various ways in other contexts. Even despite

the obscurity produced by the arbitrary being who dominates the world, the original life given by the Word is in a certain sense maintained. Somehow or another—for that is the only way we can express it, since we are not told how—men still know about the light and the life from which they draw life, and in some way they long for them. When Jesus tells them "I am the light of the world" (8:12), or when the evangelist speaks to them of "the true (real) light" (1:9; cf. 1 Jn 2:8), it is not only presupposed that men understand what light is, but also that in every possible light that they still have, they seek *the* light and ask for genuine light. The same applies to life. Man wants to live, and not merely in the most immediate sense that he does not wish to die, but also in the sense that he has a hunger and thirst for life which transcends earthly life. In this gospel he expresses that in his longing for a wonderful water of life: "Sir, give me this water, that I may not thirst, nor come here to draw", says the woman of Samaria who had misunderstood Jesus' offer (4:15). He even knows about the kind of supra-physical food which was provided for the fathers in the gift of heavenly manna in the wilderness (6:31). However much man limits and obscures life in his ideas and wishes, he is nevertheless orientated towards it. Consequently the gift of the "true bread from heaven" (6:32), of the "bread of life" (6:35, 48, 51) which is the gift of Jesus himself in the flesh, represents the decisive fulfilment of all human knowledge of life and desire for it. Men are also conscious that they need a "shepherd" and not only in Israel but also among the Gentiles, their longing is apparent for one who will lead them and defend them. So they are not unprepared when Jesus presents himself to them as really and truly "the good shepherd". It is of course true that in order to be admitted to his pasture they have to allow their ideas and desires to be radically corrected by Jesus, as John chapter 10 shows.

That falsehood, sin and death do not reduce the world to absolute darkness is made clear in yet another way in St John's

Gospel. When the manifest and definitive truth appeared in Jesus, the Word made flesh, there was, according to John, not only unbelief and rejection but also intensified restless questioning and desire for truth. That is apparent, for example, in the uncertainty of the "crowd" regarding Jesus. It is not merely that "the Jews", even the ranks of the Pharisees (12:42), are divided over Jesus and his work (7:11ff., 32, 40ff.; 9:16; 10:19ff.; 11:45f.), and that they, who represent the world, feel disturbed by him. The crowd follow Jesus, it is true, because they take him for one of the many θεῖοι ἄνθρωποι or wonder-working prophets, and regard his miracles not as signs, as pointers to a miracle of a quite different order, but as direct demonstrations of earthly welfare (e.g. 6:14ff., 24ff.; 7:11; 10:41; 11:56; 12:9). Yet they are stirred and on occasion are even moved to ask "Are you the Messiah?" (10:24). At the end of Jesus' public ministry it is seen that the crowd greets him as the Messianic king of Israel, in their sense, it is true, which Jesus at once seeks to correct (12:13ff.). Some "Greeks" also come and say "we wish to see Jesus" (12:21). This request is in fact refused, because the grain of wheat must first fall into the earth and die. Finally the Pharisees note "the world has gone after him" (12:19), though they do not in fact discern why that happened. At all events Jesus prompts questioning and disquiet and men's secret longing. However self-centred and distorted that reaction may be, however quickly it subsides, and though self-supplied answers triumph in the end, it is nevertheless an indication that man, still drawn and spurred on by the remaining traces of the strength of the primordial life-illuminating Word, rebels against his own obscuration and its power. Even Pilate who rejected the truth which was standing in front of him in the person of Jesus, and did so with the apparent superiority of someone who, thanks to the office he holds, has supposedly nothing to do with it, is nevertheless extremely disturbed by it (19:8). That behind all this there lies an inextinguishable need of man for a transcendent fulfilment, is shown by the fact that the Jews, as Jesus tells them, will continue to seek him precisely when they have killed him (7:34; 8:21). Why exactly? For they will rejoice when they are rid of him (16:20). They will seek him because the question about truth is not answered by liquidating truth. They will seek him because the quest for truth, and that means the desire for it and the will to find it, never cease. The appeal of the luminous reality of a life bestowed by the primordial Word cannot be silenced even by falsehood and its failure, sin and its offence, death and its corruption. The life-giving light continues to burn as before, and unobscured human existence in the Word shows its presence unmistakably by the fact that it remains perpetually in search of itself. What concrete form such a search actually assumes in the course of human history, is not said. It is operative not only in explicit questioning, but it also finds expression in the suffering of men who cannot or may not ask the question any more. Indeed the actual mindless vacuity of the human face produced by a heart whose only metaphysics is a technical estimation of all things with a view to immediate use, itself bears witness to the inextinguishable search for truth. But of course, the gospel does not speak of this in so many words.

But knowledge about truth and inquiring desire for it, however indelibly present in the world of man, do not rescue man from his deadly history. Man is too attached to his view and his own standards, and judges everything, man and God, as it is written, "according to the flesh" (8:15) or, "by appearances" (7:24). He is too attached to *the* interpretation of the world and himself supplied to him by the spirit of self-glorification, and he translates into action that interpretation of the world and of life. The Jews turn even their knowledge about God (5:18; 8:41; 10:33; 19:7) and their zeal for their "fathers" (8:30 ff.), for the sacred scriptures (5:39) and for the law of God (5:10 ff.; 7:19 ff., 49 ff.; 8:17 f.; [9:13 ff.];

18:28) to their own advantage and into motives for rejecting
the truth of the Word now appearing to them, made flesh in
Jesus. To such an extent are they, the representatives of men,
entangled in untruth. Their self-willed interpretation of
reality is so attentive to what is said by the autocratic being
which dominates them and the world, that they themselves
reject their own inquiry and longing for light with the asser-
tion, "We see". In that way, however, they frustrate any
decisive commitment and surrender of themselves to the Word,
that has now appeared in Jesus, any genuine obedience of
faith, which is now the way on which the light of life shines.
"Some of the Pharisees ... said to him, 'Are we also blind?'
Jesus said to them, 'If you were blind, you would have no
guilt; but now that you say, 'We see', your guilt remains'"
(9:40f.). The knowledge and longing of men, which is preserved, despite man's rejection, by that hidden indestructible
Word which is God with God, and the Son, cannot free the
world from the fundamental self-obscuration of darkness.
That can only be done by the new appearance of the Word
in the midst of this human world, the presence of the primordial
Word in the Word made flesh, and by the faith which, hearing
and seeing, opens itself to him.

CHAPTER X

The Angels
according to the New Testament

St Gregory the Great, Doctor Angelorum, writes on one occasion: "esse ... angelos et archangelos, pene omnes sacri eloquii paginae testantur",[1] but as far as the New Testament is concerned, it is not possible entirely to agree with him. It is true that every one of the New Testament writers lived with an unquestioning belief in the angels and in harmonious relations with them and their activity. Yet they are mentioned with any frequency only in the Revelation to John (which in this, as in other ways, carries on the tradition of Jewish apocalyptic), in the narratives regarding the childhood of Jesus in Matthew and Luke, in Luke's Acts of the Apostles, and finally in the first three chapters of the Letter to the Hebrews. It is true that the apostle Paul often mentions "principalities and authorities", that is to say "fallen" angelic beings, but he relatively seldom refers to the holy angels which are our theme here. John the evangelist is almost entirely silent about them in his gospel and his letters.

Another general observation must be stressed from the very start of these reflections. In the New Testament writings the angels (and for that matter the "principalities and authorities") are always mentioned merely incidentally. It is not

[1] Hom. 34 in Ev. n. 7 (*PL* vol. LXXVI, col. 1249).

that those writers are uninterested in them when they do write about them or that they pass over them hastily, but the angelic nature and activity is never the explicit theme. We nowhere find direct teaching about them or even reflection of any length on their service. Even in the first chapters of the Letter to the Hebrews, which are directed against an angel-Christology,[2] and even in the Letter to the Colossians which envisages the danger of a Gnostic cult of the angels,[3] there are no speculative considerations of any kind about the angels. People knew what an angel is.

A third preliminary remark must be added as a general guide. The New Testament speaks of the angels under a few aspects only. For its part, of course, taken as a whole it is interested only in the redemptive history of Jesus Christ and his Church. It is the book of that redemptive history from John the Baptist until the second coming of Jesus Christ. Consequently in the New Testament the angels appear almost exclusively within this redemptive history and in its service. And that fact will naturally determine the plan of any account of the angels based on the New Testament. It does not mean that we do not learn something of the nature of the angels from the New Testament. Principally, however, we shall be able to observe them in their activity and above all in their cooperation in salvation. Their nature and activity are, of course, not to be separated, particularly in their case. Consequently the two sections of our exposition should be read as far as possible in relation to one another. Scarcely more is possible than an inventory of the New Testament statements. Genuine living experience is lacking nowadays for real insights to be possible.

[2] Cf. J. Barbel, *Christos Angelos* (1941); idem, "Christos Angelos. Die frühchristliche und patristische Engelschristologie im Lichte der neueren Forschung" in *Lexikon der Marienkunde*, 21 (1957), pp. 71—96, where a bibliography can also be found.
[3] Cf. G. Bornkamm, "Die Häresie des Kolosserbriefes" in *Das Ende des Gesetzes. Paulusstudien* (1952), pp. 139—156.

I

The holy angels are called in the New Testament "the angels of God" (Lk 12:8f.; 15:10; Jn 1:51 etc.) or "the angels of the Lord" (Mt 1:20, 24; 2:13; 28:2; Lk 1:11; 2:9; Acts 5:19; 8:26 etc.). Or they may be simply called "angels" (Mt 4:11; 13:39; 26:53 etc.). The first designations chiefly point to the origin of their nature. They belong to God and are beings from his "world". That also follows from expressions such as "the angels of heaven" (Mt 24:36), "the angels in heaven" (Mk 13:32), "an angel from heaven" (Lk 22:43; Gal 1:8 etc.). They are God's heavenly beings. For that reason they are called on occasion the "holy angels", in accordance with Old Testament and Jewish usage (Mk 8:38; Lk 9:26; Acts 10:22; Heb 12:22 D*; Rev 14:10), or the "elect angels" (1 Tim 5:21).[4] Sometimes they are called simply "the saints" (Eph 1:18; Col 1:12; 2 Thess 1:10). Their natural element is the domain of God's holiness, from which they come forth and which they bring with them.

They are not, of course, emanations as it were from God, the simple radiation of his holiness. The latter has, rather, simply entered into their nature in such a way that they communicate the experience of it when they appear. They are beings created by God, produced by his creative word. That is not, as a matter of fact, stated in the New Testament of the angels themselves, but it is expressly stated on one occasion of the "principalities or authorities" (Col 1:16). And these hostile cosmic powers[5] are, of course, identical in origin with

[4] Cf. *TWNT* vol. IV, p. 190, pp. 6ff.; R. Asting, *Die Heiligkeit im Urchristentum* (1930), pp. 72f.
[5] That is to my mind how the ἀρχαὶ καὶ ἐξουσίαι are to be understood here also, for the apostle's use of this term is probably uniform and at Romans 8:38; 1 Corinthians 15:24; Colossians 2:15; Ephesians 1:20f.; 2:2; 6:12, he clearly has in mind the powers hostile to God and subjugated by the glorified Christ. It is only at Colossians 2:10 and Ephesians 3:10 that one might think of good (or "neutral") powers, but only if the context

the good angels. The angels are a part of the creation, the
invisible part which transcends the visible—flesh and blood,
as the apostle Paul calls it on one occasion (Eph 6:12), the
earthly, corporeal form of being and mode of existence. They
transcend in fact what is constitutive of the earthly creature
and its history: sexuality and time. That is most clearly recognizable from the well-known words of our Lord in Luke's
version: "The sons of this age marry and are given in marriage;
but those who are accounted worthy to attain to that age and
to the resurrection from the dead, neither marry nor are given
in marriage, for they cannot die any more, because they are
equal to angels and are sons of God, being sons of the resurrection" (Lk 20:34 ff.; cf. Mt 22:30; Mk 12:24 f.).

The transcendence of the angels is above all characterized by
the fact, to put it schematically, that they are at once personal
and impersonal beings, or, more precisely, that their impersonal nature is personally determined. We know, once again
from the case of the hostile angels, that the angels possess, in
virtue of their origin, free-will and free decision. The fallen
angels did not keep their own original position and essential
task (Jude 6; cf. 2 Pet 2:4). In obedient service of every kind,
in the manifold action and activity of the good angels, the
freedom of their nature is perpetually reflected again and
again. It is unnecessary to quote particular proofs of this from
the New Testament. But they also have knowledge and speech.
Their nature admits of word and answer. Though no details
are given in the New Testament regarding their mode of
knowledge, the communications they make as God's servants
display an insight and foresight far above human knowledge.
Here too no special references are needed. Certainly their

is left out of account. Of course at Colossians 1:16 the apostle is not considering the wickedness and hostility of the said powers, but the origin of
their being which they share with the universe, "all things", to which of
course they also belong. Hence the apparent "neutrality" at Colossians 2:10;
Ephesians 1:20 f.; 3:10.

knowledge is not unlimited. They do not know the day or the hour of Jesus Christ's second coming (Mk 13: 32 and par.). Perhaps 1 Peter 1:12 too must be understood to mean that the angels are not able to penetrate the eschatological glory which awaits the faithful. Reference is made on occasion to their tongues, i.e. to their speech. But that this is to be understood figuratively, is clear from the fact that these "tongues" are contrasted with human tongues (1 Cor 13: 1; cf. Gal 1:8; 4:20) and that, judged from a human standpoint, they contain "ineffable words, which man may not utter" (2 Cor 12: 4). The gift of tongues (glossolalia) which Paul discusses (1 Cor 14) recalls the tongues of angels. It is clear that they have a comprehensive view of what happens in heaven and on earth (1 Cor 4:9), and that they are all-seeing. For that is presumably how the remark of the Seer is to be interpreted that the "four living creatures" are "full of eyes in front and behind" (Rev 4:6). Do not let us forget one small detail: they have a measure. But it is not a man's, it is an angel's measure (Rev 21:17).

Now the New Testament says these beings are not individuals at all, but generic beings. Of the myriads of angels (Heb 12:22; Jude 14; Acts 5:11; 9:16), only two are mentioned by name in the New Testament, and these names are not proper names. Gabriel (Lk 1:19, 26) is, of course, interpreted as "man of God" (Dan 8:15 ff.), or "the strong one of God" (*Ethiopic Henoch* 40:9; *Numbers Rabbah* 2, 137 c[6]) or as "God has shown his strength".[7] And Michael[8] (Jude 9; Rev 12:7) is in fact the question: "Who (is) like to God?"

---

[6] Cf. H. L. Strack and P. Billerbeck, *Kommentar zum Neuen Testament aus Talmud und Midrasch,* vol. II, pp. 97 f.

[7] Cf. M. Noth, "Die israelitischen Personennamen im Rahmen der gemeinsemitischen Namengebung" in *Beiträge zur Wissenschaft vom Alten und Neuen Testament,* vol. III, no. 10 (1929), p. 190.

[8] Cf. W. Lueken, *Der Erzengel Michael* (1898); S. A. Horodetzky, "Michael und Gabriel" in *Monatsschrift für Geschichte und Wissenschaft des Judentums* 73 (1928), pp. 499—506.

(*Pesiqtha Rabbathi* 46, 188 a[9]). In this the peculiarly impersonal character of these personal beings is reflected. Their
nature is of course also spirit, power and radiant light and
one can almost say they move as spirit, power and radiance.
"Are they not all ministering spirits sent forth to serve, for
the sake of those who are to obtain salvation?" (Heb 1:14).
"The words of him who has the seven spirits of God and the
seven stars", says Revelation 3:1, and by that signifies Christ
who holds in his hand the seven angels of the seven communities which represent the Church, the same of which it
is reported in Revelation 4:5 "before the throne burn seven
torches of fire which are the seven spirits" (cf. 1:4; 5:6). Let
us add Hebrews 1:7 as well: "Of the angels he says, 'Who
makes his angels winds, and his servants flames of fire'"
(Ps 104:4; cf. also Rev 23:8f.). The rapid and flame-like
character of spirit belongs to their nature. On occasion the
moving character of their mode of being is referred to as fly-
ing (Rev 14:6; cf. 4:7; 8:13). Even more stress is laid on the
powerfulness of their nature. Not only does the Revelation to
John repeatedly speak of a "strong angel" and his "loud voice"
(Rev 5:2; 10:1; 18:2; 18:21; 19:6; cf. also 2 Pet 2:11)[10], but
what is implied by the very name of principalities and authorities hostile to God is also true of the good angels: they not
only have power, but they are, or to express it better, encounter
us as power and might.[11] What is expressed in Mark 13:26 and
its parallels as follows: "And then they will see the Son of man
coming in clouds with great power and glory", is formulated
in 2 Thessalonians 1:7 as: ". . . when the Lord Jesus is revealed
from heaven with his mighty angels" (cf. Mt 25:31;
2 Thess 1:9). Might is not foreign to the angels but is a feature

[9] Cf. Strack and Billerbeck, vol. III, pp. 806 f.
[10] Cf. also the πλῆθος στρατιᾶς οὐρανίου (Lk 2:13) and the ἄγγελοι of
Michael which fight against the angels of Satan (Rev 12:7 f.).
[11] Cf. H. Schlier, *Principalities and Powers in the New Testament* (1961),
pp. 19 f.

of their nature. Akin to might (δύναμις) is the splendour (δόξα) with which the angel's nature radiates. Doxa is in fact both power and radiance, might which shines forth and radiance which is power.[12] Doxa is glory. This term is frequently used in connection with the angels. "When he comes in his glory and the glory of the Father and of the holy angels", we read in Luke 9:26 (cf. Mk 8:38; Mt 16:27, differently expressed; cf. Mt 24:30 and par.; 25:31). In Luke 2:9 we read that "an angel of the Lord appeared to them, and the glory of the Lord shone around them". The cherubim are called cherubim of glory (doxa) (Heb 9:5). In 2 Peter 2:10f., and Jude 8 they are even called "glorious ones" (δόξαι). In all this, doxa always involves two things: intrinsic radiance and radiance which shines forth. Doxa sheds radiance. "His face was like the sun" the Seer says of the angel (Rev 10:1). And when the angel came down from heaven, "having great authority", it is said in Revelation 18:1, "the earth was made bright with his splendour". Similarly in Acts of the Apostles 12:7: "And behold an angel of the Lord appeared and a light shone in the cell." Hence if the appearance of an angel has to be described, mention has to be made of his "white", "bright", "shining" apparel (Mk 16:5; Acts 1:10; Jn 20:12; Acts 10:30). Of the angel at Jesus' tomb it is said that "his appearance was like lightning and his raiment white as snow" (Mt 28:3). That corresponds to the description of the changed appearance of Jesus on the mountain of transfiguration: "And his face shone like the sun and his garments became white as light" (Mt 17:2). The angels are light spreading out from the inner nature, reflected light which illuminates and irradiates. "Satan disguises himself as an angel of light" says the apostle Paul (2 Cor 11:14). And this light—true to the Old Testament meaning of δόξα—is not only a bright and illuminating light, but one which consumes. The angel is also a "flame of fire", as we have already seen from Hebrews 1:7. The angels of God,

---

[12] *TWNT* vol. II, pp. 240 ff.

the holy and elect of heaven, the invisible creation, creatures freely obedient, knowing and acting, with faces and speech, subsist innumerable and nameless as spirit, power, radiance, light and flame. That is how the New Testament sees them. And it must not be forgotten for a moment that even those statements are merely analogous.

Yet the statements about the nature of the angels would be incomplete if another fact were neglected: that, turned towards God, they surround his throne in ceaseless praise. It not only belongs to their office and charge to honour God in all their service, but it belongs to their very nature, inexhaustibly to pay him homage in unanimous, untiring praise in his sight. The angels fix their gaze always upon God. They "always behold the face of my Father who is in heaven", Jesus says at Matthew 18:10. Fascinated by him, they perceive him. To perceive him means, however, to be known and penetrated by him. And to be pierced through by his sight means to fall down before him and break out into the joy of praise. Precisely this uninterrupted and direct sight of God in which they stand, returning his gaze by their praise, is what also makes them radiant, constitutes them as splendour and light. Their radiance is but the reflection of his. And so it is said even of the face of Stephen, who "gazed into heaven and saw the glory of God and Jesus standing at the right hand of God" (Acts 7:55) that they "saw that his face was like the face of an angel" (Acts 6:15). All seeing involves being filled with what is perceived. The faces of the martyr and the angel take their appearance from what they see. If the two essential features of the angels, their essential praise and their essential radiance, are taken together, it can be said that they are radiant praise of God, and this is not merely to be understood "figuratively".

As proof that this praise belongs to the very essence of the angels, we need only refer to the Revelation to John, especially its 4th, 5th and 19th chapters. One passage at least may be cited in lieu of the rest: "And when he had taken the scroll, the four living creatures and the twenty-four elders fell down before the Lamb, each holding a harp, and with golden bowls full of incense, which are the prayers of the saints; and they sang a new song, saying, 'Worthy are thou to take the scroll and to open its seals, for thou wast slain...' Then I looked, and I heard around the throne and the living creatures and the elders the voice of many angels, numbering myriads of myriads and thousands of thousands, saying with a loud voice, 'Worthy is the Lamb who was slain, to receive power and wealth and wisdom and might and honour and glory and blessing!' And I heard every creature in heaven and on earth and under the earth and in the sea, and all therein, saying, 'To him who sits upon the throne and to the Lamb be blessing and honour and glory and might for ever and ever!' And the four living creatures said, 'Amen!' and the elders fell down and worshipped" (Rev 5:8—14). Just as the nature of the visible creation is such that from its created being there issues a stream of secret exultation, so it is with the invisible creation, the angels. To unite them all and men with them in jubilation for ever, is the goal of the raising up of the Lord Jesus Christ. And so the Church hymn, which the apostle has incorporated into his Letter to the Philippians, ends: "...that at the name of Jesus every knee should bow, in heaven and on earth and under the earth, and every tongue confess that Jesus Christ is the Lord, to the glory of God the Father" (Phil 2:10 f.; cf. also Heb 1:6). That this adoration of God concerns all angels, even those who are sent to serve men, and that therefore it belongs to the very essence of angels, can be seen from a slight turn of phrase in the mouth of Gabriel when he introduces himself to Zechariah: "I am Gabriel, who *stand* in the presence of God; and I was *sent* to speak to you" (Lk 1:19). And so too "the seven angels who *stand* before God", the seven who blow the trumpets, and unloose the sevenfold judgment on the cosmos (Acts 8:2, 6 ff.),[13] are described as envoys. Finally it is said of

---

[13] Cf. J. Michl, *Die Engelvorstellungen in der Apokalypse des Heiligen*

the angels in heaven who are assigned to the little ones on earth, that they "always behold the face of my Father who is in heaven" (Mt 18:10). Adoration and joy inseparably accompany such standing in God's presence and sight of his face.

Finally the fact and manner of angelic appearances indicate their nature. One can see an angel in a dream in which he "appears" (ἐφάνη; cf. Mt 1:20, 24; 2:13, 19, 22). The Seer of the Apocalypse sees the mighty angels in his visions which transcend time and place. But even in the present the angel is met with, visible and audible, in various ways. In the New Testament it is taken for granted that an angel can seem completely like a human person (Acts 12:15; Gal 4:14; Heb 13:2). Usually, however, something remains unconcealed of his awe-inspiring majesty and transcendent nature, and this is reflected in his "appearance" (εἰδέα; Mt 28:3), of which we have already spoken. "And there appeared to him an angel of the Lord standing on the right side of the altar of incense. And Zechariah was troubled when he saw him, and fear fell upon him" (Lk 1:11 f.; cf. 2:9 f.; Acts 10:4; Mk 16:5, 8; Mt 28:4, 5, 8; Heb 2:2; 12:20 f.; Rev 19:10; 22:8). At any rate the appearance of the angel is always felt to be a mysterious incursion from the invisible, so that on occasion the same word may be used to characterize it, namely ὤφθη (Lk 1:11; 22:43; Acts 7:35), as is otherwise used in regard to the resurrection appearances (Lk 24:34; Acts 13:31; 1 Cor 15:5 ff.), of the glorified Christ (Acts 9:17; 26:16; 1 Tim 3:16) and of the second coming (Heb 9:28). That does not mean that in each of the two sets of cases it is a question of an appearance in the same sense and mode, but it does mean that the angelic appearances fall into the general category of epiphanies.[14] And so on the one hand

Johannes, vol. I, "Die Engel um Gott" (1937), pp. 112—210. Michl gives detailed reasons for identifying them with the seven spirits of Revelation 1:4; 3:1; 4:5; 5:6 and the seven angel princes.

[14] Cf. on the angelophanies of the New Testament E. Pax, "Ephiphaneia": _MTS_, vol. I no. 10 (1955), especially pp. 171 f.; pp. 188 f.

there may simply be mention of a coming in (εἰσελθεῖν: Lk 1:28) and of an approach (ἐπιστῆναι: Lk 2:9; παραστῆναι: Acts 27:23), and on the other hand it may be said that the person approached by the angel "sees" (ὁρᾶν: Lk 1:22; cf. 24:23) a "vision" (ὀπτασία). And while Cornelius himself says: "behold, a man stood before me in bright apparel" (ἔστη ἐνώπιόν μου: Acts 10:30; cf. 11:13), the account given by the author of Acts himself reads: "he... saw clearly in a vision an angel of God coming in..." (εἶδεν ἐν ὁράματι φανερῶς... ἄγγελον... εἰσελθόντα: Acts 10:3; cf. also Lk 24:4 with 24:23). The angel's appearing is only known in a "vision".

II

The angelic nature is ordained by God to serve the world and mankind. There is little mention in the New Testament of creation and creatures as such having their angels. But it is not overlooked. To my mind the four "living creatures" (ζῷα) of Revelation 4:6 ff.; 5:8; 19:4 are not only to be regarded as prominent angels in a general sense[15] but[16] as special angels of the creation, the higher "powers which bear the world",[17] realities in which what is created is protected and praises God.[18] On occasion the Apocalypse refers to angels "at the four corners of the earth holding back the four winds of the earth, that no wind might blow on earth or sea or against any tree" (7:1), which therefore preserve earth and sea and their produce from harm (7:2; cf. 9:15). Not to be forgotten either, is the angel who has power over fire (14:18) and the angel of water (16:5).

---

[15] So W. Bousset, E. Lohmeyer, J. Bonsirven on the passage.
[16] Especially in view of Revelation 5:13 f. and 6:1, 3, 5, 7, 10.
[17] A. F. Ch. Vilmar; cf. A. Bisping, E. B. Allo, A. Wikenhauser on the passage.
[18] The interpretation of these as referring to the four evangelists is of course found as early as Irenaeus, Adv. haer. III, 11, 8.

According to John 5 : 4 (Vetus latina), the water of the pool of Bethzatha owed its healing power to an angel.[19]

Man too has his angel who keeps him under his protection. We have already mentioned Acts 12 : 15 f. "It is his angel", the disciples thought when the maid Rhoda recognized Peter at the door by his voice. In Luke 16: 22 it is said of the dead Lazarus that, "The poor man died and was carried by the angels to Abraham's bosom". Men found him repugnant and certainly would not throng to his funeral, yet in him it is every poor man whom the angels carry to where the just sit down at table with Abraham. But that carrying is only the last moment of the secure care of creatures in general, of which the tempter in Matthew 4: 6, mingling truth with lies, reminds Jesus: "For it is written, 'He will give his angels charge over you', and 'On their hands they will bear you up, lest you strike your foot against a stone'" (Ps 91 : 11 f.). The angel is God-given support.

In addition to this relation of the angels to creation and creatures, which is only occasionally referred to, the New Testament chiefly describes their cooperation in the action of God and Christ in the history of redemption. Looking back to the Old Alliance, Stephen mentions the help which Moses received from the angel (Acts 7: 30, 35, 38). It was he—but God was his surety—who appeared in the burning bush and whose pillar of flame guided Moses on the way as "ruler and deliverer" of his people. It was with him that Moses spoke on Mount Sinai and received from him instructions for Israel, the Law (Acts 7 : 53), which of course in Hebrews 2 : 2 is also called "the message declared by angels" (ὁ δι' ἀγγέλων λαληθεὶς λόγος).[20]

---

[19] The view that they are only representatives of the creation and not personal angels is opposed by J. Michl, *Die Engel um Gott*, pp. 74 ff. But there is no incompatibility between the two. They are personal angels in such a way that they represent the creation, and they represent the creation by being personal angels.

[20] At Galatians 3 : 19 the ἄγγελοι are evil powers, inasmuch as there the

In the Law the voice of the angels also is heard. The archangel Michael still protects the very body of Moses from the devil (Jude 9).

But Moses is only a type of Christ. And the Law is only a pointer to the righteousness of grace in which it is fulfilled. The angels' service to Moses and the Law, to the envoy and to the word, is only an advance sign of the service which they will give to Jesus and through him to the salvation effected by God. Thus the narratives regarding the birth of Jesus repeatedly speak of the service performed by the angels. Matthew sees it chiefly as guidance of Joseph and protection of the child. Luke represents the angels as heralds preparing the way for the child in the hearts of men and as interpreters of the salvation that has come with him. Protection and manifestation of the "Son of the Most High" on earth constitute, therefore, their function, in general. And by that they serve not only him, but the salvation of men. But even the Father is linked with the Son through angels. That is what is meant by Jesus in the Gospel according to John when he declares, with an allusion to Jacob's ladder, "Truly, truly, I say to you, you will see heaven opened, and the angels of God ascending and descending upon the Son of man." They are the bearers and intermediaries of Jesus' uninterrupted communion with God, the powers of heaven open above him even when on earth. By their service they cause him to know by experience what on occasion he says: "I am not alone, for the Father is with me" (Jn 16:32; cf. 8:16, 29) and "I and the Father are one" (Jn 10:30). Such attendance of the angels conveying to him God's close presence is also mentioned in the synoptic gospels at three other characteristic moments of Jesus' earthly existence. After Jesus had victoriously withstood temptation by the devil, Matthew notes: "Then the devil left him and

law is regarded not as God's beneficent guidance for life, but a law of achievement abused by sin and provoking to sin. Cf. H. Schlier, *Der Brief an die Galater.* Krit.-exeget. Kommentar über das NT, 7. Abt. (12th ed. 1962), pp. 104 ff.

behold, angels came and ministered to him" (Mt 4:11; cf.
Mk 1:13). Disobedient Adam was driven from the Garden of
Eden by the angel; the angels are subject to the obedient
Messiah Jesus.[21] God through them ministers to the man who
has proved himself in God's service. Another time Jesus himself
mentions their protecting power, once again in connection with
his obedience which in this case is actually shown by renouncing their assistance. "Do you think that I cannot appeal to my
Father, and he will at once send me more than twelve legions
of angels? But how then should the scriptures be fulfilled, that
it must be so?" (Mt 26:53 f.). The holy angels do not impose
their protection, they cannot and will not extend it against the
will of the Son and the Father. Their service is always a mission.
God's will is always involved. God does not leave the Son in
the lurch in such obedience. And so the angels are mentioned a
third time during Jesus' activity on earth, when on the Mount
of Olives he had consented to his Passion. "And there appeared
to him an angel from heaven, strengthening him. And being in
an agony he prayed more earnestly; and his sweat became like
great drops of blood falling down upon the ground" (Lk
22:43 f.). His prayer, "Thy will be done", brought the angel. The
angel, did not take away his suffering, did not take away the
mortal anguish, which in this *praeludium mortis* (A. Bengel)
was like his death agony. But the angel did not allow him to
collapse in fear of suffering. He "strengthened him". In this
way Jesus in his obedience experienced through angels at the
beginning and end of his earthly work—mention is not often
made of it—God's encouraging and strengthening presence.

At the birth of Jesus the angels of God protect and proclaim
the child. At the beginning and end of his earthly work they
serve him in his obedience. For the risen Christ they are witnesses and interpreters and open out a path for the Gospel
concerning him. An "angel of the Lord" descends from heaven

[21] Cf. J. Schniewind, *Das Evangelium nach Markus* (6th ed. 1952), pp. 48 f.

and gives access to the empty tomb, from which he proclaims the first Gospel: *resurrexit,* which, however, only repeats what Jesus said: *sicut dixit.* The angel, however, the first envoy, also serves the mission. He does not send the women as Jesus later sends his apostles. But he sends them to the disciples and the disciples by them to the risen Christ so that he may send them as witnesses (Mt 28:7). And in Matthew the angel sends the women on the strength of his own word: "Lo, I have told you" (Mt 28:7); in Mark (16:7) and Luke (24:6), however, he simply recalls Jesus' words: "as he told you". The angel serves the Gospel and the apostolate as one who in the first place is fulfilling Jesus' words. We might say that the testimony and purpose of the resurrection is still high above, in the angelic sphere. John 20:12 also confirms this. There the two angels who, we may suppose, are keeping watch over the place of death, only go as far as the question to Mary Magdalen, "Woman, why are you weeping?" Then Jesus, appearing to her unrecognized, takes over the question from the angels and announces himself to her as bodily present. The ascension of our Lord, seen from the earth, as it were, is the completion of his resurrection until his second coming. And so at the ascension too, the angels are interpreters, not of their own knowledge but recalling the words of the Lord himself (Acts 1:10f.). It is they to whom, according to the hymn in 1 Timothy 3:16, Jesus, ascending into heaven, "appeared" before he was preached by the apostles to the nations: "appeared to the angels, preached among the nations".[22]

They now, however, also serve the advance of the Gospel and cooperate actively in the foundation and consolidation of the Church. The centurion Cornelius of what was called the Italian cohort in Caesarea, is instructed by an angel of God to send for Peter. And so the first baptism of a pagan comes about by

---

[22] Perhaps at Ephesians 2:17f. the same passage is in the background. Cf. H. Schlier, *Der Brief an die Epheser* (3rd ed. 1963), pp. 136ff.

angelic mediation (Acts 10:3 ff.). An angel frees the apostles from prison to preach afresh (Acts 5:19; 12:7; cf. 16:26). An angel convinces Paul that he will stand before the emperor (Acts 27:23). But it is before the eyes of the angels and not only before those of men that the apostle has to play the painful role of his preaching: "We have become a spectacle to the world, to angels and to men." The divine worship of the assembled congregation takes place under the protection and with the help of the angels, in proportionate harmony with their heavenly praise of God and their eschatological joy. Their presence at divine worship which requires women to veil their heads, is mentioned at 1 Corinthians 11:3 ff., whatever interpretation of this obscure passage is adopted. According to Revelation 5:8; 8:3, they carry the prayers of the faithful up to God. In the glossolalia, which is akin to the speech of angels, there is even a danger to the congregation, if it does not serve to "edify" and is not interpreted (1 Cor 14). In its liturgy the earthly *ekklesia* is perpetually travelling towards the heavenly Jerusalem, constantly approaching "innumerable angels in festal gathering, and the *ekklesia* of the first-born who are enrolled as citizens in heaven, and God the judge of all, and the spirits of just men made perfect and the mediator of the new covenant, Jesus..." (Heb 12:12 ff.). It has its exemplar in the heavenly liturgy of which the Revelation to John gives us a glimpse, and which the earthly liturgy emulates. The "rejoicing", the ἀγαλλίασις and the ἀγαλλιᾶσθαι which is the result of being penetrated by the awareness of the overwhelming presence of God in Jesus Christ, and which echoes his redemption, is a characteristic of the earthly (Acts 2:46) and of the heavenly community (Rev 19:7). But the local churches themselves, as well as the individual believers, each have an angel. For so, in my opinion, the ἄγγελοι are to be understood, for whom the glorified Lord dictates letters to the Seer: they are not to be interpreted as bishops. Apart from any other reasons, ἄγγελος would be a strange name for them and one which is not used anywhere else.[23] These angels assigned to the seven churches, which taken together represent the whole Church, are held as seven stars in the right hand of the Son of man on high who is to be seen among the seven lampstands, the seven communities (Rev 1:13, 16, 20; 2:1; 3:1). The angels of the churches which there surround Christ with light, stand in the defending power of the risen Lord and, as the protected and protecting spirits of the churches, transmit to these consolation and admonition. But it is the Seer who is to instruct the churches in the person of their angels.

The faithful as individuals also have their angels, because they are lowly and dependent in every way upon God. What Jesus says at Matthew 18:10 is a proof of this: "See that you do not despise one of these little ones; for I tell you that in heaven their angels always behold the face of my Father who is in heaven." These "little ones" are not primarily the children, not even in the mind of Matthew, who alone hands down this saying and has placed it with other sayings about authentic greatness. As can be seen from Matthew 18:6 in agreement with Mark 9:42 and Matthew 10:42, they are the simple and insignificant, the negligible, lowly disciples, the "babes" of Matthew 11:25 and Luke 10:21, the "poor in spirit" of Matthew 5:3.[24] Their angels stand in the perpetual sight of God, contrary to the Jewish conviction that only the highest order of the throne angels are permitted to see God's face. They themselves, however, the poor and insignificant disciples, are protected and preserved with God through their angels' having that vision of God. God guards them in their angels, who are his own, from men's contempt, for example. What is small and insignificant is, in the

---

[23] Cf. TWNT vol. I, pp. 85 f. (G. Kittel) on Revelation 1:20. A different view is taken by T. Zahn, W. Hadorn, A. Wikenhauser.
[24] According to Luke 17:2, it is perhaps poor and lowly people in general who are meant; cf. Lk 6:20; cf. TWNT vol. IV, pp. 652 f. (O. Michel); J. Schmid, Das Evangelium nach Markus (3rd ed. 1954), pp. 181 f. on Mark 9:42; J. Schniewind, Das Evangelium nach Matthäus (7th ed. 1954), p. 199.

angel, open to God and stands in his sight. So it is not surprising that the angels are also concerned in penance. Their joy rests on the sinner and welcomes those who repent. "I tell you there is joy before the angels of God over one sinner who repents" says Jesus in the parable of the prodigal son (Lk 15:10). "Are they not all ministering spirits sent forth to serve, for the sake of those who are to obtain salvation?" the preacher of Hebrews justly asks (Heb 1:14).

Nor is the world abandoned by the angels in the age when its history no longer consists of anything but the decision for or against the returning Lord.[25] They are chiefly at the service of the judgment which is accomplished in it. According to the Revelation to John, their service began in the moment when Michael and his angels threw Satan and his angels down to the earth (Rev 12:7 ff.). But now other powerful angels of history also help to make way for the coming of Christ in triumph in the world which is more and more simply an obstacle to him that has to be destroyed. That occurs in three ways. The angels announce the final accomplishment of the judgment on this earth and its powers in mighty words and signs (Rev 8:3; 10:1 ff.; 14:6 ff.; 18:1 ff., 18, 21). Sometimes it happens in conjunction with the words of consolation and admonition of the "eternal gospel" to the faithful. This history resounds with the mighty call of the angels that "there should be no delay" (Rev 10:6 f.) and that the great Babylon is fallen (14:8; 18:1 f.). The angel of history is heard when the proximity and hidden advent of its end are perceived.

Angels also actively provoke history, however. God produces eschatological events of history—and all history now is eschatological history—through his angels. What occurs is in response to the call of angels. That is true not only of the ground of events, inasmuch as the glorified Lord, who of course alone is worthy and able to make all history plain, steps forward at

---

[25] Cf. H. Schlier, *Die Zeit der Kirche* (3rd ed. 1962), pp. 265—274.

the question of a strong angel: "Who is worthy to open the scroll and break its seals?", and receives the book of history from the hand of God (Rev 5:2 ff.). Even in details the eschatological event is represented as the answer to an angelic command. "And another angel came out of the temple, calling with a loud voice to him who sat upon the cloud, 'Put in your sickle and reap, for the hour to reap has come, for the harvest of the earth is fully ripe.' So he who sat upon the cloud swung his sickle on the earth, and the earth was reaped" we read in Revelation 14:15 f. (cf. however also 7:2; 14:17 ff.; 19:17). What happens in this age of history, the age of judgment, happens as an echo of angelic summons.

But angels are also themselves the controllers and active agents of the eschatological event. The trumpet blasts of the "seven angels who stand before God" unleash catastrophe after catastrophe (Rev 8; 9; 10:7; 11:15). From the bowls of another seven angels the wrath of God is poured onto the earth (Rev 15; 16). The perpetually increasing eschatological judgment in the catastrophes of world-history, in which Christ makes his way, bears within it the power of the holy angels, whom God has appointed for this. It is an angel from heaven, too, who has power over the pit and who binds Satan in it (Rev 20:1 ff.). God is master of all the abysses of this history and governs the abyss of history itself through his angel.

It is Christ's parousia, however, after his birth and his resurrection from the dead, as the third great and definitive redemptive decision of God, which once again assembles the angels round the Lord as heralds and executors of his will.[26] It is the voice of the archangel, the trumpet of God, which announces the descent of the *Kyrios* (1 Thess 4:16). His "mighty angels" accompany him (2 Thess 1:7; cf. Mt 16:27 and par.; 25:31; 1 Tim 5:21), and as his envoys carry out the judgment. "The harvest is the close of the age and the reapers are angels"

[26] Cf. B. Rigaux, *Saint Paul, Les Epitres aux Thessaloniciens* (1956), pp. 623 ff.; *TWNT*, vol. I, p. 83, pp. 25 ff.

(Mt 13:39). Together with Christ they form the tribunal: "And I tell you, every one who acknowledges me before men, the Son of man also will acknowledge before the angels of God" (Lk 12:8f.; cf. also Rev 3:5; 14:10). The gathering and separation (Mt 13:41f., 49f.) and the gathering of the "elect" "from the four winds, from one end of heaven to the other" (Mt 24:31), is described as the angels' office. They bring about the irrevocable. For that reason on the gates of the new, heavenly Jerusalem there stand the names of the twelve tribes of Israel, of the eschatological People of God, but they are also occupied by twelve guardian angels. The heavenly city is entrusted to their protection. To their protective nature God has committed even what is definitive.

These are the main features of the description given in the New Testament of the angels' service. As personal powers of heavenly life and light they have their innermost essence in rejoicing at the sight of God, and before God's face carry out the liturgy of preserving the creation and the creatures. Their service gave Jesus in his days on earth protection and refreshment. From their mouths, the heavenly witnesses who surrounded his birth and his grave, the earliest message of salvation went forth. They serve the mission and the apostolate. They are close to the Church gathered together on earth for worship, and whose communities and faithful have each an angel in whom they face God and the Lord. The angels are heralds who proclaim the judgments of history and are active in them. They appear as the glory of the coming Lord and also serve him in the final decision. They watch eternally over the heavenly city.

Yet however mighty the angels may be in the power and light which God has granted to man through them, the New Testament is conscious that for all their superabundance they have a limit. The Son, Jesus Christ, is superior to them, he is also *their* Lord. The Son is not an angel. He is the Lord. "He sat down at the right hand of the majesty on high, having become as much superior to angels as the name he has obtained is more

excellent than theirs", says Hebrews 1:3 f. (cf. Phil 2:11).
However great the majesty of the angels may be, so that, as the
remarkable text Jude 9 indicates, its glory still rests even on
the devil, and although God may have made the Son "for a
little while lower than the angels", this same sentence does not
end there and goes on to say "thou hast crowned him with glory
and honour, putting everything in subjection under his feet"
(Heb 2:7). And in this the faithful share, those whom he is not
ashamed to call "brethren" (Heb 2:11). Certainly the angelic
mode of being surpasses the human so much that only those
raised from the dead and transfigured will be "like the angels"
(Mt 22:29 f.). And certainly in unfailing adoration of God they
are unfailingly holy and perform unfailingly perfect service.
Yet "it is not with angels that he is concerned but with the
descendants of Abraham" (Heb 2:16). And by concerning himself in the excess of his grace with these fallen and sinful creatures, he prepares for them joys "into which angels long to
look" (1 Pet 1:12). And if the holy angels assist and serve in
the tribunal of the Son of man, those "called to be saints" are
asked by the apostle: "Do you not know that the saints will
judge the world? ... Do you not know that we are to judge
(the fallen) angels?" (1 Cor 6:2). In the order of grace and by
grace, men are more than the angels. It is in the light of the
greatness and limits of the angels that the scene must be understood which the Seer describes at the end of his book. When he
had seen and heard everything through the angel, "I fell down
to worship at the feet of the angel who showed them to me"
(Rev 22:8; cf. 19:10). But the angel would not permit this.
"But he said to me, 'You must not do that! I am a fellow
servant with you and your brethren the prophets, and with those
who keep the words of this book. Worship God'." The angels'
nature and service make the faithful honour and love them.[27]
But worship belongs to God alone.

[27] Cf. Augustine, *De vera religione* 110 (*PL* vol. XXXIV, col. 170).

CHAPTER XI

The Unity of the Church according to the New Testament

The New Testament shows that the question of the unity of the Church preoccupied Christians from the beginning. The unity of the Church was in fact threatened from the beginning. It was endangered by the controversies, extending to the very roots of faith, between Christians who had been Jews and Christians who had been Gentiles, regarding the significance of the Law for salvation. It was no less shaken by the Gnostic tendencies of certain enthusiasts which in Corinth, for example, led to the formation of conventicles even inside the actual local Church. There it was a question of the significance for salvation of individual experiences of the Spirit. Similar endeavours in heretical circles, often of a more theological character, are visible in the later letters of the New Testament, for example in the seven letters of the Revelation to John or in the pastoral epistles. The unity of the Church was never uncontested. And the New Testament writers were convinced that it never will be uncontested. As time advances its unity will in fact be ever more seriously imperilled. That is part of the sufferings of the Last Days, which have already begun. It will also be manifested more and more in the coming divisions and schisms of the Church. "I know", the Acts of the Apostles describes Paul as saying to the elders of the Church at Ephesus (Acts 20: 29 f.), "that after my departure, fierce wolves will come in, not sparing the flock; and from among your own selves will arise men speaking perverse things, to draw away the disciples after them. Therefore be alert...". And 2 Peter 2:1 says, "But false prophets also arise among the people, just as there will be false teachers among you, who will secretly bring in destructive heresies". Those are not the only warnings of that kind in the New Testament, which is aware both of the unity of the Church and of the forces which perpetually endanger it. It fights for the unity of the Church. For according to the New Testament unity is not merely a great benefit, it belongs to the Church's very essence. If it is abandoned, the Church is abandoned, for the Church is one or simply does not exist.

What unity is meant, then? We shall attempt to make clear the main features of the answer which the New Testament gives.

I

The unity of the Church ultimately has its ground in the one God. He is the one real God among many so-called gods. All that is and happens is due to him as the one Creator and the master of history. To him as the one Lord, we are all orientated (1 Cor 8:6). He wills to restore and unite all things in Christ (Eph 1:10). He is the one God who in fact justifies Jews *and* Gentiles by faith (Rom 3:29f.), the one God and Father who rules over all those he has justified, who acts through all and dwells in all (Eph 4:6). He releases forces, gifts and energies of many kinds in the community of believers and these serve their unity (1 Cor 12:6). It is in this unifying unity of the one God and Father that the unity of the Church has its ground. To divide the one Church would be nothing less than to resist the unifying will and operation of the one God.

The one God who wills and produces unity has in Jesus Christ revealed himself and his unity to a mankind torn by hostile divisions, and has bestowed on it in him a new basis of unity. And so the New Testament repeatedly refers to the crucified, risen and glorified Lord Jesus Christ when it is speaking of the unity of the Church. It expresses the situation in various ways. It was Jesus Christ who broke through the wall of separation between God and man on the one hand, and between men, that is between Gentiles and Jews, on the other and made Jews and Gentiles into "one new man", reconciling "both to God in *one* body (i.e. in his body) through the cross" (Eph 2:15 f.). By the fact that he "died for all" and they all "died in him", "they (all) live no longer for themselves but for him who for their sake died and was raised" (2 Cor 5:14f.; Rom 14:7 ff.). Through him and in him all men who enter into relation with him are now once again open to God and to one another in a unity of freedom and responsibility (Gal 5:1, 13; 2 Cor 5:10; Rom 14:10). The Cross of the risen and exalted Jesus Christ, therefore, has disclosed the ground of the unity of the Church in history. That unity rests on the Cross on which he "welcomed all for the glory of God" (Rom 15:7).

The Gospel according to John does not envisage the basis in sacred history of the unity of the Church any differently, but it also points to the relation of the Son to the Father: "that they may all be one", it describes our Lord as saying in his sacerdotal prayer (17:21, 23), "even as thou, Father, art in me, and I in thee, that they also may be in us ...". This unity of the Father with the Son and of the Son with the Father in mutual love opened out once again to all men the glory of the one loving gaze of the Father, from which they received life and light. "The glory *(doxa)* which thou hast given me I have given to them, that they may be one ..." (17:22). That gaze uniting all men, however, was bestowed by Jesus in his words and signs and finally in the word and sign of his sacrifice for them in death. Caiaphas as high priest said, deliberately yet not knowing what he was really saying, "It is expedient for you that one man should die for the people and that the whole nation should not perish". The evangelist regarded that as a prophecy "that Jesus should die for the nation, and not for the nation only, but to gather into one the children of God who are scattered abroad" (Jn 10:50ff.). According to John's Gospel, too, the unity of the Church has its foundation in the all-embracing and supporting love of the Lord raised on high through the Cross.

That unity founded by Jesus Christ and present in him, unfolds itself, according to the New Testament, in the Holy Spirit. Access to the unity of the Church is, therefore, to be found in the unity of the Holy Spirit. The apostle teaches us that God makes us know himself and all his saving gifts through his Spirit (1 Cor 2:10ff.). Christ himself causes us to know him in his Spirit (cf. Rom 8:10f.). In this sense, "the Lord is the Spirit" (2 Cor 3:17; cf. 1 Cor 6:17). In his Spirit which is God's Spirit, the power and might of God's self-revelation, Christ also manifests himself as the ground of all unity. And so the apostle Paul can say: "Through him (the crucified and exalted Lord) we both (Jews and Gentiles and, therefore, all men) have access *in one Spirit* to the Father" (Eph 2:18). And so he can also name the *one* Spirit as the foundation of the unity of the Church which is to be maintained and tested (Eph 4:4). And once again the matter is really no different in the Gospel according to John. There Jesus says: "And I, when I am lifted up from the earth, will draw all men to myself" (12:32). In what way does that happen? Through the Spirit, the "other helper" (Jn 14:16; cf. 14:26; 15:26; 16:7; 1 Jn 2:1), in whom the glorified Jesus comes again and is present (cf. 7:39; 14:16f.; 16:12—15 etc.). *He* is Jesus' unifying influence towards himself. And so we see that when the New Testament speaks of the unity of the Church, it means a unity which is grounded in the will and operation of God. God gave rise to it in Jesus' crucified body that was the bearer of all, and revealed it in the Holy Spirit who summons all to it. To disregard or harm that unity means to act against the one God, the source of unity operative in Christ Jesus through the Holy Spirit. When the apostle Paul learnt of the discord and conventicles in the Corinthian *congregation,* he reproachfully asked the Christians of Corinth: "Is *Christ* divided?" For he considered that if the Church, even the local Church, is divided, then Christ is divided. He meant this really, not just figuratively. But when he goes on to say: "Was Paul (to whom one part of the congregation was attached, whereas others preferred Peter or Apollos) *crucified* for you? Or were you *baptized* in the name of Paul?" (1 Cor 1:12f.), he brings us to another aspect.

II

So far we have been inquiring into the ground of unity. We must now consider the ways and means by which unity is manifested. The New Testament names the Gospel, baptism and the Lord's Supper and, from another point of view, the apostolic ministry and the charismata or gifts of the Spirit.

The unity of the Church willed by God in Christ through the Holy Spirit finds expression in the one Gospel. This is not uniform. Each of its apostolic preachers sets out the one Gospel under one particular aspect. While, for example, the Gospel according to John emphasizes the glory of the Incarnate Word in Jesus manifested in words and signs, the evangelist Luke is concerned to present the events concerning Jesus in the context, and in the very centre, of a great history of redemption which also includes the history of the foundation and spread of the Church as far as Rome. Similarly each of the other New Testament writers had his own perspective and tendency. Yet for all that, it is the one Gospel by which the Holy Spirit summons men into the unity of the Church and so produces the unity of the Church. We know with what determination the apostle Paul defended the unity of the Gospel. Against Jewish Christian opponents in the Galatian communities he stressed with particular emphasis that there is only *one* Gospel. "I am astonished"—he writes to the Galatian Christians (1:6 ff.)—"that you are so quickly deserting him who called you in the grace of Christ and turning to a different gospel—*not that there is another gospel*, but there are some who trouble you and want to pervert the gospel of Christ. But even if we, or an angel from heaven, should preach to you a gospel contrary to that which we have preached to you, let him be accursed." And because there is only *one* Gospel, Paul submits his Gospel, which he of course had received by revelation from Christ and which was not a human one, and had not, therefore, sprung from his own mind, to the original apostles in Jerusalem who had preached the Gospel before him. The agreement of the two manifested the inner unity of the one Gospel which the two sides had certainly preached each in their own way and from their own particular point of view. Its truth appeared as a unity. As Paul could later express it, "There is *one* body and *one* Spirit, just as you were called to the *one* hope that belongs to your call" (Eph 4:4).

It must not be forgotten that the Gospel is one in another respect. It is one despite the great variety of its form and of the ways in which it is proclaimed. It is expressed orally or in writing, in catechetical, homiletic or liturgical traditions of the most varied kinds. We are thinking for example of the kerygma of the apostle Paul, of the *paratheke* or apostolic legacy in the pastoral epistles, of the *homologia* of the Letter to the Hebrews, the tradition in the First Letter of John, which are all shown to be the basis and criterion of faith, as opposed in particular to beliefs which threaten the one truth and true unity. The influence of the one Holy Spirit uses the one Gospel in proclamation, scripture and rule in order to bring men into contact with Jesus Christ and, in him, with the ground of all unity.

But in the centre of the Gospel, illumined by it and in its turn bringing fulfilment, and impressing its mark, there appears what we call "sacraments", especially, according to the New Testament, baptism and the Lord's Supper. By baptism, in virtue of its very source, the Holy Spirit orientates all who submit to it in faith, towards the unifying unity, and incorporates all believers in virtue of its very basis, into the unifying unity of the Church, "... by *one* Spirit we were all baptized into *one* body, Jews or Greeks, slaves or free, and all were made to drink of one Spirit..." says the apostle Paul at 1 Corinthians 12:13. Baptism, which incorporates into the one Christ, renders irrelevant every difference of sex, class and origin, by bringing them all into the unity of the same hope. "For in Christ Jesus you are all sons of God, through faith. For as many of you as were baptized into Christ have put on Christ. There is neither Jew nor Greek, there is neither slave nor free, there is neither male nor female; for you are all one in Christ Jesus. And if you are Christ's, then you are Abraham's offspring, heirs according to the promise" (Gal 3:26 ff.). Because they "have heard the word of truth, the gospel of your salvation and have believed", even those who were formerly pagans have been "sealed with the Holy Spirit" and thereby (in baptism) have been incorporated into the unity of the Body of Christ (Eph 1:13; 3:6; 4:30). And so Ephesians 4:5 lists with the one Lord and the one faith, the one baptism as the means which effectively confers and promotes unity as well as being its sign.

The unity of the Church constituted in baptism in virtue of the Holy Spirit, is strengthened anew and rendered visible in the Lord's Supper. Here all the baptized, far from the "table of devils", visibly share the "Lord's table" (1 Cor 10:21) and (as Israel had prefigured) all eat "the same spiritual food" and all drink "the same spiritual drink" (1 Cor 10:3 f.). And so it is particularly at the Lord's Supper that the division and secret schism in the Church of Corinth was brought to light. The one eucharistic bread had lost its true sacramental significance in the eyes of the Corinthian enthusiasts and consequently its power to unite the congregation, just as the unifying proclamation of the death of the Lord and the unifying kerygma generally had already lost theirs. And so the unity of the one Body of Christ, the Church, was really threatened.

Once again the apostle Paul is almost the only one to testify to this connection between the unity of the Church, Gospel and sacraments. Nevertheless the evangelist Luke alludes to it when in a brief picture of the Jerusalem Church he describes as follows the life of the newly-converted, and by implication, that of all the faithful. "So those who received his word were baptized, and there were added that day about three thousand souls. And they devoted themselves to the apostles' teaching and fellowship, to the breaking of bread and the prayers" (Acts 2:41 f.). This text, however, takes us further. We see that in addition to baptism, teaching and Eucharist, two other factors are referred to, which have to be taken into account in dealing with the question of the unity of the Church: the apostles and prayers. That reminds us that according to the New Testament the apostolic office and the charismata have their importance for the unity of the Church. Not as though both were actual means of salvation and as such constitutive of the unity of the Church; but the holders of office and in another sense the recipients of charismata are *mediators* (and guardians) of the saving unity of the Church. At the service of the one Gospel in the building up of the one Church there stands, we hear again and again, in the first place the one apostolic ministry, though this again is diversified and develops. It has its roots in the "Twelve" who were called (Mk 1:16 ff.; Mt 4:18 ff.; cf. Lk 5:1 ff.) and appointed (Mk 3:13 ff.; Lk 6:12 ff.) by Jesus as the future rulers and judges of the eschatological Israel (Mt 19:28; Lk 22:28 ff.) to gather together the people of God in the Last Days. They are the unifying core of this people of God which is already assembling. In themselves they also represent a quasi-institutional unity which in Simon Peter has its responsible head who is at the same time the foundation of the Church (Mt 16:17 ff.; Lk 22:31 ff.; cf. Jn 21:7 ff., 15 ff.). Authorized, equipped and sent by Jesus to represent and extend his service

on earth (Mk 6:6ff.; Mt 10:1ff.; Lk 9:1ff.), confirmed in
this mission by the risen Christ (Mt 28:16ff.; Lk 24:47f.;
Acts 1:2ff.; cf. Jn 20:21ff.), they are definitively empowered
by the Spirit of the glorified Christ to exercise their apostolic
office (Acts 2 etc.). According to Luke, as the "Twelve" they
extended the Jerusalem "jurisdiction" to the Church which was
spreading over Samaria among the Gentiles (Acts 8:14ff.;
15:1ff.). According to Acts, the exceptional apostle, Paul, was
only carrying out the mission to the Gentiles inaugurated by
Peter, and his measures required confirmation by the apostolic
college (cf. Acts 10; 13; 15). Paul himself, of course, knew that
he owed his service to the revelation of the glorified Christ who
personally had sent him to preach the Gospel (Gal 1—2). But
as the original apostles with Peter at their head were there before
him, and as he too recognized them as apostolic authorities, the
same problem arose for him in regard to the apostolate as there
did in regard to the Gospel, and he solved it in the same way.
The unity of the apostolate was manifested by the agreement of
authorities mutually recognizing each other. In such unity of
the apostolate the apostle Paul himself, like each of the other
apostles, was then, of course, the force which formed, promoted
and preserved the unity of the Church in his missionary
territory. His Churches are his "workmanship in the Lord"
(cf. 1 Cor 9:1), the building on the foundation he has laid
(1 Cor 3:10ff.), the letter which he, or rather Christ through
him, has written (2 Cor 3:2f.). He is their father, and became
their father in Christ Jesus through the Gospel (1 Cor 4:14f.),
the mother who bore them (cf. Gal 4:19), the nurse who feeds
them (1 Thess 2:7). His Churches are under his authority and
his instructions are their unifying guide in dogma, liturgy and
ecclesiastical law. And so we find repeatedly in his letters
formulae such as these: "I commend you because you remember
me in everything and maintain the traditions even as I have
delivered them." Or, "If any one is disposed to be contentious,
we recognize no other practice, nor do the Churches of God."

Or, "But in the following instructions I do not commend you."
Or, "About the other things I will give directions when I
come"—all statements from the 11th chapter of the First Letter
to the Corinthians (cf. also 1 Cor 4:21; 5:3 f.; 6:1 ff.; 7:17;
14:36 f.; 2 Cor 10:5 f., 8; 13:10). It is the apostle's awareness
that in virtue of the one Gospel and the one apostolate he is an
instrument of the Church's unity that explains his numerous
visits to the Churches, his letters to them, and his sending his
disciples and representatives to them. That cannot, however, be
gone into here.

From the apostolic ministry derive, according to Acts, the
local Church offices (cf. Acts 6:1 ff.; 13:23). They too tend,
as the personal position of James in Jerusalem shows (Acts 12:17;
15:13; 21:17 f.; 1 Cor 15:7; Gal 2:9, 12), towards unity at the
summit. The apostle Paul is shown in Acts as handing over
expressly to those whom the Holy Spirit has appointed as
overseers, the leadership and protection of the community. Such
a commission also gives them charge of the unity of the local
ekklesia (Acts 20:28 ff.). That is already indicated in Paul's
letters when he gives his disciples and representatives a share in
the responsibility and care for the local Churches of his missionary territory (e.g. 1 Cor 4:17; 16:10) and when in his epistles
he calls upon the members of those Churches to obey those who
have devoted themselves to the service of the saints and to all
who have worked with him in the cause of the Gospel
(1 Cor 16:15 f.; cf. Heb 13:1 f.). "But we beseech you, brethren,
to respect those who labour among you and are over you in the
Lord and admonish you; and to esteem them very highly in
love because of their work. Be at peace among yourselves"
(1 Thess 5:12 f.). And so the apostle, in a glance back over
the whole building up of the Church, sees that among the
"gifts" of the glorified Lord the local "pastors and teachers"
must also be counted and they too have to serve in building up
the one Body of Christ with the apostles, prophets and evangelists (Eph 4:11). According to the pastoral epistles, not only

the apostle himself but, by succession in his ministry, his representatives and followers also, care for the unity of the Church or, as the case may be, of a certain Church territory. That care extends to doctrine, worship and discipline. They transmit these—rather like apostolic delegates and metropolitans, as it were—to the presbyters and bishops of the local Churches. Finally, in the Johannine writings, as is well known, ministry retreats very much into the background, despite the importance of the mission. Yet the "disciples", who are usually identified with the Twelve, are the "witnesses from the beginning" (Jn 15:26; 17:18), sent by Jesus into his eschatological "harvest" (Jn 4:34 ff.). As such they are the bearers of the word which produces the unity of the faithful and as a consequence the unity of the world (Jn 17:20 ff.). In the epilogue to the gospel (Jn 21), Simon Peter who stands out among the Twelve in the gospel itself (Jn 1:42; 6:68 ff.; 13; 18; 20:1 ff.), in a symbolic scene brings the fishes to the risen Christ in his net (Jn 21:10 f.), and Jesus solemnly commits the "flock" to him to pasture. The Church is one; it is the Church of Peter; and the risen Jesus has committed to him (in the midst of the Twelve) the harvest, the draught of fishes and the feeding of the flock. In the Johannine letters, too, care for the unity of the Church is apparent (1 Jn 2:18 ff.; 4:1 ff.; 5:5 ff., 21; 2 Jn 7 ff.; 3 Jn 9 f.).

According to the New Testament, however, the Holy Spirit has yet another possibility of bringing about and strengthening the unity of the Church given by God in Jesus Christ. From the beginning there were not only apostles but also prophets in the Church, and these too served unity by their spiritual gifts. The prophecy of Agabus prompted the collection for Jerusalem in the Church of Antioch, a proof of fraternal solidarity (Acts 11:27 ff.). Through prophets and teachers in the same Antioch, the Holy Spirit sends Barnabas and Saul on the mission (Acts 13:1 ff.). Once again the apostle Paul is clearer. The prophets whom God has appointed in the Church (1 Cor 12:28 f.; cf. Eph 3:5), serve to build up the one Body of Christ

(Eph 4:11). It is expressly said at Ephesians 2:20 that the heavenly edifice of the Church is "built upon the foundation of the apostles and prophets, Christ Jesus himself being the cornerstone, in whom the whole structure is joined together and grows into a holy temple in the Lord...". From the start, therefore, the prophetic spirit is a spirit of unity. And it is perpetuated in the Churches by spiritual gifts all of which promote unity. It is true that these are only enkindled by the apostolic testimony which is the basis and agent of unity (1 Cor 1:7). Consequently they find their measure in that testimony i.e. in the faith of the Church, and may not leave that ground if they are to be genuine charismata. A standard example is provided by Paul's controversy with the Corinthian enthusiasts (cf. also Rom 12:6). As genuine charismata, however, they are gifts of the *one* Spirit, bestowed in order to cause the unity of the Church to be vitally experienced. "Now there are varieties of gifts but the same Spirit; and there are varieties of service but the same Lord; and there are varieties of working but it is the same God who inspires them all in every one. To each is given the manifestation of the Spirit for the common good... All these are inspired by one and the same Spirit who apportions to each one individually as he wills", says the apostle Paul (1 Cor 12:4 ff.). "For the common good" means: to build up the one Body, whose members by their gifts enlighten, encourage, instruct, forgive, guide, strengthen and help one another in need (cf. 1 Cor 14; Rom 12:6 ff.). So the charismata permeate the one Church giving light and life, and, the Holy Spirit working in them, cause its unity to become visible and continually give new strength.

III

The unity of the Church, as the New Testament understands it, has its ground in the one Jesus Christ in whom God confers unity in the power of the Holy Spirit; through the Gospel he announces it and summons men into it, seals those called as its members through the unity of baptism and continually renews unity through the unity of the Eucharist. That Gospel is served by the one apostolic ministry and, in their own way, by the free gifts of the one Spirit. In that way is formed the one people of God and the Body of Christ. We must now give our attention to these, for most light is thrown on the fact that the Church is one, and on the meaning of its unity, by these two designations, to which perhaps a third may be added, that of temple of the Holy Spirit.

The Church, the New Testament tells us, is the people of God. But there is only *one* people of God in the world. That is very full of meaning, in two ways. It is well-known that *ekklesia tou theou*, which we translate as "Church of God", is a name for the assembly of the Old Testament people of God which has been transferred to the Christian community. By *ekklesia tou theou* the New Testament denotes sometimes one particular local Church or congregation (e.g. Acts 5:11; 8:1, 3 etc.; Rom 16:23; 1 Cor 14:4, 23 etc.) or even a house gathering (e.g. Rom 16:5; 1 Cor 16:19; Philem 2), sometimes the Church as a whole (e.g. Acts 9:31; 20:28?; 1 Cor 12:28; 15:9; Gal 1:13; Phil 3:6; Colossians and Ephesians passim; 1 Tim 3:5, 16). What is notable in that respect is that the Church as a whole is not merely the sum of the local communities and the local Churches are not merely parts of the whole Church, so that the latter in the last resort could subsist in its parts. The relation of the two is of a different kind. According to the New Testament, the entire *ekklesia* is present in the particular community. In each local Church *the* people of God is manifest. For the apostle Paul there is no doubt at all that "all Churches [of the Gentiles]" (Rom 16:1, 16; 1 Cor 4:17 etc.), do not form merely a derivative or consequent unity, but form a unity from the very start. The individual congregation is simply the form in which the whole Church is locally present. The salutation of the First Letter to the Corinthians, for example, "... to the church of

God which is at Corinth . . ." is to be taken in its full meaning.
That there is only one people of God, with a people's concrete
reality, not only means that this people, the Church, at present
scattered throughout the world, is represented at this or that
particular place as the case may be, but also that it reaches back
through the ages and is identical with the people of God of the
Old Testament. The one people of God, the Church, is of course
a continuation of Israel and is the manifestation and fulfilment
of Israel, to the extent that Israel, not only was called but
actually accepted its vocation: Israel's "remnant" (Rom 11:1 ff.),
in its root, the patriarchs who form its basis, and the Israelites
who attained faith (Rom 11:13 ff.). In the people of God, the
Church, the "Israel of God" (Gal 6:16) is present, the "spiritual
Israel" (cf. 1 Cor 10:18), "the circumcision" (Phil 3: 3), "the
children of Abraham" (Rom 4:10 ff.; 9:1 ff.; Gal 3:15 ff.,
26 ff.; 4:2 ff.), God's "growth" (cf. 1 Cor 3:6 ff.; Rom 11:17 ff.;
cf. Is 5:1 ff.; Jer 2:21; 12:10; Ps 80:15 ff.), and it also brings
together the *klete hagia* (*miqra qodesh* Ex 12:16; Lev 23:2 ff.;
Num 28:25), the holy convocation (cf. *kletoi hagioi* 1 Cor 1:2;
Rom 1:7). In the one Church, the New Testament sees the fulfilment of the Old Testament and Jewish expectation of the
eschatological assembly of the scattered nation or even the
eschatological re-unification of the twelve tribes which are also
joined by the Gentiles. In the prophet Isaiah, God says to his
Servant, "It is a small thing that thou shouldst be my servant,
to raise up the tribes of Jacob and to convert the dregs of Israel.
Behold, I have given thee to be the light of the Gentiles, that
thou mayst be my salvation even to the farthest part of the
earth" (Is 49:6). And so, as the evangelist John says (11:52),
Jesus was to die "not for the nation only, but to gather into one
the children of God who are scattered abroad". So too in John 10
and elsewhere in the New Testament, the image of the "flock"
and its "pastor", widespread in the Old Testament and in
Jewish apocalyptic (cf. for example 1 Henoch 90:32 ff.), is
employed to signify the Church and its unity. "And I have

other sheep that are not of this fold; I must bring them also, and they will hear my voice. So there shall be one flock, one shepherd", says Jesus at John 10:16. The Messianic people of God is one. It has its provisional realization in the Church. Consequently the Church cannot not be one.

The one people of God is, however, also the one people of Christ. That is indicated in expressions like "all the churches of Christ" (Rom 16:16), "the churches of Judea in Christ" (Gal 1:22) or even "the churches of God in Christ Jesus which are in Judea" (1 Thess 2:14). Paul then expressively calls this people of Christ "the Body of Christ". Whatever the origin of this term, and whatever may be the precise content which it comprises, it expresses at all events the essential and at the same time concrete unity of the Church. We remember that at 1 Corinthians 12:13 it is said: "For by one Spirit we were all baptized into one body ... and all made to drink of one Spirit", and at 1 Corinthians 10:17: "Because there is one bread, we who are many are one body" (cf. also Eph 4:3 f.). This body is one because it is the body of the one Christ (the head) and so it is Christ in his body (1 Cor 12:12; cf. 1:13; Eph 1:22 f.; 4:12, 16; 5:22 ff.; Col 1:18; 2:19). It is also one, however, because its members are related to one another by the *pneuma* of baptism and live for one another in the same *pneuma* (cf. 1 Cor 12:14 ff.; Rom 12:4 f.; Eph 4:1 ff., 11—16; Col 3:5). The unity of this Body of Christ is antecedent to the unity of its members. The latter do not create it, it is a prior datum for them in Christ. But precisely that antecedent unity of the Church as the Body of Christ demands harmony among the members and is manifested in such harmony. And if the concept of the one people of God denotes unity with the Israel which heard the promise and, consequently, the unity of the people of God of sacred history in the midst of world history, then the concept of the Body of Christ points to the unity of humanity which is comprised in it. On the Cross, in Christ's crucified body, as Ephesians 2:15 says, "one new man" has been created out of mankind divided between Jews and Gentiles. Christ is the "last Adam", the second man, who like the first, founds, comprises and gives rise to a new mankind, in fact the new and final mankind (cf. Rom 5:12 ff.; 1 Cor 15:21 f.; 15:44 f.; Eph 3:18; 4:13).

The term Body of Christ alternates with that of a "building" or "temple", which also has a long history behind it. It also serves vividly to picture the essential unity of the Church, of the people of God, of the Body of Christ, this time as an eschatological sanctuary marked out from the world (cf. Mt 16:18; Acts 9:31; 20:32; Rom 9:32 f.; 15:2, 20; 1 Cor 3:9 ff., 16 f.; 14:3 ff., 12, 26; 1 Cor 6:16 ff.; 12:19; Eph 2:20 ff.; 4:12 ff.) and as a heavenly palace. The one "building" is the eschatological Church of Christ, as Matthew 16:18 shows, in virtue of his word founding it on Peter. It is the one "temple" as is shown particularly in 1 Corinthians 3:16 f. and Ephesians 2:20 ff., in virtue of the one Spirit which builds it up out of the faithful as "God's dwelling in the Spirit" so that in unity and harmony they may once again preserve the one Spirit who pervades that building and that temple. Both the eschatological Church of Christ founded on Peter and God's temple pervaded by the Spirit of God belong together, or rather, are one and the same. The two constitute the one Church.

IV

But how does such unity come about on the part of men? How do they fit into that unity and preserve it? The answer of the New Testament in general terms is: by becoming Christians and by being Christians. To be a Christian and to be a member of the one Church are the same thing according to the New Testament.

Man enters this unity through faith. The unity of the Church is the unity of faith. Faith answers the one Gospel in which

God expresses his summons through Christ in the power of the Holy Spirit. On that all the New Testament authors are agreed. "And they will *heed my voice.* So there shall be *one* flock, *one* shepherd" it is said in John 10:16. "I do not pray for these (his disciples, the Twelve) only, but also for those who *believe* in me through their word, that they may all be one", says Jesus at John 17:20. Faith leads to baptism, which stamps all with their unity in Christ Jesus (cf. Acts 2:41 f. and Gal 3:26 ff.). Faith, however, also accepts that being one in Christ Jesus which has come about in baptism from the new basis of existence, and maintains itself there. Whatever its more specific nature, for the New Testament faith always consists of obedience to the one Christ, in obedient abandonment of self-confident thought and self-righteous achievement, in unselfish acceptance of the wisdom and righteousness of Christ, in radical rejection of all "boasting" as the apostle Paul says, of glorying in origins, works and gnosis, which sets men at enmity; and in unifying submission to God's glory (cf. Rom 5:11; 1 Cor 1:29 ff.; 4:7; Gal 6:14 etc.).

To the obedience of faith, which springs from hearing the Gospel and is conscious of its submission to the Gospel, there accrues, from the Gospel and what it teaches, a knowledge that belongs to faith and a doctrine of the faith. These too are modes and guarantees of the unity of the Church. According to Ephesians 4:13, the glorified Christ sent apostles, prophets, evangelists, pastors and teachers for the building up of the one Body of Christ, the one Christ, "until we all attain to the unity of faith and of the knowledge of the Son of God". The knowledge of faith, however, relates to the confession of faith and finds expression in it. Faith is in principle inseparable from *homologia* (Rom 10:9 f.), which is the corporate, public and obligatory assent of faith to the one apostolic faith which takes form in the Church. The Church's insight presses forward to a common profession, a unified assent and consent of believers to the one faith. The unity of the Church in its receptivity to faith is also a unity of hope. This is one aspect of faith. Those who (through baptism) are justified in faith (Rom 5:1), "wait for the hope of righteousness through the Spirit, by faith" (Gal 5:5; cf. Rom 8:24 f.; 12:12; 15:13). They await it in "fear and trembling", for of course the definitive verdict "before the judgment seat of Christ" has still to come (Phil 2:12; 2 Cor 5:10; Rom 14:10 f.). And such hope which (therefore) does not exclude but includes fear of God, is explicitly brought into connection with the unity of the Church: "One body and one Spirit, just as you were called to the one hope that belongs to your call" (Eph 4:4). The one call of the Gospel has opened out one vista before those called. To live with such a perspective, to hope, involves entering into a unity and maintaining it. The vista which Christ has created and which the Gospel has opened out before us *is* as it were the perspective in depth of the unity of the Church. Division of the Church is always a result of hopelessness, as the Corinthian Gnostics show, for whom everything seemed to be fulfilled in their individual spiritual experiences. That there is this connection between unity and hope is shown by Romans 15:13. There Paul concludes his urgent exhortations to the members of the Roman congregation to accept one another (and so preserve the unity of the Body of Christ in Rome), with the prayer that "the God of hope" might fill them with all joy and peace in believing "so that by the power of the Holy Spirit" they might "abound in hope". It is only in the joy and peace of hope which God grants through the Holy Spirit that unity is found.

The unity of the Church is, however, above all attained and maintained by love. For love, of course, simply accepts the unifying love which Christ showed for us (cf. Rom 5:5; Eph 5:2; Jn 13:12 ff., 34; 15:9, 12, 17; 1 Jn 4:10 f. etc.), and to which he called us and set us free (Gal 5:1, 13). In it faith is operative in hope. In it sight and will are open and ready for one's neighbour. In it I seek not my own but another's (cf. 1 Cor 10:24). In it, therefore, we attain and live a life for one another and in relation to one another in which we live in the unity of the Body of Christ. Love, not loveless gnosis, "builds up" (1 Cor 8:1; 10:23; 13:5). In its truth the unity of faith and of the knowledge of the Son of God is perfected (Eph 4:12 f., 15). Here John is in agreement with Paul. Only those branches remain in the vine which is Jesus, and therefore in his society, who bear fruit in love and keep his commandments (Jn 15:1 ff.). This love manifests itself of course in many forms according to the particular personal situation of each and their encounter with their fellow-men. Its general form in the Church and beyond it, is "brotherly love" which is repeatedly referred to in the New Testament (Rom 12:10; 1 Thess 4:9; Heb 13:1; 1 Pet 1:22; 2 Pet 1:7; 3:8) and inculcated (cf. for example Gal 6:9 f.; 1 Thess 5:15; 1 Jn 3:16 ff.). It is expressed by mutual sympathy and help, by communication, visits, inter-cession and care and also, for example, by collections. Its power to unite the Church was shown in particular in the Pauline missionary territories by the great collection made by the Gentile Christians for the mother-Church in Jerusalem. The Jewish Christians of the mother-Church who had given the Gentile Christians throughout the world a share in their spiritual goods, and by so doing had already foreshadowed the unity of the Church, were to accept thanks in material form in order to confirm and strengthen this unity (cf. Rom 15: 25 ff.; 2 Cor 9:13 and 2 Cor 8—9 generally; also Gal 2:10).

There is a special relation between humility and the unity of the Church. According to the apostle Paul, humility was lacking to those Jewish Christians infected with Gnosticism who caused disturbances in the Pauline Churches in Galatia and also in Philippi and, for a time, in Rome. Dissensions were sown above all by those who boasted of belonging to the nation privileged by God, who trusted in their moral achievements, and through such self-righteous confidence did not bear their neighbour's burden, but, instead of instructing him, judged him (cf. Gal 6:1 ff.; Phil 3:2 ff.; 2 Cor 10:12 ff.; Rom 16:17 ff.). Equally dangerous is the pride of those who withdraw from the

unifying kerygma—dogma, as we would say—and give themselves over to the apparent superiority and freedom of self-
centred knowledge which has its limit and norm only in the
plenitude of personal experiences. Enamoured of their own
experiences and "inflated" in a sort of snobbish Christianity,
these people strong in knowledge paid no heed to the "weakness of the weak" (Rom 14:1; 15:1 f.), and there was no
question of their outdoing "one another in showing honour"
precisely to those who were religiously inferior (Rom 12:10).
In that way, as the example of Corinth shows, they prepared
the way for schism and heresy. For only "lowliness and meekness with patience" and "forbearing one another in love" as
Paul shows (Eph 4:1 ff.), are able to bear the tensions to which
the Church too is subject, and are able "to keep the unity of
the Spirit in the bond of peace". Only humility accomplishes
by imitation the humility of Christ in which the Church has its
foundation, for Christ "did not please himself", but "welcomed"
us (Rom 15:3, 7). The apostle Paul speaks repeatedly of this
connection, a sign how important it is for him. We will quote
only one admonition: "So if there is any encouragement in
Christ, any incentive of love, any participation in the Spirit,
any affection and sympathy, complete my joy by being of the
same mind, having the same love, being in full accord and of
one mind. Do nothing from selfishness or conceit, but in humility
count others better than yourselves. Let each of you look not
only to his own interests, but also to the interests of others. Have
this mind among yourselves, which was in Christ Jesus..."
(Phil 2:1 ff.; cf. Rom 14:1 ff.; 15:1 ff., 7 ff.; 1 Cor 8:9;
Eph 4:32—5:2). The unity of the Church, based on the Cross
of Christ, is ultimately preserved only by accepting the Cross
of Christ which Christians lay on one another's backs. In the
judgment of the apostle Paul, that was precisely what those
zealous for the Law, and the enthusiasts in Galatia and Corinth,
were not willing to bear (cf. Gal 5:11; 6:11 ff.; 1 Cor 1:17 ff.).
For that, something is required which is particularly difficult

for those who are "haughty", as Paul calls them (Rom 12:16): they must not overstep "the measure of faith which God has assigned him" (Rom 12:3), but must have "sober judgment". Humility is required so that the gift of faith may not be exaggerated in the presumption of pious ambition and impose this on itself and others through its own exaggeration. It was being "puffed up" as Paul calls it, in that way, which caused the Corinthian Gnostics to despise the apostolic ministry, the kerygma and the sacraments, to esteem showy gifts too highly, to misunderstand hope, to put love in the background, to split into little groups of pious superiority and by all these things to threaten the unity of the one Body of Christ.

We see that the New Testament expresses the unity of the Church from a number of points of view. They are not all which we should have liked to see the New Testament give. For example, there is practically nothing said about the limits of unity. It is of course clearly recognizable that limits exist. With the Church are contrasted, though without pride, "those outside", and this term "outside" has a concrete meaning. "Those outside" are partly those who do not accept the Gospel, partly those who have separated themselves from it and its apostolic teaching (cf. Mk 4:11 par.; 1 Cor 5:12f.; Col 4:5; 1 Thess 4:12; Acts 22:15). It can also be gathered from the New Testament that decision about belonging to the unity of the Church lies in the hands of the apostles, their representatives and successors, and the community (cf. Mt 16:19; 18:15 ff.; 1 Cor 5:1 ff.; 2 Thess 3:14f.), and that such decisions are not taken lightly, but after several attempts to correct those in error and fault (cf. Mt 18:15 ff.; 2 Tim 2:23 ff.; Tit 2:9 ff.; 3:10f.). Finally it is evident that the limits of unity become apparent where those factors which bring about the unity of the Church and preserve it historically are distorted or not respected, in other words, where it is a question of the Gospel, the sacraments and the ministry (cf. for example 1 Tim 1:18ff.; 2 Tim 2:17; 4:14).

Even if these and other questions are not really answered, the foundations and fundamental characteristics of the unity of the Church are clear and we may finally summarize them as follows. Its unity is the outcome and reflection of the unifying unity of God. It is offered to men and bestowed on them in the one Body of Christ on the Cross. It develops in the power of the one Holy Spirit. It grows through the means of salvation and the gifts of which God makes use in Jesus Christ through the Holy Spirit: the one unifying word of God, which takes form in the one faith of the Church; the one unifying baptism and the one unifying Lord's Supper. These are served by the one ministry and also by the charismata which nourish and animate unity. Unity presents itself in the Church as the one people of God in which Israel also is fulfilled, as the one Body of Christ comprising the one mankind of Jews and Gentiles, as the one eschatological temple in which the one Spirit breathes. Such unity is inaugurated and confirmed and maintained in the faith, hope and charity of those who are incorporated into it by baptism, but in a special way by humility which accepts the measure of faith bestowed by God, and shows a loving forbearance towards other members of the Body of Christ.

In that way the unity of the Church according to the New Testament shows itself in the first place to be always a prior datum, not something that has to be brought about; secondly it is present and not merely future; thirdly it is concrete and historical and not merely ideal or interior; fourthly it is a unity which has to be grasped ever anew and preserved by the individual Christian. Consequently Christians can certainly leave the unity of the Church or even return to it once more, but they cannot take it with them. There can certainly be groups which split off from the unity of the Church, but there is only *one* people of God. The Body of Christ, which is one, is indivisible. The Holy Spirit dwells only in the *one* temple of God.

CHAPTER XII

The State
according to the New Testament[1]

All the New Testament authors were convinced that Christ was not merely a private individual and that the Church is not merely a voluntary association. And so each in his own context and form his own angle reported the encounter of Jesus Christ, and of those who bore witness to him, with the political world of the state and its authorities. None had so profound a grasp of that encounter as the evangelist John. Even in his general perspective he regarded the story of Jesus as a case brought, or intended to be brought, against Jesus by the world, represented by the Jews. This action reached its public, judicial decision before Pontius Pilate, the representative of the Roman state and holder of political power. Consequently if we study what is said in the 18th and 19th chapters of St John's Gospel,

---

[1] Of the more recent literature on this subject, see J. Schmid, "Der Antichrist und die hemmende Macht" in *TQ* 129 (1949), pp. 323 ff.; W. Schweitzer, *Die Herrschaft Christi und der Staat im Neuen Testament* (1949); H. v. Campenhausen, "Zur Auslegung von Römer 12: Die dämonische Deutung des ἐξουσία-Begriffes", *Festschrift für A. Bertholet* (1950), pp. 97 ff.; J. Blinzler, *The Trial of Jesus* (1959); S. G. F. Brandon, *The Fall of Jerusalem and the Christian Church* (1951); R. Bultmann, *Das Evangelium des Johannes* (1953), pp. 501 ff.; O. Cullmann, *The State in the New Testament* (1957); A. Strobel, "Zum Verständnis von Römer 13" in *ZNW* 47 (1956), pp. 67—93; J. Blank, "Die Verhandlung vor Pilatus Joh. 18 : 28 — 19 : 16 im Lichte johanneischer Theologie" in *BZ* 3 (1959), pp. 60 ff.; E. Käsemann, "Römer 13 : 1—7 in unserer Generation" in *ZTK* 56 (1959), pp. 316—376.

we shall attain fundamental insight into the nature of the state as this appeared to the New Testament.

I

The argument between Jesus and the Jews or the world which will not give itself to God, is in general at an end. There has been fulfilled what was said in the prologue: "He came into his own and his own received him not." And it has also been confirmed that: "To all who received him, he gave power to become children of God" (Jn 1:11 f.). Now Jesus is apprehended with the help of a detachment of Roman soldiers and some police officials of the Jewish Sanhedrin. They lead him to Annas who was not the actual high priest, as the evangelist expressly states. The proceedings, or rather interview with this influential man who no longer held an official position, however, simply brought to a conclusion what had occurred until then. Annas asked Jesus quite generally "about his disciples and his teaching". And Jesus pointed out to him that he must know about it, for "I have spoken openly to the world; I have always taught in synagogues and in the temple where all Jews come together . . ." (Jn 18:20). In the spiritual and religious sphere, everything has been said and done. Consequently the political authority must now speak. Proceedings before the high priest Caiaphas are passed over in this gospel. The political authority is the Roman procurator Pontius Pilate. As the highest official of the emperor in the procuratorial province of Judaea, an annexe of the imperial province of Syria, he held the highest jurisdiction and power of life and death even over the natives of the province. The Jews recognized that. The initial situation, therefore, is characterized in this way: the representative of political power faces the world and its representatives. To be sure the political power is a secular one, and even a pagan, Roman power, not a sacred one—the sacred power is accused in the person of Jesus—, nevertheless it confronts the world at this trial, in which all are unmasked by the accused.

The informatory process of the trial begins. Immediately the ambiguous position of Jesus' accusers comes to light. The procurator's pertinent inquiry, "What accusation do you bring against this man?" (18:29), is dismissed by the Jews: "If this man were not an evildoer, we would not have handed him over" (18:30). And after another pertinent retort by the procurator, they make it plain that they have already given their verdict and only wish to make use of the judge to carry out the sentence of death which they have already passed. "The Jews said to him, 'It is not lawful for us to put any man to death'." How will Pilate react? He does not break off the hearing. He intends to get to the bottom of the case. So he goes into the praetorium to the accused and assails him suddenly with the question, "Are you the King of the Jews?" This question indicates the first of the limits of his understanding. For that, of course, is a question about the political claims of the accused. It is true that by it Pilate also showed that he was remaining within the framework of his office, which was political in scope. But his office reached the limits of its power to comprehend, precisely in this matter. Jesus wants to make Pilate realize what he had meant by his question. So he inquires, not like an accused man at all, but more like the judge, how Pilate had arrived at his question. "Do you say this of your own accord, or did others say it to you about me?" (18:34). And he receives the admission that in this matter the role of judge has been imposed on the procurator by the world. "Am I a Jew? Your own nation and the chief priests have handed you over to me" (18:35). He shows that things of that kind are forced on the state. He is on the defensive from the start.

Then Pilate goes on with the hearing of the case. He now asks Jesus more generally, "What have you done?" In that way, as the evangelist sees it, he is framing the question as it would often be put to Christians later on. They will then reply with a profession of faith, just as their Lord "in his testimony before Pontius Pilate made the good confession", as 1 Timothy 6:13 says. The present gospel regards that confession of the Lord as being made at this point. With a certain solemnity, but at the same time as something that is taken as a matter of course, Jesus bears his decisive witness before the political tribunal: "My kingship is not of this world; if my kingship were of this world, my servants would fight that I might not be handed over to the Jews; but my kingship is not from the world" (18:36). Pilate learns, therefore, that it is possible to speak of a *basileia*, a kingly rule, of Jesus. But this kingship does not have its origin in the world; it does not draw its origin from the world. It does not use methods of worldly force to affirm itself against the will of the world. Pilate learns that there is another rule in the world besides the legitimate political rule of the Roman emperor. State rule is not alone in the world. And Pilate learns that beside his legitimate state authority, another rule, namely that of Jesus, the accused, has appeared, which claims to be essentially superior to the rule of the state. For "not of this world" means, of course, in Johannine terms, "from above", and "from above" means "from God". With Jesus there appears beside the rule of the state, the rule of God, which as regards the means of establishing itself, does not even enter into competition with earthly rule. So far is it from standing on the same plane.

But that is only a negative indication of the kingship which the state finds itself faced with. When Pilate, impeded by his political categories asks: "So you are a king?", Jesus answers yes. For he is "a king", since he possesses a royal rule. But he explains his answer, as regards its positive aspect this time: "For this I was born, and for this I have come into the world, to bear witness to the truth. Every one who is of the truth hears my voice" (18:37). It can be seen that Jesus not only discloses word by word the nature of his rule, but in doing so presses his judge hard at each step. Perhaps Pilate's political perspective can after all be widened. Yes, I am a king, Jesus says to the representative of the state. And my royal claim does not come from the world but from above. It is of course expressed through the mouth of a man—"for this I was born"—but this man is different from all others because he can also say of himself: "I have come into the world", and is therefore sent and authorized by God as the legitimate bearer and revealer of truth: "to bear witness to the truth". Truth, however, is the enlightening and liberating reality of God. That is what he has the responsibility of vindicating in this world. And that is happening now in this suit which the world has instituted against truth before the tribunal of the state and its lawful magistrate. And he, God's witness, is maintaining the rights of truth even in the face of the state and its representative. For Jesus is of course also and at this point chiefly, addressing his claim, which is that of truth, to Pilate, when he says: "Every one who is of the truth hears my voice." In those words there is contained, even for the representative of the state, the summons to be of the truth and to decide for the truth. There is contained the warning affirmation that even political authority must recognize truth and its sovereign question. Certainly, from the political viewpoint, truth is a powerless thing, something which is held prisoner by men and, ultimately, by the state. Yet everything nevertheless depends on what attitude the representative of political power adopts to the question truth puts. Does the state allow itself to be questioned by the truth in Jesus or not? Its representative should certainly not allow his political office to be taken from him by the forces of a world that is hostile to truth and which assail the state itself. He possesses his office legitimately. But there is one thing he should do: set truth free and maintain its freedom against all the attacks of its enemies. By that he would demonstrate that in his function and as the representative of the state, he has heard and acknowledged the royal claim from above. Thereby it would be shown that he does not regard his political office, and the state which he legitimately represents, as something self-contained and autonomous and as the final judge of all things even of truth, but as a power and authority questioned, like everything else, by God.

What will Pilate do in regard to Jesus' question and testimony? It is remarkable that he evades it. He declares that in his judicial office and in the situation which is before the court truth does not concern him at all. That is what is meant by Pilate's famous question: "What is truth?" (18:38), which is not at all an expression of philosophical scepticism. Procurators are seldom philosophers. Nor does it reveal, as Spengler thought, a political realism which takes account of the world of facts, but not of the world of "truths", as Spengler misleadingly puts it. Pilate's question is, rather, as Bultmann with greater justification explains, "an expression of the neutrality of the state which as such is not concerned by the question of the reality which forms the basic reality of his life" (*Das Evangelium des Johannes* [1953], p. 507 note 8). We must only correct this, in accordance with the sense of the evangelist, into: It is the expression of an ostensible neutrality which he thinks he can maintain in the face of the truth standing in front of him. Pilate is clearly convinced, like so many after him, that for the holder of political power there exists in principle a third possibility—in addition to those of rejecting truth or acknowledging it—namely, that of exercising political office and of making the decisions it calls for, appropriately, that is, in accordance with political requirements, apart from and without regard to the sovereign claim of truth. He overlooks what the Jews in their way did not, for of course they were attempting to kill truth, namely that "neutrality" in regard to truth is always simply a step towards its rejection. He does not know that rejection of the possibility of being called in question oneself leads to regarding oneself as unquestionable, and that for the state, its function and action to be unquestionable, destroys the state. That becomes strikingly apparent in the second part of the Johannine account of Jesus' trial.

At first sight, of course, it looks as though nothing was changed by Jesus' having disclosed his own special claim to rule and by Pilate's having set it aside as without interest. Pilate appears really to prescind from the claim of truth and to be able to carry the hearing to a conclusion in an objective manner. What he had already surmised becomes a certainty after his conversation with Jesus, and he therefore openly attests the political innocence of the accused: "I find no crime in him" (18:38 b). But why does he not set him free at that point? For now comes the strange and unexpected fact that his acknowledgement of Jesus' innocence is followed by a reminder of the customary right of the Jews to have a prisoner released as a favour at the Passover, and he asks the Jews: "Will you have me release for you the King of the Jews?" (18:39). Why does he make Jesus' release an act of grace, when it would after all have simply been in accordance with the law he himself recognizes? And why does he again speak of the "King of the Jews"? Is he being ironical about the Jews and Jesus? Has his irony some hidden meaning? It is meant to veil the fact that the procurator who is "neutral" in regard to truth can no longer administer his office neutrally, even in the sense of being impartial and independent? Does the whole strange procedure reveal the fact that political authority, when it no longer openly decides for truth, can no longer freely decide in accordance with law? The effect of his yielding to the pressure of the world, unjustifiable even from the political point of view, is absurd, though only to be expected: "They cried out again, 'Not this man, but Barabbas!' " Barabbas was "a robber", the gospel laconically remarks (18:40) and means by that a Messianic revolutionary. Is his politically correct judgment forsaking Pilate? Of course the Jews do not choose the man they mortally hate. And so they, who are accusing Jesus of a political crime, do not even shy at asking for the release of a political criminal. And Pilate, the protector of the Roman state against political intrigues, satisfies their demand which from the political point of view is an impossible one.

It quickly becomes clear that the rejection of the question of truth not only weakens official authority, and not only falsifies political action, but leads to injury to the state. It is clear that "neutral" political power, apparently independent of truth, has not the force to resist the subversive will of the masses and their leaders.

It is true that Pilate does not give way immediately. He tries in another way to save Jesus and the authority of the state — these are suddenly both on the same side. But what Pilate undertakes now shows even greater confusion of his political judgment. Pilate has Jesus scourged, though he has just proclaimed his innocence. He clearly wants to rouse the compassion of the crowd for the "King of the Jews" beaten and mocked by the anti-Semitic Roman soldiery, always inclined to brutality. With the words "Here is the man!" he presents Jesus to the Jewish crowd after the scourging. But he has been mistaken in his political tactics. He overestimates the effect of a humane appeal to the mob. It is not moved by the sight of Jesus at all. It already senses, of course, that power and authority are slipping from the procurator. And so its only answer is: "Crucify him, crucify him!" (19:6). What Pilate answers sounds helpless: "Take him yourselves and crucify him, for I find no crime in him" (19:6). But of course Pilate also knows that because of their political status the Jews may not put anyone to death.

The Jews know this too and so, in order to advance their ends, they employ a new device. They make the submission to Pilate: "We have a law, and by that law he ought to die, because he has made himself the Son of God" (19:7). According to the principle of Roman provincial administration, the Roman officials were supposed to be accommodating to the native population in religious matters. The Jews had found a masterly formula, as can be seen from the effect of their demand on Pilate. "When Pilate heard these words, he was *the more* afraid" (19:8). He had therefore been afraid before. The political

authority which regards itself as unquestionable, is afraid!
Afraid of the mob and of something uncertain but imminent.
Now "he was even more afraid", clearly because the Jews had
stirred his pagan dread of uncanny suprahuman beings, such
as the sons of gods, for instance. This terror of the possible
immensity that may be concealed behind Jesus and to which
the politician who was ostensibly not to be affected by the
question of truth involuntarily succumbs, drives Pilate back
to Jesus with a question which reveals quite plainly his helplessness and fear: "Where are you from?" (19:9). Jesus gives
him no answer. He had of course already given an answer and
he will not for the sake of his salvation free the procurator from
the only genuine anxiety which he perhaps still has. And when
Pilate suddenly recalls his power to set free or crucify the accused,
who has already been scourged, Jesus no longer refuses to speak
to him but states the true situation: "You would have no power
over me unless it had been given you from above" (19:11). It
is not Pilate's power but God's will and dispensation which place
him in Pilate's hands. Of course that does not abolish the procurator's responsibility, nor that of the Jews, and does not lessen
his, and certainly not their, guilt.

Pilate can make nothing of the accused in this case. Unusual,
impenetrable things are afoot. He therefore makes yet another,
last attempt to escape from the horns of the dilemma which his
flight from truth has presented to himself, to his office and to the
Roman state. "Upon this Pilate sought to release him" (19:12a).
But he no longer succeeds in doing so. He has already renounced
his political freedom of action by renouncing an open attitude to
truth which would have preserved it for him. And now the
Jews have recourse to a means which is always effective when
the authority in a state knows it is no longer firmly based and
is consequently being abandoned piecemeal to the crowd. They
drop any show of subordination and threaten the procurator
with denunciation to the emperor. "If you release this man,
you are not Caesar's friend." And covertly but effectively

accusing him of connivance with a political criminal, they also add, "Every one who makes himself a king sets himself against Caesar" (19:12). This decides the matter for Pilate. For where political power is not based on truth, it is no longer a question of holding office but of holding on to a position.

The trial is over. The verdict follows. But does it really follow? Pilate ascends the judgment seat and addressing the crowd says, "Here is your King!" (19:14). The answer of the crowd is, "Away with him, away with him". And when he asks, "Shall I crucify your King?" the spiritual leaders of the nation utter the momentous words, "We have no king but Caesar" (19:15). By that the Jews through their spiritual leaders abandon their Messianic hope. They link it to Caesar, the emperor. The world sets its hope on Caesar's empire, ultimately out of hate for Jesus. "Then he handed him over to them to be crucified", the last sentence runs (19:16). The roles are reversed. It is not the Jews who are delivering up Jesus to the state; the state is delivering up Jesus to the world. There is no longer a state. By declaring itself uninterested in truth, it has delivered itself to the world, which links all human prospects with Caesar. By rejecting truth, the state has delivered up its authority and right to the forces for which Caesar is the sole salvation and hope.

We can see that John the evangelist was in fact thinking of the problem of the state while he was describing the trial of Jesus. He clearly recognized that the political power represented by Pilate has its "own sphere and the possibility of freedom in relation to the world" (cf. Bultmann, *Das Evangelium des Johannes* [1953], p. 513, note 2 a), although it is of the world. It has legitimate *auctoritas* and *potestas*. But there appears with Jesus, in addition to the state, another dominion which does not take its origin and therefore its nature from this world, but is from "above". It is the dominion of truth, which claims a hearing from the state itself. Neutrality on principle towards the testimony of truth destroys the state and the action proper to it. It gives rise to the fear which makes its official duty uncertain and political action no longer objective. It necessarily delivers the state to forces which abuse it to destroy truth and hand over all Messianic hopes to Caesar. It lays the foundation of a "sacred" state which in its political, intellectual and metaphysical totality is an embodiment of untruth.

II

These views on the nature of the state which, like everything else, becomes plain in the presence of Jesus Christ, can be confirmed and elucidated from the rest of the New Testament, and we shall pursue this, retaining the points of view which we have just indicated.

1. The evangelist Luke also indicates in his two works that political authority is opposed in principle to the world and its forces. It is true that he does not think out the political phenomenon as thoroughly as John, but he devotes more attention in detail to it. We have in mind, for example, his well-known synchronization of the saving-event in Jesus Christ with the dates of political events in the Roman Empire and in the Jewish client states (Lk 1:5; 2:1 f.; 3:1 f.). Ultimately, he too holds that there are two counterparts in the world, Christ and his apostles on the one side and the Roman emperor and his officials on the other. Luke too considers that decisions in the world are the legitimate concern of the political authorities. Consequently in Luke Jesus does answer the Roman procurator (the emphasis is different in Mark and Matthew), and his statement makes it possible to "establish the objective juridical findings, and that is at once done *ex officio*" (M. Conzelmann, *Die Mitte der Zeit* [1954], p. 72). For Paul in Acts also the procurator is the correct and proper place for Christ to defend himself (cf. Acts 24:10; cf. 26:2). Finally it is by God's providence that Paul comes to Rome, because the emperor lives there. As a Roman citizen Paul can have resort to him as the ultimate court of appeal from

a Roman procurator who is seeking to hand over the accused to the Jews (Acts 25:9 ff.; 26:32).

Luke goes further, however. Caesar or the imperial authority, and Jesus Christ and his Church, are fundamentally not enemies but in principle can live with one another because they are interrelated for their mutual benefit. That is the particular contribution of this evangelist to our present question. There is a fundamental possibility, even for the pagan Roman state, through its representatives, to be open to the claim of Jesus as *Kyrios* and *Soter*. This need not be regarded merely as the well-known "apologetic" tendency of Luke. Or rather, we must inquire into the actual meaning of such apologetic. It consists in the conviction that the co-existence of the Roman state and the Church was a practical possibility based on a fundamental and enduring relation between political authority and Gospel. Luke has no illusions about the state and its representatives. John the Baptist does not, according to him, reject the profession of arms i.e. the professional use of force, but knows of its abuse and rejects this (Lk 3 : 14). The way in which Jesus, in a passage peculiar to Luke, judges Herod Antipas (Lk 13:31 ff.), or speaks of Pilate's action (13:1 ff.), and, according to Luke, appraises in his parables or elsewhere rulers great and small (Lk 22 : 25; 19 : 11 ff., 14, 31 peculiar to Luke) shows that the evangelist Luke who records this tradition regarding Jesus, does not intend to hide from his readers what happens in politics. Moreover the way Luke in Acts portrays the proconsuls Sergius Paulus and Gallio (13:7; 18 : 17) and the procurators Felix and Festus, and of course Pilate (Acts 24:25, 26, 27; 25:9; 26:24; Lk 23:12, 24 f.), not to mention Herod, indicates quite clearly that he is not idealizing actual political conditions. Finally it is Luke who regards the era of the Church as fundamentally a time of suffering, the temptations and sorrows of which will only cease at the end of time (Lk 8 : 13; 21:28). And the political authorities contribute largely to these sufferings. It is Luke, too, who transmits to us in Acts the Church's prayer in which we read : "The kings of the earth set themselves in array and the rulers were gathered together, against the Lord and against his Anointed—for truly in this city there were gathered together against thy holy servant Jesus, whom thou didst anoint, both Herod and Pontius Pilate, with the Gentiles and the peoples of Israel, to do whatever thy hand and thy plan had predestined to take place" (4:26—28). But the evangelist Luke also emphasizes the following. (1) These Roman officials were under pressure of all kinds from the mob to take the steps they did. It is remarkable how in Acts the pagan masses are continually stirred up against the apostles by the Jews (13:50; 14:5f., 19; 17:13; 18:6), while the latter then denounce the apostles to the Roman authorities (Acts 17:5 ff.; 18:12 ff.). And in the trial of Jesus itself, Pilate could no longer resist the shouts of the angry Jewish mob and so delivered up Jesus to them. According to Luke he did not condemn him nor have him put to death (Lk 23:23—26a; Acts 13:27—29). (2) The Roman authorities for the most part were not only personally reserved towards Jesus and his apostles, but administered the law correctly, and on occasion did so in the interest of the accused. The procurator Festus appears as a political hypocrite, it is true, but what he says to King Agrippa may well, to Luke's mind, have been put into practice as a general maxim: "It is not the custom of the Romans to give up any one before the accused meets the accusers face to face, and has opportunity to make his defence" (Acts 25:16). (3) The Roman magistracy was also in a position, according to Luke, to recognize Jesus' innocence and to see through the calumnies alleged against him. The words of Pilate to the chief priests and leaders of the Jewish people are very definite: "You brought me this man as one who was perverting the people; and after examining him before you, behold, I did not find this man guilty of any of your charges against him; neither did Herod, for he sent him back to us. Behold, nothing deserving death has been done by him" (Lk 23:14 f.). The procurators make quite similar declarations in Acts about Paul's case (cf. 18:14 ff.; 23:29; 25:18, 25;

26:30 ff.; 28:18). In these and similar observations two things emerge which are fundamental for Luke's judgment of the state. The pagan Roman state was in principle capable of recognizing at least the political harmlessness of Christianity. Moreover, the political freedom from guilt of Jesus and his apostles indicates that the cause they represent is entirely in harmony with the interests of the state. But of course, the fact that powers are at work in the world striving to prevent the co-existence of the two, is just as little to be overlooked as the human weakness and malice of the high officials of the state. "This is your hour, and the power of darkness", Jesus says to the Jewish authorities when he is arrested (Lk 22:53 b).

The apostle Paul shares the Lucan view of political authority as an element of order in face of the destructive powers of the world and his view of the possibility of collaboration between the political authorities and the preachers of the Gospel. He sees this very clearly, though he personally must have had many experiences which contradicted it. As a theologian he also finally gives us the reason for this peculiar special position of a secular phenomenon. Within his paraenesis in the Letter to the Romans we find in the 13th chapter verses 1—7, the well-known words about political authority which have received many interpretations and have been often misinterpreted and misused. In one point these can take us beyond what we have noted so far from the New Testament. In itself what the apostle writes is clear provided we do not try to turn it into a handbook of political theory. "Let every person be subject to the governing authority" it begins. The *exousiai hyperechousai* were, according to the current use of the term, the political authorities, "kings and all who are in high positions" as it is expressed in 1 Timothy 2:2, "the emperor, governors" as 1 Peter 2:13 puts it. They are not on the same level as the citizen of the state, the *civis romanus,* but "superior", and so make plain the contrast between them and the world, of which we have spoken. What is the basis of this superiority? We are told here: God's ordi-

nance. "For there is no authority except from God, and those
that exist have been instituted by God" (Rom 13:1). Their
ministry is not founded, as Greek sophist theories held, in a
human convention, however much the practical shape their
form takes is subject to the changes of history. Nor is it based
on the actual personal gifts of the bearer of such sovereign power,
however great the importance of such charismatic endowment
may be for the performance of political tasks. Political authorities—not some ideal authorities or other, but as Paul says, "those
that exist"—ultimately have their mandate, authority and
dignity from God who has instituted them. So the apostle calls
them "God's servants" (13:4) and even "ministers of God"
(Rom 13:6). Consequently he deduces, "Therefore he who resists the authorities resists what God has appointed" (Rom 13:2).
He also indicates the purpose for which God established them:
the political authority "is God's servant for your good". That
means, then, that "If you do wrong, be afraid, for he does not
bear the sword in vain; he is the servant of God to execute his
wrath on the wrongdoer" (Rom 13:4). Before this, Paul had
said that "rulers are not a terror to good conduct but to bad.
Would you have fear of him who is in authority? Then do what
is good and you will receive his (official) approval" (Rom 13:3).
Of course the paraenetic sense of these sentences must not be
overlooked, for they are intended in the Rome of Nero to warn
Christians, who perhaps to some extent were still animated by
Jewish resentment against the Roman state, against feelings of
hostility to the state, and against an attitude which forgot the
eschatological character of the present epoch and of Christian life
generally. This admonition of the apostle, it is not to be denied,
stands in a context which begins with the call to the Christians in
Rome not to be conformed to the pattern of his world—and to
be hostile to political authority belongs to the pattern of this
world—and ends with the reminder that the day is at hand and
consequently the hope of it should already make us wake from
the sleep in which Caesar appears to us as a nightmare. But even

apart from this, in the mind of the apostle Paul what has been said about the basis and significance of political office is objectively valid even for the state under Nero, and even as regards him the apostle takes it for granted that in a certain way he is still fulfilling the function which God assigns to political powers. How and to what extent remains obscure, just as it is not of course made clear what his functions and powers in principle are. It is only indicated that they are to be sought in the sphere of the "sword" and of the "taxes" (cf. Rom 13:4, 6 ff.) and 1 Timothy 2:1 f. shows that the Pauline tradition envisaged them as extending to enabling the Christians and all men to "lead a quiet and peaceable life, godly and respectful in every way".

If, however, political power is bestowed by God and ultimately derives its authority and dignity from his mandate, and if it is given by God for "good", we shall scarcely be wrong in regarding it as being, in the apostle's view, on the plane of what he calls the "law" which, according to him, in some way even the pagans know and administer (cf. Rom 2:12 ff.). The connection of Romans 13 with the Jewish Pharisee tradition regarding the state, supports this conjecture. On that basis we can see why Paul calls upon the Christians to obey political rulers not only out of fear of punishment but also "for the sake of conscience" (Rom 13:5) and "for the Lord's sake" as 1 Peter 2:13 says. It is also clear why the holders of political power are expressly and in all cases placed under the protection of "honour" (Rom 13:7; 1 Pet 2:17) and committed to the Christians' prayers (1 Tim 2:2). All this moreover in the face of an authority which was certainly often incapable and unjust and even inhuman and which in addition was already beginning to persecute Christians for their name's sake. On the basis of the connection of political authority with the law of God, however, it can also, on the other hand, be understood why the action of the state for Paul (and for the whole New Testament) is never assimilated to a salvific action. The future of *God* is not in the earthly *polis* but is comprised in the heavenly *politeuma* (Phil 3:20 f.).

Because, however, the state belongs to the sphere of the law, obedience can be given it in truth only by those who wish, and are able, to obey God thereby. But they are those who have been transformed by the renewal of their mind (cf. Rom 12:1 f.).

2. This state whose function implies a partner, the world, because as we have now seen, it is ordained by God for "good", itself possesses a vis-à-vis and this confronts it with the superior claim of truth to sovereignty. This point of view is confirmed for us by the well-known incident of the "coin of the tribute" which is told by the first three evangelists (Mk 12:13—17 and par.). Jesus and his opponents are engaged in discussion. The opponents are Pharisees, who begrudged paying the poll-tax which the Roman administration collected in the provinces in Roman currency, and Herodians, adherents of the ruling house of the Herods who simply accepted it because they were collaborators of the occupying power. These opponents put the question to Jesus: "Is it lawful to pay taxes to Caesar or not? Should we pay them or should we not?" By this question they wanted to "entrap" Jesus, to elicit an answer from him which either way would compromise him. If he says Yes, he brands himself as a collaborator; if he says No, they can denounce him to the Romans as a zealot. Jesus, however, tears apart the threatening snare. Moreover, he unmasks their "hypocrisy". The question they put has already been decided by their actions. The coin bearing the image of the emperor is current in the country. By having a coin brought and making his opponents state the image and inscription, he forces them to contradict themselves, at all events to bring out the fact that Caesar is the ruler of the country. In that case, however, the requirement is simple, "Render to Caesar the things that are Caesar's", that is, the tax. But the emperor is not alone in the country, for Jesus of course continues his sentence, "and to God the things that are God's". The rule of this God is now at hand. In Jesus it is close at hand. They do not see that. The hypocrisy of these opponents is profound. Ostensibly out of regard for the honour

of God they ask whether taxes should be paid to the emperor. They completely overlook and ignore the fact that God is there in the man whom they are questioning and that he is making a quite different, much more important and urgent demand than the one they are concerned about, namely that they should give themselves wholly and entirely to him. Understood in this way as the summons of the rule of God now appearing within the horizon of the world in Jesus, this pericope in fact confirms what we have learnt from John, namely that the claim of the state is now limited by the quite different claim of a quite different rule, which is now being made in the midst of the world itself by God.

This sovereign claim of God through Jesus will be taken up and continued to be made by his disciples. On their lips too it will be a testimony which political authorities cannot evade. "And you will be dragged before governors and kings for my sake"—states a saying of our Lord which has been handed down in different forms (Mt 10:8; cf. Mk 13:9; Lk 21:12 f.)—"to bear testimony before them and the Gentiles". The apostle Paul too, as the Acts of the Apostles describes, bore his witness, which is that of the Lord and his rule, "to small and great" (Acts 26:22). When King Agrippa, whom the procurator invited as an expert to Paul's interrogation, declares ironically, "In a short time you think to make me a Christian!" the apostle admits: "Whether short or long I would to God that not only you but also all who hear me this day" (therefore in the first place the procurator) "might become such as I am except for these chains" (Acts 26:29). The Gospel does not halt in face of Agrippa. Therefore outside St John's Gospel also, it is acknowledged or implied that the state has a relative claim on men. But as the New Testament sees it, the state itself is summoned by the overriding claim of God's rule which appeared on earth in Jesus and continues to be encountered in his disciples and apostles. Precisely that summons, addressed to the state by God's rule present and at hand in a hidden way in Jesus and in those who are his, provokes the strange and terrible course of history which leads to the totalitarian state, the deformed caricature of the state, when men shut themselves off from God's rule.

3. We may remember the third point of view which emerged from the account of Christ's trial in St John's Gospel: the state which evades the question of truth in ostensible neutrality, delivers itself into the hands of the world which acknowledges Caesar and his rule as its ultimate salvation. The so-called Apocalypse of John, the title of which is really the "Revelation of Jesus Christ to his servant John", warns the Christians against such a degenerate state.

The possibility of such a state was confirmed for the New Testament writers by the experience of a state which made a god of itself in the emperor-worship which developed in the second half of the first century. But for the Seer of John's Apocalypse, this state which paid homage and worship to itself is not merely a particular historical phenomenon, but a potentiality of the state in general and, we must not hide the fact from ourselves, a vision of the future. Not only did Jesus Christ force the state, in the person of Pontius Pilate, to decide, and the decision was made in such a way as to hand over political authority to the powers of a self-sufficient world, but Jesus Christ on high will continue to urge the state to ever new decision, through his Church and particularly through its saints and martyrs, and the state, as the prophet sees it, will increasingly deprive itself of the receptive attitude towards God which is its life, and as a consequence, will corrupt itself and political authority. The Revelation to John is not alone in this conviction. The omnipotent divinized state had already weighed with crushing force on wide circles of later Judaism. In the early Christian community a mysterious apocalyptic saying was current as a saying of Jesus. It had been phrased under the influence of Daniel 9:27 and other texts: "But when you see the desolating sacrilege set up where it ought not to be . . ." (Mk 13:14 par.). The setting up of the altar to Zeus in the Temple of Jerusalem by Antiochus Epiphanes in 168 B.C. was an event which had assumed eschatological proportions for the Jews themselves. For Jews and Christians it became a symbol of the active hostility to God of the totalitarian state of the future.

Even the apostle Paul who wrote the 13th chapter of his Letter to the Romans knew this aspect. For him too, the Antichrist is a political phenomenon. It is not certain, but to my mind it is still a well-founded interpretation of 2 Thessalonians 2:1 ff., that the state, to the extent that it is still a state, stands opposed there to the state whose authority is degenerate. This is precisely what is represented in the time of apostasy by the "man of lawlessness", "the son of perdition, who opposes and exalts himself against everything that is called God or held sacred, so that he takes his seat in the temple of God, proclaiming himself to be God" (2 Thess 2:3 f.). His parousia, as it is called by analogy with the parousia of the emperor or of his representatives in the provinces, and in deliberate contrast to the parousia of Christ, will take place "by the activity of Satan with all power and with pretended signs and wonders and with all wicked deception" (cf. 2 Thess 2:9 f.).

What Jesus' saying and the apostle Paul point to, becomes the theme of the Apocalypse. The apotheosis of the state which no longer recognizes any derivation of political authority from God's mandate; which as a state closes itself to the testimony of the truth and persecutes it; which does in fact even in its perversion contain some elements of real political dominion and even in its caricature of the authentic state gives some idea of the majesty of genuine power; and whose limit will no longer be the witnesses and the Church on earth, but the end of all things and the last judgment—that state is represented in visions of the Apocalypse chiefly under two forms, that of the beast in chapter 13 and that of the great harlot in chapters 17 and 18. The imagery is fantastic and brings together all the forebodings of the prophets and apocalyptics. But they are fantastic only because the reality which will come upon the inhabitants of the earth will be fantastic. Only the main features of this reality can be indicated.

From the abyss (11:7; 17:8) but also from the sea of peoples
and multitudes, nations and tongues (13:1; 17:15), the "beast"
emerges above the horizon of history. It is an indescribable
monster, the sum of all the past animals or realms of the world
(13:2). The kings of the earth give over their power to it and
they themselves only have power as its satellites (17:12 f.).
It is always present because its mortal wounds heal (13:3, 12, 14;
17:8, 11). It has a name, but it is better to conceal it when
speaking of it (13:17 f.). It is the name of a man (13:18). Even
this monstrous state does not derive its power from itself. But
it does not have it from God. It receives "power, throne and
great authority" from the "dragon" (13:2). This is the ideogram
of Satan, who had already pursued the woman and the child
which was snatched from his mouth up to God's throne (12:4 f.).
He now, thrown down to earth, has little time left. In his
"wrath" he finds political expression for himself in the totalitarian state (12:12). His activity has one aim: "to make war
on the saints and conquer them". The totalitarian state is essentially both an anti-God and anti-Christian state (cf. 11:7;
12:17; 16:13 f.; 20:7 ff.). He cannot endure the name of Christ
(cf. 14:1; 15:2). Blasphemy is written on his brow (13:1). An
essential attribute is his "mouth". This is given him to utter
"haughty and blasphemous words..." (13:5 f.). The contemporary experience from which the Seer drew the material
for his visions is still clearly recognizable. The emperor Domitian
styled himself not only *potens terrarum dominus* but also
dominus ac deus, which gave offence even to pious pagans who
had still some remnant of common-sense. The inscription on a
coin from Temnos: *Theon Domitianon Autokratora*, or another
from Alexandria, which as well as the usual *Sebasto* also bears
Theou Hyios, clearly expresses the fantastic and impious opinion
the emperor had of himself. And since he was greeted as *terrarum gloria* and *salus mundi*, and was hymned by Statius and
Martial as *Aion*, it is quite clear what the actual experience was
to which the Seer owed his visions. But they are visions, and see

the monster only just appearing; henceforward it will never die but will fill the world until the end.

The first beast is joined by another which is smaller but without which its power is not complete. This is the "false prophet" (16:13; 19:20; 20:10). In him the state has its philosopher and theologian. But philosophy and theology in his service are simply propaganda. He shapes the mind of the state and the heresy of the state. Of this second animal it is said that by signs and wonders (13:13) it persuades men to make an image for the beast and worship it (13:12). It takes care of the necessary official opinion, the right state ideology. The image is a speaking image. The political symbolism, which now turns into a symbolism of worship, becomes so powerful that an offence against it leads to death. The spirit of the totalitarian state also causes all the inhabitants of the earth "to be marked on the right hand or the forehead, so that no one can buy or sell unless he has the mark, that is, the name of the beast or the number of its name" (13:16 f.). That is the anti-Christian *sphragis*, the sign of the state party, as it were the secularized seal of baptism which levels all differences between men and only distinguishes between friends and enemies of the ruling system. Those who refuse the new metaphysical slavery are deprived of their economic foundations. Even economic life is directed by the spirit of the beast.

In chapters 17 and 18 we find yet another symbol for the degenerate state. This is the Babylon of the prophets in the form of the splendidly adorned, great harlot in a world wilderness (17:3 f.). She is the world-state in the form of a degenerate city which rests on the world-empire (17:18; cf. 17:3, 9 ff., 12, 16). She is irresistible to the dwellers on the earth. She puts on the glitter of luxury and is very rich and wanton. She cultivates the festivities and arts of civilization. She deceives all nations with her sorcery (18:23; cf. 18:3, 9, 14, 22). She is full of hubris. She repeats "in her heart" the old saying of Babel: "A queen I sit, I am no widow, mourning I shall never see" (18:7).

It is a characteristic of this state that suffering is taboo, death explained away and the illusion of perpetual happiness is the official line. But Babylon falls. Its fall is accompanied by a great lament of those who dwell on the earth. The "merchants of the earth" (18:11) lament, "who gained wealth from her" (18:15), and so do the "shipmasters and seafaring men" (18:17, 19). Political splendour was also to the advantage of international traders. "Thy merchants were the great men of the earth" (18:23). Before all else, however, there resounds the lament of the "kings of the earth", those who owed their little power to Babylon. She made them drunk with the wine of her fornication (17:2, 4, 5; 18:3, 9; 19:2). The international relations between these small states and this cosmopolis are only established in intoxication and, in sober terms, are prostitution. This Babylon is drunk in another sense also. "And I saw the woman, drunk with the blood of the saints and the blood of the martyrs of Jesus" (17:6; cf. 18:24; 19:2). This blood intoxicates the political power, which can no longer even punish but can only murder or, as it is twice said, "slay" (18:24).

What will Christians do in this situation? Not very much is said on the subject. They will no longer want to have any part in this caricature of a state; they will "go out". They hear the voice from heaven: "Come out of her, my people, lest you take part in her sins, lest you share in her plagues" (18:4). They will simply be outlawed and persecuted. There will be no longer any talk of a Christian world, but only of scattered saints and witnesses who will then constitute the Church. It will be very difficult to be a Christian. Even then the Christians will not say a word against God's creation and providence but as before will give praise: "Great and wonderful are thy deeds, O Lord God the Almighty! Just and true are thy ways, O King of the nations" (15:3). They will raise no sword against the monster, this "mystery of lawlessness". "If any one is taken captive, to captivity he goes; if any one is to die by the sword, with the sword he must be slain. Here is a call for the endurance and faith of the saints" (13:10; cf. 14:12). That is their solution. They will not worship the beast. They will think of Jesus' judgment on the lukewarm and cowardly (3:15 f.; 21:8) and seek to "conquer" by testimony and death (2:7, 26 f., etc.), in order to obtain what is promised to those who "conquer". They will know that they conquer and die "in the Lord" (14:13). The ultimate is not, of course, so they believe, the beast which crawls out from the pit, but the rider on the white horse who rides out from heaven. "And the name by which he is called is The Word of God" (19:13). Nor is the ultimate the hard-pressed and grievously wounded Church on earth, but "the holy city" which comes down out of heaven from God (21:10). Something of this can be descried even within the walls of affliction, when we hear the word of the Spirit and the song of the martyrs, which fill the Apocalypse and those days.

It can be seen that the third point of view which we derived from St John's Gospel is confirmed and elucidated by the rest of the New Testament. The domination of the state by the forces of the world which place all their hopes in Caesar, is at all times a danger for the political domain. One day it will finally determine a political reality which will close itself to God and Christ. The state which in itself has a limited mission from God, and which must and can hear the claim of God's rule, will, if it does not accept the latter's validity, change into the totalitarian, anti-Christian and anti-God contrary of the state. At the point in history where the state rejects God's claim, Christ will drive out Antichrist. Antichrist, however, is an intellectual and political phenomenon. With him the state even as state will be destroyed. Even in that it is shown once again, this time negatively, that the state which is the counterpart of the world, thanks to God's commission, and even has a counterpart in Jesus Christ and his lawful witnesses, needs Jesus Christ and his Church in order to persist in its own nature. It is true of course that the inhumanity of the degenerate state will also be an indication of the proximity of the Son of man.

CHAPTER XIII

The Baptism of Jesus
as Presented by the Gospels

All four gospels contain the report of Jesus' baptism. The actual act of baptism is of course simply mentioned or presupposed. The interest of the evangelists is directed to what happened in connection with the baptism. Obviously that is what expresses what they think is important in this mystery of salvation. Consequently that is what we shall focus our attention on, when on the octave day of the Epiphany the Gospel of Jesus' baptism is announced to us in the celebration of the liturgy.

Each of the evangelists reports the events connected with Jesus' baptism in his own way, each bringing out a different aspect of the matter. The Church has not felt that to be a disadvantage but an enrichment. In that way the saving event finds expression from a variety of points of view and the Gospel itself unfolds for us the multiple sense implicit in it. Certainly the Gospel is one, and only one. But it is the *one* Gospel "according to Matthew", "according to Mark", "according to Luke" and "according to John". The fact that there is more than one of these gospels reminds us of the inexhaustible plenitude of Jesus Christ's saving action.

Mark in the first place reports simply and objectively that "in those days"—that is, when the Baptist appeared and called to penance—Jesus of Nazareth in Galilee "came and was baptized by John in the Jordan". The matter could hardly be

related in fewer words. But that of course is only the introduction to what Mark finds worthy of reflection: that at this
baptism there occurred the first epiphany of the Messiah—Son
of God who is the Servant of God. The first epiphany of the
Messianic king, not the first vision of the prophet Jesus! For
Mark lays no weight on the fact that Jesus "saw", and he makes
no mention of his hearing the voice. What interests him above
all, and what he wants to proclaim to Christians is, that "the
heavens opened, and the Spirit descended upon him like a dove
and a voice came from heaven, 'Thou art my beloved Son; with
thee I am well pleased'".

Since Ezekiel (1:1) the heavens' opening signified the occurrence of a divine revelation. Heaven is no longer closed to earth.
God opens his own world, precisely at this point when the Son
comes up from the baptismal water to go forward to his work
on earth. God's open world becomes visible, to him in the first
place, but through him to us also. Perhaps Mark is also allud-
ing to something else as well. He actually says "and immediately
he saw the heavens torn", just as the "curtain of the temple was
torn in two" (15:38) and the way to the Holy of Holies was
clear when Jesus died on the Cross. Perhaps the tearing open of
heaven here and the torn curtain there were linked in Mark's
mind, so that here he is pointing to the beginning of what was
completed on the Cross: access to God has been opened through
Jesus.

This thought suggests itself because of course, from the opened
heaven, the Spirit appears and descends on Jesus. It is the Spirit
which, according to Luke (3:22) is the Holy Spirit, *the* Spirit
therefore which gives access to the opened heaven of God. He
descends "like a dove". That recalls that he is the Spirit of the
Creator and of the Redeemer in one. For according to the
Jewish exposition of Genesis 1:2, the Spirit of God broods over
the surface of the water like a dove over her young and "the
voice of the turtle dove" (Song 2:12) is sometimes described as
"the voice of the Holy Spirit of redemption". The Spirit, under-

stood in this sense, descends on Jesus and joins him from whom he will one day come once more, that is, when Jesus is raised on high through the Cross (cf. Jn 7:39; Acts 2:33).

The heavens above Jesus are torn, the Holy Spirit appears upon him, but the signs are not yet at an end. God also sends forth his voice to Jesus. In that way he inaugurates, as it were, the Gospel, which of course has no other meaning than to make it clear who this Jesus is who is coming from his baptism. The psalmist and the prophet (Ps 2:7; Is 42:1; 44:2) had foreseen and proclaimed what the Father here states, that he is the Messiah-Son of God of the Last Days, the Servant of God, whom God has chosen for his work.

That is Jesus' baptism as the evangelist Mark understands and proclaims it on the basis of the divine signs: the appearance of what still lies hidden in the future but which is beginning to be disclosed in this very moment as Jesus comes from the water of baptism. God's heavens open, the Holy of Holies; the Holy Spirit reveals himself as the Spirit of Jesus and comes with him; the eternal Gospel of the voice of God surrounds him and is inaugurated with him, God's Gospel which shows him to be the beloved Son, the Messianic king and the Servant of God. Jesus' baptism is, according to Mark, his appearance among the signs of the saving gifts which he will bring. Even now when all is still hidden, these appear above him and for him and so permit the still hidden Servant of God, who is hastening towards the obscurity of death, to be recognized as the Messianic king. The significant event of Jesus' baptism is, according to Mark, the epiphany of the hidden Son of God at the moment when he sets off on the road to revelation through death, that is, the road of his life-history.

The evangelist Matthew (3:13—17) discerned the significant baptism event in the same circumstances. But he did not see in them solely the epiphany of the hidden Messiah. In Mark no word of Jesus is reported, only his silent gaze, and the fact of baptism is simply mentioned, and appears almost incidental. Matthew, however, not only tells of Jesus' intention to be baptized by John—"Then Jesus came . . . to be baptized by him"—but also refers to a conversation with the Baptist. And precisely this conversation, together with the reference to Jesus' intention of receiving baptism, reveals a little of the hidden Messiah Jesus. At the same time it directs our attention to an aspect of the baptismal event which had not yet found expression in Mark.

John does not want to baptize Jesus. He recognizes in him—how and in what sense, the evangelist does not tell us—the man who will "baptize with the Holy Spirit and with fire" (3:11), who will judge the world and bring it to its consummation. His reply to Jesus' request is that he, John, must be baptized by Jesus. But the latter who is in fact, though this is still hidden from the eyes of the world, the ground and occasion of all ultimate decision, insists on his request, his mysterious command to John to confer on him also the baptism for sin, the baptism of conversion to God. And he gives the reason for this request in the mysterious statement, "for thus it is fitting for us to fulfil all righteousness". By having himself baptized, he fulfils in obedience to God "all righteousness", that is, the righteousness demanded by God's Torah as it was originally, when unfalsified and rightly understood (5:17), and which, therefore, is "more" than the righteousness of the scribes and Pharisees (5:20). But how does he fulfil this righteousness by baptism? To the extent that by the latter he, the obedient, places himself with sinners, he who comes from God and abides with God, with those who must turn to God. Now at the beginning of his way, on which time and time again he will stand "with" sinners, in order to grant them the righteousness of his presence, he joins them in the baptism which he asks of the Baptist. From then on, he who always comes to them as one who already stands with them, becomes more and more profoundly involved in such standing with them until it is manifest on the Cross as his dying for them. And so this baptism in water by John becomes the anticipatory sign of that baptism which is his death on the

Cross. Mark (10:30) and Luke (12:50) also speak of this as a baptism.

In that way the first evangelist's presentation brings into focus one side of the baptism event which Mark leaves in the background. This Messianic king and Servant of God, as the voice of God proclaims him to be, is the righteous Servant of God who stands in solidarity with sinners and by his baptism already enters into his sufferings for them. We cannot say that Mark knew nothing about this. If he knew of the Servant of God—and the "with thee I am well pleased" reminded him of that figure, of course—then he knew about his sufferings. But we can say that Matthew emphasized this feature of the epiphany just as, of course, in the original community they certainly pondered more and more the meaning of Jesus' baptism by John. In Jesus' baptism even more was manifested than the mysterious Son of God accompanied at the beginning of his course by the signs of his saving gifts. Matthew proclaims that there the Son of God appeared who from the beginning willed to go among sinners, though just, and in this baptism willed to begin and foreshadow his future baptism on the Cross. On that basis, the epiphany of the opened heaven, from which the Holy Spirit descends on Jesus and the heavenly voice acknowledges the Son of God, should be understood as a divine answer and confirmation. The two must be taken together, because both belong together: the obedient Servant of God who, for sinners, in the first baptism itself is already hastening towards the second, the Cross—and what came by him, heaven opened by the power of the Holy Spirit and by means of the Gospel. Both of these, Matthew affirms, taking a unified view of the whole, as he generally likes to do, are already apparent for those who have eyes to see, in Jesus' baptism.

The evangelist Luke (3:21—22) primarily follows the Marcan tradition and makes little change in it. Nevertheless small differences from Mark show from what angle he envisaged the tradition and how he understood the baptism event and wanted it understood. It is true that he too speaks of Jesus' coming to baptism "when all the people were baptized". He is therefore aware of Jesus' solidarity with sinners who are converted. But he does not elaborate on this. His thoughts dwell exclusively on the significant events which Mark had related and in the light of which the mysterious Messiah-Servant of God is manifest. Certainly in Luke they do not occur in such an unprepared way, nor in a way so apparently unconnected with Jesus. For in Luke we read: "when Jesus ... had been baptized and *was praying*, the heaven opened ..." It is Jesus' prayer, which Luke on other occasions also emphasizes more than the other evangelists (e.g. 5:16; 6:12; 9:18, 28, 29; 11:1), which causes the heavens to open, the Holy Spirit to descend upon him and the divine voice to address him. And so he brings this epiphany into connection with another, that on the mountain of the transfiguration, which also took place when Jesus was praying (9:28 ff.). And that is an anticipation of the glorification of the risen Christ. Clearly Luke sees in Jesus' baptismal epiphany, in addition to the Servant of God's solidarity with sinners (which he does not, however, develop as Matthew does), a reference to Jesus' glorification. From the very beginning of his journey to Jerusalem, which of course is his "taking up" (9:51), Jesus sets out on it as one already secretly marked out in baptism for glorification. In that way Luke comes a little closer to the view of the fourth evangelist, to whom we now turn.

What John reports of Jesus' baptism might be compared with the last notes of a bell, which bring out its full tone more clearly because they stand out against the background of what has preceded them. Jesus' baptism is no longer narrated for its own sake, but in the framework of the testimony of John the Baptist and for the sake of that testimony.

In 1:29 a second phase of the Baptist's testimony begins. It is primarily a question of making plain who it is that the Baptist has previously spoken about so mysteriously. It is like a mediaeval painting. In the foreground there still stands the

Baptist. Around him but, so to speak, lower than he, are the
people, scarcely noticeable, however, because, of course, the
forum which he is addressing is the whole world. The Baptist
is gazing into the middle distance. There Jesus appears and
comes towards John the Baptist. Where he comes from, no one
knows. It is enough that he *is* coming, coming nearer. It is not
stated where he comes from. Obviously it is in order to motivate
the testimony of the Baptist, which is the essential. And this
testimony starts: "Ecce agnus Dei . . ." There is already a liturgical ring about it. He who is coming towards the Baptist is
immediately attested as "the Lamb", the sacrificial lamb on
which the sins of the world are laid so that it may bear them
away. The Servant of God of Isaiah 53 appears in the light of
the Cross. And "this man", who bears the burden of the sins
of the world, is the eternal Word. With him, who appeared
chronologically on the stage of history after the Baptist, there
has come he who is at all times, and with whom the beginning
and origin of all things appears (cf. 1:15). He is the eternal
Logos, made flesh. But John the Baptist must confess, and he
confesses for us all, "I myself did not know him". For in order
to recognize the eternal Word, the origin and the beginning, in
Jesus who is the Lamb of God who takes away the sins of the
world, a revelation is needed which opens the eyes of our hearts
to the flesh which brings the glory closer and at the same time
hides it.

But this revelation took place. The Baptist, as he himself
confesses, baptized for no other purpose than to bring it about.
For at the baptism there occurred that epiphany of Jesus narrated in the tradition which John himself had read. And it
happened so that it might figure in John's testimony and so that
Jesus might appear to Israel through this testimony. One essential point of view, therefore, from which John the evangelist
regards Jesus' baptismal epiphany is that the latter inspired
the testimony of the Baptist, that is, the very first testimony
to Jesus. The list of witnesses to his glory does not begin with

those who saw the risen Christ, but with the witness of his baptism, John the Baptist. For if on the one hand we may say that the Word was made *flesh* and that the flesh conceals the radiance of the Logos, it is also possible to say—and this is the view proper to the evangelist John—that the *Word* was made flesh and the flesh mediated his glory to us from the beginning, and his glory was recognized by those who "received" him, and was testified to by those who allowed its light to shine into their hearts. The first of these was the Baptist. And the first rays of the glory of the Word made flesh shone at the baptism.

Another point of view is also important for John the evangelist. From all that was related by tradition about Jesus' baptism, he emphasizes only one thing: the descent of the Spirit from heaven like a dove and his remaining on Jesus. For him, however, the "Spirit" is naturally the Spirit about whom Jesus will say so much in his farewell discourses, the Spirit of truth, who is advocate and comforter and witness in one, the Holy Spirit whom the glorified Christ will send in his place so that the Church will not be orphaned but will be guided into all truth. That Spirit descended from heaven on Jesus at his baptism, on the Lamb who bears the sins of the world, never more to be separated from him. From now on, Jesus comes *with him*. Then, however—in the epoch of the Church—the Spirit comes *with Jesus,* comes as *his* Spirit, from him and in his place, bearing witness to him and glorifying him. Jesus, when glorified, comes in the Spirit. That is therefore the other side of Jesus' epiphany at his baptism, as the Baptist, and the evangelist with him, testify: Jesus appears and with him the Spirit who "remains". That Jesus appears who is the Jesus of the Spirit, who later guides the Church. The Spirit appears who is later the Paraclete of those who are his own, inseparably linked with Jesus, the Spirit of Jesus. The heavenly voice discloses that to the Baptist. For the union of Jesus and the Spirit, of Jesus the Lamb of God who bears the sins of the world, and the Spirit who now remains united with Jesus, is also acknowledged by man only if God opens his eyes. "This is he who baptizes with the Holy Spirit", says the heavenly voice, taking up a phrase of the Baptist which tradition reports to us in Mark (1:8). This is John the Baptist's baptizer in the Spirit, he on whom the Spirit rests and who will "baptize" with the Holy Spirit in a quite different way from what John had imagined.

Anyone who hears, can also "see". And anyone who "sees" can also be a witness. The Baptist allowed his unseeing eyes to be opened by listening to the divine voice and so he "sees" and testifies that this man and no other is the Lamb of God who bears the sins of the world, the Word of God with whom the beginning comes once again anew, Jesus with whom the Holy Spirit has now united himself enduringly, "the Son of God". Thereby he is everything which the Baptist was not and refused to claim to be, the evangelist thinks: the Elias, the prophet, the Messiah and even more. Finally, for the fourth evangelist, the baptismal event is the first epiphany of the Son, whose Sonship appears in the gospel in ever new epiphanies of his glory through word and signs.

We see, therefore, that in fact what happened at Jesus' baptism is mirrored in a variety of ways in our gospels: as the appearance of the mysterious Messiah-Servant of God with the revealing signs of the salvation which he will bring; as the appearance of the righteous Servant of God who places himself with sinners and so enters on the road to his baptism on the Cross, but whom God acknowledged as his beloved Son; as the appearance of the Son, who by his prayers brought about his first glorification; as the appearance of him who, as the Lamb of God, the Word of eternal renewal, from the beginning preserves the Spirit in whom he will one day come to his own in order through him to abide with them—and who in this way enters from the beginning into the testimony of the witnesses, of whom the first is John the Baptist. This complexity of aspects mirrors the multiplicity of the occurrence which was clearly handed down as a unity to the evangelists, but which they interpreted in each case in the perspective of their whole view. Taken together, they gradually manifest all that it states and signifies. The unity of the event and its tradition also provides the basis for the unity of its manifold presentation by the four gospels. All proclaim Jesus' baptism as the epiphany of what is still hidden but will one day emerge: the Cross, the glory, the Spirit, the heavens opened, and all this in him who is the Servant of God and the Son of God.

CHAPTER XIV

The Call of God

(Matthew 22:1—14)

The parable of the royal marriage feast makes it clear that we enter heaven only if we listen to God's call.

God's summons calls forth everything that exists. That is why the apostle Paul on one occasion calls God him "who gives life to the dead and calls into existence the things that do not exist" (Rom 4:17). Our parable is not concerned with the call to which we all, in fact, whether we like it or not, owe our life. It refers to the call by which the dead, who refused the call of the Creator, are brought back to life. It signifies God's redemptive call.

In the first place it means the call to Israel. It is the members of this nation who are first called, "invited", to the "marriage feast". They are those whom God had already said in the book of Isaiah, "But you, Israel, my servant, Jacob, whom I have chosen, the offspring of Abraham, my friend; you whom I took from the ends of the earth, and called from its farthest corners, saying to you, 'You are my servant ...'" (Is 41:6). But "they would not come". "They made light of it", says the parable. And now God gathered once again all his calls in a single final, ultimate call, to which all previous ones had been merely pointers and to which they had been merely guides. This was the call which he sent forth "in" Christ. He is God's call in all he said, did, suffered and was, from the very centre of his history, his Cross and resurrection from the dead. But his "deed-word" (ῥῆμα: Rom 10:17) as the apostle once calls this histor of his which is a summons, has passed from this history into a multiform "message". His epiphany found expression in the "holy call" of the Gospel, was handed down to human history in a "tradition" which the Holy Spirit entrusted to the Church. Now Christ's call rings out from the Church, from its hymns and prayers, its teaching and preaching, from each simple statement of the catechism, even from each good example and mark of love on the part of its members. Now it continues to call indefatigably into all the recesses of the heart and of the earth. One day this call will fall silent, when the sound of the trumpet takes its place. Then the period of God's "patience" will be at an end and the reckoning will begin.

But what does this call of God which, finally, went forth once and for all "in" Jesus Christ—"Their voice has gone out to all the earth, and their words to the ends of the world" (Rom 10:18)—say to men? What does it throw open to them so that they may go in? For it must be noted that the messengers in the parable do not merely convey a piece of information. They summon those who are invited and so open for them the door leading to the marriage feast. But this marriage feast is the sum of all communion with God and of all fulfilment which it confers on men. "Blessed are those who are invited to the marriage supper of the Lamb", we read in the Apocalypse (19:9). In God's call, which has now gone forth in Jesus Christ, we hear of a blessed happiness.

But what exactly does that mean? In the first place it means that God "called you out of darkness into his marvellous light" (1 Pet 2:9). In God's call, darkness gives way and light appears. "Again I am writing you a new commandment which is true, in him and in you, because the darkness is passing away and the true light is already shining" (1 Jn 2:8). God's call admits us to the light which appears in it and illumines the life of those who hearken to it. "Thy word is a lamp to my feet and a light to my path" (Ps 119:105). The life enlightened by God's call, however, shines and gives light to others. It is only through men of light that the world becomes light.

Light appears in this call because hope emerges in it. "Just as you were called to the one hope that belongs to your call" says the apostle Paul (Eph 4:4). The call in fact announces the prospect which has been opened to us by the death and resurrection of Christ. This vista opened out by the call is that of the glory of God on the face of Christ. "To this he called you through our gospel, so that you might obtain the glory of our Lord Jesus Christ" (2 Thess 2:14). The glory is the power and radiance of his face which is turned towards us once more in Christ.

Such a prospect brings peace. In God's call peace speaks to us. "He is our peace" (Eph 2:14). In the light of the prospect of the regard which God bestows on us once again, I abandon all anxieties about the regard in which I am held and all trust in my own worth. That, however, ultimately dissolves all enmity among men and of men towards God, and peace spreads. "And let the peace of Christ rule in your hearts, to which indeed you were called in one body" (Col 3:15).

In the peace of the new outlook opened to us by God's call, we also become free. Freedom meets us in it. "For he who was called in the Lord as a slave is a freedman of the Lord" (1 Cor 7:22). It is the immense freedom from attempting to affirm, secure and advance myself, freedom from desires and needs, fears and cares which debar me from peace. Consequently it is freedom from men and what they can give or refuse me. Yet I am also inclined to affirm, secure and advance myself by pious achievements before God. This freedom therefore is also freedom from the law, which perpetually tempts me astray into pious achievements intended to justify me. "For you are all called to freedom" (Gal 5:13), that is, to the great freedom of loving God for God's sake and the neighbour for his sake and not both for our own sake. Safe in the call which inspires hope, we can at last be rid of ourselves and be available for God's claim. "For God has called us to holiness" (1 Thess 4:7). Holiness is the accomplishment of freedom. It is the proof of release from ourselves, of detachment from ourselves even in the most secret domains. The saint is not only not unrighteous, he is not self-righteous either; he is not self-seeking in any way.

There is a final point. If God's call attracts and urges us into light, hope, peace and freedom, it also brings those who open themselves to it into joy. "May the God of hope fill you with all joy and peace in believing so that by the power of the Holy Spirit you may abound in hope", the apostle Paul prays for the Christians in Rome (Rom 15:13). Life which in hope is alight with peace is permeated with joy. It has set out for the presence of the Lord, or rather, by his call the presence of the Lord has already surrounded it. "Rejoice in the Lord always; again I will say, Rejoice ... The Lord is at hand" (Phil 4:4 f.).

There is one thing we have not mentioned. In God's call, grace is offered and summons men to itself: "... who called you into the grace of Christ" (Gal 1:6). Grace is God's self-giving for us in Christ, offered and conferred. The call of grace is the offer of God's self-giving bestowed on us in Christ. Grace is self-giving, a gift absolutely. And all that takes place in its call is purely a gift. "What have you that you did not receive?" (1 Cor 4:7). That life receives light and darkness is scattered, that the outlook broadens and we revive under the loving gaze of the Lord, that the spell of fear and self-seeking breaks, that the blessing of peace grows and joy blossoms,—all is grace, all takes place by gift.

But let us return to the parable. God's call has been uttered. It is one which contains implicitly an appeal: "Behold ... everything is ready". Will it be heard? And that means, will it be heard as a summons to make use of what God has prepared? "What no eye has seen, nor ear heard, nor the heart of man

conceived, what God has prepared for those who love him"
(1 Cor 2:9). Israel, the parable says, did not accept this offer
and command. "They would not come." "They made light of
it." "The rest seized his servants, treated them shamefully and
killed them." It is the continual story of the Passion of God's
call among his people. In it, too, something like the pattern of
the fate it meets with in the world generally can be perceived.
Not to want to come, to treat the call lightly because of the
mass of other business, finally in a rage to shut the mouths of
his messengers; who cannot recognize the answer of all the ages
to God's summons? "Now these things happened to them as a
warning, but they were written down for our instruction, upon
whom the end of the ages has come" (1 Cor 10:11).

The parable, of course, also speaks directly of "us". We
Christians from among the Gentiles are those who without
historical preparation were called from the thoroughfares of the
world, after Israel as a nation had refused itself to God. We
came and filled the hall—good and bad. But how did many of
us think we could come? The Lord makes it clear by the case
of one of us. He had followed the call. We could say, he was
baptized. He stood in the hall of the king, where the marriage
feast was to take place; in fact he had already sat down to table.
The king noticed him and was on the point of greeting him as
his guest. But he was not wearing a wedding garment. "And he
said to him, 'Friend how did you get in here without a wedding
garment?'" He had accepted the invitation, but nothing indicates that he prepared himself for it. He comes to the feast, but
nothing shows he adorned himself for it. Outwardly he is standing as a guest in the room but at heart he is clearly still occupied
with his affairs. Or should we say that at heart he is taking
part in the meal but outwardly he does not give expression to
that fact? Both can be said. Before God, and therefore in truth,
however, interior and exterior belong together, and neither can
exist without the other. What is inward must become outward
and what is outward must be inward. The wedding garment is

not something merely external. Dress is a sign and expression of my inner self. The everyday garb of the man who has been called from the street to the Son's marriage shows that he has not yet heard the call, that he has become aware of it but has not accepted it, has not committed himself to it. If he had accepted what was offered and commanded, he would have put on a new garment, a festive garment. He would have put on the festive garment of joy. For in the context it is the wedding garment of joy that must be thought of. "Can the wedding guests mourn as long as the bridegroom is with them?" (Mt 9:15). Many of us—that is made clear by this one guest—do not enter into the appeal of joy which surrounds us since the Lord is at hand. For many come to the marriage feast closed against God and their neighbour, fundamentally closed, in fact, against themselves, sad from perpetually keeping God and their neighbour at a distance and from the labour of perpetual self-affirmation. Many remain in the gloomy narrowness and anxiety of an unrighteous and self-righteous life and do not enter into the radiant expanse of the joy of those who are free. Many hear the call, but they do not perceive that it is the offer and bidding of him who will also greet those who come: "Well done, good and faithful servant; enter into the joy of your master" (Mt 25:21, 23).

In order to be able to hear that, preparation is needed to enter into God's call. Let us consider what that means. Because the parable says nothing about it, let us reflect again with the help of the wisdom of the apostles who know a great deal about it. Of this only a little can be pondered. Let us remember Abraham. "By faith Abraham obeyed when he was called to go out to a place which he was to receive as an inheritance; and he went out, not knowing where he was to go" (Heb 11:8). God's call summons to a strange land. To accept the call means to go out into a strange country, yet one which is home. No one of himself knows where it lies, no one knows where the path to it leads. Only the call is there, which knows, and leads us. To hear it and hold to it and to trust it more than any other call in life, to trust it blindly, that is, to enter into it and as it were go through it into the strange land which is home.

That is not done without struggle and decision. There are of course throughout life so many other and, as it seems, more attractive and promising calls which seek to hold us back and draw us away from the path into the strange land. That is why the apostle Paul reminds his pupil Timothy: "Fight the good fight of the faith, take hold of the eternal life to which you were called..." (1 Tim 6:12). This fight requires on occasion the following (it can only be one example out of many): "To this (i.e. to glory) he called you, ... brethren, stand firm and hold to the traditions which you were taught by us" (2 Thess 2:14 f.). To stand firm and to hold fast, in the Spirit, the "tradition" in which the Lord communicates himself to the world from the Cross and resurrection to the end of the world, that also belongs to following God's call.

Only we must reflect that the call goes through the heart and is established in the heart. "Let the peace of Christ rule in your hearts, to which indeed you were called" (Col 3:15). With the heart one abides in the call. "It is well that the heart be strengthened by grace..." (Heb 13:9). The heart itself stands firm, however, when it allows the call which it guards, and which guards it, to penetrate even into its "works" or even into "the members". *They* must put themselves at the disposal of the call so that it may dispose of them and so fit us for heaven. The "holy nation"—they are the "saints who are called"—will "declare the wonderful deeds of him who called you out of darkness into his marvellous light". How will it declare the "wonderful deeds" of God? By itself being "holy" in all its conduct, as he who called it is holy; through hope in the grace which one day will dawn clearly and finally (1 Pet 1:15; 2:9).

Much might still be said, but we will refer to only two of the apostle's remarks. The first occurs at the beginning of the fourth chapter of the Letter to the Ephesians, where he exhorts us "to lead a life worthy of the calling to which [we] have been called, with all lowliness and meekness, with patience, forbearing one another in love, eager to maintain the unity of the Spirit in the bond of peace". Here the connection between God's call and our life is evident. God's call has been uttered. It has opened up a single and unifying hope, a prospect among the "angels" (Eph 1:18 f.). The opening out of such a vista demands a way of life that corresponds to it, one which is accomplished with that hope in mind and maintains hope in that hope. So, for example, it is one of humility, meekness, patience and mutual forbearance. All that shows that one in fact has hope and that one's outlook has a divine scope. Anyone who has the appeal of this heavenly prospect singing in the ear of his heart will be able to ignore all the hopeless self-assurances and the hopeless building up of self which a life without prospects so much needs. He will be able to commit himself to Christ's care, who has already provided for our life, and to Christ's glory, which is what builds us up. Secure and esteemed, he can be generous with the generosity of love.

What does such a life of commitment to and trust in God's call look like when viewed as a whole? It has a remarkable dynamism. The apostle shows this in the third chapter of the Letter to the Philippians. "Not that I have already obtained this or am already perfect; but I press on to make it my own, because Christ Jesus has made me his own. Brethren, I do not consider that I have made it my own; but one thing I do, forgetting what lies behind and straining forward to what lies ahead; I press on towards the goal for the prize of the upward call of God in Christ Jesus" (3:12). The life of one who is "called" consists in being stirred by the call of Christ, leaving self and all that belongs to self as a mere obstacle, and hastening unceasingly towards the goal. The call has been uttered, it has taken hold of me, and in it, the Lord himself. But since he is the call from on high, the call is not only behind me but also always in front of me for me to grasp. I am surrounded by the call, which no longer leaves me. I cannot escape from it any more. I cannot linger in ignorance among the calls of the world. This call is always coming to me. God's future calls me and so I throw myself towards it until I reach him who is calling, until he emerges from his call face to face with me. To commit oneself to God's call means to be on the way from light to light, from hope to hope, from peace to peace, from freedom to freedom, from joy to joy—from grace to grace.

At the end of our parable there is a sentence in which we probably should hear the evangelist speaking: "For many are called, but few are chosen". In this statement, the apostle Matthew mentally considers the innumerable crowds hurrying to the Church. Many are called and in baptism are irrevocably submitted to this call. Among these crowds, however, there are few whose life is impelled and carried by this call to what it announces to us, to joy. The one man who did not wear a wedding garment is a symbol of the many. We know what happens with him. Under the king's gaze and at his question, he does not know what to answer. "And he was speechless. Then the king said to the attendants, 'Bind him hand and foot, and cast him into the outer darkness; there men will weep and gnash their teeth.'" That is the contrary of the joy of the Lord, the antithesis of peace, freedom, hope, light and the call. It is lamentation, horror and fear, unfreedom, absence of any prospects, darkness, speechlessness. It is to be cast out into the night. Anyone who does not accept the call of God, who does not submit to its dynamism, in however small an impulse towards the light, anyone who shuts himself off and becomes numbed in impenitence so that no call affects him any more, anyone who will not put on the wedding garment of joy, but is attached to his old garb and is satisfied with the dreariness of his own self-seeking, may have come once, but will not stay. We can also say, that anyone who remains what he was, will one day definitively be what he wills to be.

"Who then can be saved? But Jesus looked at them and said

to them, 'With men this is impossible, but with God all things are possible'" (Mt 19:25 f.). We understand why the apostle Paul prays "that our God may make you worthy of his call, and make efficacious your joy in all good and the work of faith in power" (2 Thess 1:11). He prays with confidence in the Lord in God's fidelity. "May the God of peace himself sanctify you wholly; and may your spirit and soul and body be kept sound and blameless at the coming of our Lord Jesus Christ. He who calls you is true, and he will do it" (1 Thess 5:23 f.).